THE BEAUTY OF THE HOURI

THE BEAUTY
OF THE HOURI

Heavenly Virgins, Feminine Ideals

NERINA RUSTOMJI

OXFORD
UNIVERSITY PRESS

Oxford University Press is a department of the University of Oxford. It furthers
the University's objective of excellence in research, scholarship, and education
by publishing worldwide. Oxford is a registered trade mark of Oxford University
Press in the UK and certain other countries.

Published in the United States of America by Oxford University Press
198 Madison Avenue, New York, NY 10016, United States of America.

© Oxford University Press 2021

Library of Congress Cataloging-in-Publication Data
Names: Rustomji, Nerina, author.
Title: The beauty of the houri : heavenly virgins, feminine ideals / Nerina Rustomji.
Description: New York : Oxford University Press, 2021. |
Includes bibliographical references and index.
Identifiers: LCCN 2020058292 (print) | LCCN 2020058293 (ebook) |
ISBN 9780190249342 (hardback) | ISBN 9780190249366 (epub) |
ISBN 9780190249373 | ISBN 9780190249359
Subjects: LCSH: Paradise—Islam. | Islamic eschatology.
Classification: LCC BP166.87 .R87 2021 (print) | LCC BP166.87 (ebook) |
DDC 297.2/3—dc23
LC record available at https://lccn.loc.gov/2020058292
LC ebook record available at https://lccn.loc.gov/2020058293

DOI: 10.1093/oso/9780190249342.001.0001

9 8 7 6 5 4 3 2 1

Printed by Sheridan Books, Inc., United States of America

To
Shehriyar
and
the city of New York

CONTENTS

List of Illustrations   ix
Acknowledgments   xi

Introduction   1
1.   The Letter   13
2.   The Word   43
3.   The Romance   63
4.   A Reward   93
5.   The Promise   123
6.   The Question   149
      Conclusion   165

Notes   *171*
Bibliography   *193*
Index   *221*

ILLUSTRATIONS

1.1.	Four-page handwritten letter	15
2.1.	*The Great Odalisque*, Ingres	57
2.2.	*The Turkish Bath*, Ingres	58
3.1.	*Leila*	75
3.2.	*Zuleikha*	76
3.3.	*The Touch*, Maurin	80
3.4.	*The Dream*, Maurin	81
3.5.	*Islamic Paradise*, Jazet	82
3.6.	*Star of Love*	88
5.1.	*Lesser and Greater Signs of the Hour*	128
5.2.	*Women of the People of the Fire*	129
5.3.	*Women of the People of the Garden*	130

ACKNOWLEDGMENTS

I HAVE BENEFITED FROM ALL kinds of support at many stages.

Librarians provided access and encouragement. Carmen Ayoubi at the American Center of Oriental Research in Amman, Jordan, assisted at an early stage of the project. Jay Barksdale at the New York Public Library, where I worked in the Wertheim Study and Soichi Noma Reading Room and participated in the MARLI program, was also an early supporter. My interview with him and subsequent tea service reminded me of the civic value of the public library system whose librarians, including Melanie Locay and Carolyn Broomhead, made this book possible. Ray Pun has been an all-around media resource.

Colleagues offered useful references and made helpful suggestions. I would like to thank Dick Bulliet, Ayesha Jalal, and Denise Spellberg for their early and continued support for the project. Scholars of Islamic history, Islamic religion, and Muslim societies have helped me expand my ideas. They include Durre Ahmed, Dana Burde, David

Cook, Adam Gaiser, Matthew Gordon, Sebastian Günther, Kathryn Hain, Juliane Hammer, Amir Hussain, Akbar Hyder, Pernilla Myrne, Lisa Nielson, David Powers, Frances Pritchett, Tahera Qutbuddin, Dagmar Riedel, Walid Saleh, Eric Tagliacozzo, SherAli Tareen, Shawkat Toorawa, and Jamel Velji. Scholars of American and English history have guided me through contexts and literatures and have offered useful advice. They include Dohra Ahmad, Jacob Berman, Hasia Diner, Kathleen Lubey, Todd Fine, Mitch Fraas, John Gazvinian, David Grafton, and Christine Heyrman. Other scholars have helped me interpret traditions of the ancient Near East, late antiquity, comparative religion, and South Asia. They include Amy Allocco, Carla Bellamy, Richard Davis, Lynn Huber, Cecile Kuznitz, Ruth Marshall, Scott Noegel, Shai Secunda, and Joel Walker. Indispensable assistance with du Loir and his context was provided by Michael Harrigan, Ioanna Kohler, and Michael Wolfe. I benefited from the intellectual community of academic list-serves, including Adabiyat, H-Atlantic, H-Islamart, H-Mideast-Medieval, H-Mideast-Politics, H-World, and Islamaar. My anonymous reviewers offered useful advice and constructive commentary, and I am grateful for their suggestions.

Generous listeners at presentations and conferences asked sharp questions and shared valuable insights. These exchanges took place at the American Council of Oriental Research, Bard College, Barnard College, Columbia University, City University of New York Graduate Center, Cornell University, Franklin and Marshall College, George Mason University, International Congress of Medieval Studies, Katholieke Universiteit Leuven, Middle East Studies Association, New York Public Library, Organization of

American Historians, University of Göttingen, University of Pennsylvania, University of Texas, University of Washington, and Yale University. Additionally, I would like to thank Cindy Postma for inviting me to King's College, where questions from members of the audience challenged me, gave me much to reflect upon, and showed me the value of intellectual exchange that bridges the divide between scholarly and popular worlds.

Institutions provided vital support. The book started with an American Council of Learned Societies fellowship in 2007–2008. Additionally, I held a research fellowship at the American Center of Oriental Research, and thank Barbara Porter for her wonderful engagement over the years. While the idea of the book started while I was working at Bard College, the book was researched and written at St. John's University where I held a Summer Research Fellowship in 2011. My students at St. John's University shared meaningful perspectives during classroom discussions. I also benefited from the counsel of History Department colleagues, including Dolores Augustine, Frances Balla, Mauricio Borrero, Elaine Carey, Shahla Hussain, Tim Milford, Phil Misevich, Lara Vapnek, and Erika Vause.

Friends and strangers were part of the process of researching and writing the book. There are more houri jokes in the universe than one can imagine, and over the years I have heard many of them, thanks to enthusiastic interlocutors. My research may have started with the inventory of Internet jokes, but a joke does not make a book. I would not have completed the manuscript without the generosity and assurance of Kristen Demilio, Jean Ma, and Laura Neitzel who helped me refine my thinking, edited drafts, and encouraged at every turn.

The book is made possible because of Oxford University Press. My editor, Cynthia Read, has been a steady champion, and her insight and judgment have been invaluable. Zara Cannon-Mohammed, Cameron Donahue, Marcela Maxfield, and Christian Purdy have been helpful collaborators. Dorothy Bauhoff, Julie Goodman, and Cynthia Read edited the manuscript with keen eyes.

I was able to research and write the book because of the bracing love of Aban, Purvez, and Arish, the witty joy of Shehriyar, and the whimsy of Azad and Tahmir. I was also inspired by the city of New York, whose beauty is expressed through verve, humor, and civic connection. The beauty of the city was visible on September 11th when the world was watching, and it is present today when no one is looking. This book was motivated by that day, drafted in city libraries, shaped by city students, and encouraged by city neighbors. It could not have been written, with such resonance, anywhere else.

INTRODUCTION

THE HOURI IS AN UNKNOWABLE, otherworldly beauty. All faithful Muslim men are said to be awarded these female companions—*hur al-ʿin* in Arabic, houris in English—in the ineffable realm of paradise. Since the houri is not an earthly being, lived experiences cannot attest to her beauty. She remains a cosmic promise. Writers attempted to explain her large dark eyes and her virginal, untouched purity. Their imaginings of her physical form demonstrated a fascination with the ultimate gendered reward—a female companion for a male believer. What makes the houri an ideal beauty, by contrast, is far more complex than a list of her attributes.

This is my September 11th book, but I did not know it until 2004. I opened *The New York Times* to find an opinion piece by Nicholas Kristof entitled "Martyrs, Virgins and Grapes." The column linked the figure of the houri with the lack of freedom of speech in Muslim societies. It argued that houris are really white grapes, but that most Muslims are unfamiliar with this interpretation because they are not free to question their religious texts. The column referred to the theologian al-Suyuti, who died in 1505. I was struck by this reference. As a new assistant professor, I questioned what students needed to know and why they needed to know it. I wondered whether *The New York Times* readers had encountered al-Suyuti before, and why they needed to learn of him that day. I recognized a tension. The houri is often referenced in popular texts, but there was not a developed scholarly literature that explains her significance. This book began as an attempt to address both scholarship and popular discourse about the houri. It has expanded into a larger examination of the houri by theologians, grammarians, travelers, journalists, intellectuals, and bloggers. The question that has guided me is not whether Kristof's argument about scriptural interpretation was correct, but why references to these heavenly virgins would have been recognizable to his readers at all. I wanted to understand how "Islamic virgins" have become part of the American vocabulary about Islam.

As I began to study the prevalence of the houri in print and online media, I became aware of a vast and complex set of historical reflections about the houri. Houris appear in genres of Arabic theology and Arabic and Persian poetry, but they were also frequently found in English and American literature until the early twentieth century. The history of the houri, then, is not an exclusively Islamic history. The figure of the houri inspired writers, readers, artists, and viewers in many different times and contexts. This chronicle of inspiration is not a continuous narrative. It has multiple beginnings, some lulls, and no clear end. Yet, at each point of development, the houri is a topic of fascination. She is a cosmic being, but she also presents an image of human feminine perfection. That promise of perfection transformed the houri into a model that had potential to inspire both men and women.

The book ranges from the seventh to the twenty-first century, but its starting point is found in the recent American past of September 11, 2001, which for many readers may mark their first encounter with the image of the houri in popular media as a heavenly virgin waiting to reward the perpetrators of the attacks on the World Trade Center, the Pentagon, and United Airlines Flight 93.

This book uses theological and literary sources and analyzes them through discursive and contextual analysis. It also examines contemporary media representations of the houri that have emerged on online digital platforms such as YouTube in the last two decades. The sources often took forms that I did not anticipate. A letter said to be written by September 11th hijacker Mohamed Atta was a dramatic piece of evidence offered by the Federal Bureau of Investigation and subsequently was published by newspapers to account for evidence of and motivation of the hijackers. Now it is a small, mostly ignored display in the National September 11 Memorial and Museum in New York City. The videos made by jihadi groups and globally disseminated via YouTube were evidence of a vibrant traffic of jihadi recruitment efforts. Now that technology companies have become more circumspect about content, the circulation of such videos has been reduced. In fact, some videos in my research can no longer be accessed. While I have studied many of them, I only discuss the ones that I was able to archive digitally. Meanwhile, other sources that demonstrate the American and English fascination with houris await consideration.

The houri originated in Islamic texts, developed in European ones, and gained a new life in digital media. When we survey the writings about houris, we see creative interpretation and engagement across times, cultures, writers, and texts. If there is a significant limitation of the book, it is that it studies the written productions of urban people. The texts were designed for theological elite in Islamic circles and cosmopolitan elite in Europe and the

United States. Similarly, the videos considered here are designed for digitally connected people. While accessing digital productions today may not require the same networks of power as accessing the texts of the past, the digital productions do require the capacity to use technology and be connected to the web. Even with this limitation, the Internet offers the potential to record attitudes, assumptions, thoughts, reactions, and prejudices for digitally connected populations.

A QUESTION OF ORIGINS

Scholars have tried to understand the houri through comparison with other religious traditions. The quest for origins is challenging since it is unclear what a houri really is. Assumptions about the purported source of origin lead the argument, rather than close textual study. In these modes of reasoning, scholarship points to origins in Zoroastrian, Jewish, and Christian eschatological traditions. In the Zoroastrian religion, after believers die, they are said to cross the Chinvat Bridge. As the soul crosses, the soul learns of its everlasting place. If met by a beautiful female, the soul sees the embodiment of its good deeds, or Daena, and earns a place in paradise. If met by an ugly hag, the soul sees the embodiment of its bad deeds and earns a place in hell. Some scholars suggest that the houri may have been borrowed from this Zoroastrian belief.[1] Another theory locates the origin of the houri in early stages of Jewish eschatology when sexual pleasures were part of paradise.[2] In both the Zoroastrian and Jewish origin theories, the feminine beings have a spiritual and an aesthetic dimension.

Theories that involve Christian origins depend on different assumptions about the material world. One theory turns toward ideas about angelology or the heavens, where the houri is a celestial being who is spiritually pure and without the capacity for physical beauty or the desire to please.[3] The houri, in effect, is equated with a feminine angel. The theory focused on the Syriac texts of St. Ephrem accords a more material dimension to paradise and links the houri with the image of a paradise garden.[4]

Charles Wendell refreshingly argues for an Arabian origin and suggests that the houri is the "most Arabian" feature of Islamic paradise.[5] He argues against foreign origins of the houri, noting that it is worth looking for parallels. For example, if the Zoroastrian religion was the inspiration for the figure of the houri, then the dichotomy should also be carried over, and an ugly hag should appear in Islamic eschatology as the antithesis of the houri.[6] Wendell suggests instead that the origin may be found in Arabian taverns or drinking houses, and he turns to Arabic poetry to explain the meaning of the houri.

Interestingly, the theories about the houri's origins often misrepresent the relationship between the material and spiritual world in Islam. The houri is misunderstood either as a sensual being, at the expense of spirituality, or as an angel without any physical capacity. Scholars who make these linkages understand the houri through her physical, sensual, or sexual meanings, but their theories do not account for the nature of aesthetics in the Islamic afterworld. Their discussions either center on physical form without acknowledging spiritual perfection or invalidate the possibility of any physicality at all. They read the houri primarily as a woman designed for men's pleasure rather than a feminine being who exemplifies the possibilities of an aesthetically and spiritually pure realm. The scholarship on the houri sheds light on the frameworks that scholars brought to understand a feminine being who was never fully defined in the Qurʾan and Islamic theological texts.

CHAPTERS

The six chapters of *The Beauty of the Houri* offer two developing perspectives. The first perspective focuses on the European, English, or American views of the houri from the sixteenth to the twenty-first century. The second perspective offers a view of classical and contemporary Islamic uses of the houri from the seventh century to the present. These two perspectives are not in opposition. There is not one definitive meaning of the houri in either European and American or Islamic literature. Instead, there are a number of meanings that lead to different driving questions. The clustering of the chapters is an organizational scheme to account for change in context and genre and to appreciate how contemporary thinkers draw on different sources to present visions of a twenty-first-century houri.

The book starts with discourse after September 11th and ends with contemporary Muslim discourse on the Internet. In between, the chapters show the antecedents of these two modern discourses in earlier European, American, and Islamic histories. The first three chapters introduce the American viewpoint and its legacies and suggest that the fascination with the houri involves using feminine models to determine and judge the value of Islam. The houri became a distinctly European and American symbol that may have been developed from Islamic texts, but far exceeded their parameters and significance. The final three chapters present an Islamic perspective of the houri and suggest that there has always been an ambiguity about the houri in the Qur'an and Qur'anic commentaries. It is precisely the lack of clarity about the meaning of the houri that has led to such vivid depictions in historical accounts, theological texts, online videos, and contemporary discourses. Unlike the writers who claim that Muslims lack a tradition of scriptural interpretation, Chapters 5 and 6 show that there is vibrant Islamic discourse about the meaning of the houri in the twenty-first century. This discussion suggests the possibility of gender parity in paradisiacal rewards in which Muslim women are promised a reward equal to that of Muslim men who are granted houris.

Chapter 1, "The Letter," studies the most consequential recent mention of the houri, the purported letter of September 11th hijacker Mohamed Atta, and shows that media fascination with the houri is related to American reactions to the events of September 11th. It looks at the function of the houri in the letter and then turns to how media have understood the passages about the houri. It introduces two related arguments commonly found in US news media. The first is that Islam needs a form of scriptural interpretation so Muslims can be able to live in free, secularized societies. The second is the white grape theory, the argument that references to houris are really references to white grapes or raisins, and not to female companions awaiting men in paradise. In tracing the impact of the theory, the chapter turns to the diffusion of the houri in comedies, satires, and novels.

Chapter 2, "The Word," shows how the English and French fascination with Islam involved interpretations of the houri and her meanings. The chapter surveys sixteenth-century polemics about Islam, seventeenth-century French travel writings, and eighteenth-century English literature about the Muslim East. In describing these early modern exchanges, which involved Turks in England and the English and French in the Ottoman Empire, the chapter depicts the widening of the English and French worldview. By the eighteenth century, "houri" was used as a way to describe superlative feminine beauty, even while views of Islam and Islamic empires were ambivalent.

Chapter 3, "The Romance," demonstrates how nineteenth-century literature transcended religious frameworks and questioned the nature of male authority and feminine purity. This chapter shows that, although the houri may have been based on assumptions about Islam, the term eventually was applied to Jewish and Christian women. In Romantic tales and poetry and captivity narratives, the houri appeared in different forms. There is a Byronic houri, a Victorian houri, and even a Kentucky houri. In these texts, the houri signifies the ideal female, irrespective of religion or region.

Chapter 4, "A Reward," presents Islamic theological and historical texts about the houri and argues that the houri is an ambiguous reward of paradise that has developed multiple meanings. At the most basic level, the houri is a companion, and the chapter elucidates the concepts of companionship and labor in the afterworld by comparing the houri to male companions in paradise. The houri is also a pure companion, and the chapter surveys explicit and implicit Qur'anic verses and Qur'anic commentaries that grappled with the houri's meaning and her relationship to purity and earthly wives. In eschatological literature, the houri becomes a more sensual reward for individual believers. This sense of individual reward is highlighted in manuals about jihad, where marriage to the houris is discussed. The chapter also assesses the houri as entertainment, and demonstrates that the houri provided inspiration for singing slave girls. These singing slave girls, in turn, may have influenced descriptions of houris who became known for their melodious voices. Since the chapter focuses on the developing tradition of the houri, it treats mainly Sunni texts and does not explore fully traditions of paradise and the houri that may be found in Shiʿi and even Bahai texts.

Chapter 5, "The Promise," explores websites and new media that use the houri. The chapter looks both to reformist Sunni websites where tours of paradise are presented as a form of education and also to jihadi videos that aim to develop affective bonds in recruiting in online communities. The chapter focuses on the videos of Anwar al-Awlaqi, the leader of al-Qaʿida in the Arabian Peninsula, who used the houri to represent the wonders of paradise and to recognize the injustices of this world and the superlative nature of the cosmic world.

Chapter 6, "The Question," brings together American and European perspectives and also classical Islamic and contemporary Muslim perspectives, presenting answers to a critical question in online communities about the houri: "If men receive houris, then what do women receive?" After assessing the assumptions built into the question, the chapter presents four different answers: Muslim women receive misogyny; they receive eternity with their husbands; they obtain higher status than the houris; or they receive male houris of their own. The chapter concludes by suggesting that the question is evidence of an Islamic scriptural tradition in the twenty-first century that fuses American, European, and classical Islamic interpretations of the houri.

TERMS AND DATES

The houri is identified by different terms. Variations for houri in the singular and the plural can be found in Arabic and Persian. These include the plural terms *hur'in* in the Qur'an and *hur al-'in* (with the definite article "al") in Islamic theological texts. They also include the singular *ahwar* and *hawra'*, which do not appear in the Qur'an and only sometimes in theological texts. I generally use the term "houri" for the singular and "houris" for the plural since they have been English words since the eighteenth century. I highlight specific variations in the text, such as *hora, horhin, hur, hur'in, hur al-'in,* and *al-hur al-'in,* when their appearance is significant. Additionally, I have reflected the varied English orthography of the eighteenth and nineteenth centuries.

The book argues that the houri can be seen both as a being and an object. In the former case, the houri is identified within the context of companionship and marriage and is seen as an active character. The latter recognizes the houri's physical composition as one of the rewards in the landscape of paradise and sees her as an inactive object. Reducing the houri to one or the other misses the multiple dimensions of the houri's constitution in paradise.

The book follows the *International Journal of Middle East Studies* transliteration guidelines; however, all letters are not transliterated fully with diacritical marks. The Arabic letter of ʿayn is expressed by ʿ and hazma is expressed by ʾ. Arabic proper names of twentieth- and twenty-first-century individuals either adopt their preferred spelling or commonly accepted English spelling. Finally, the book uses the Gregorian calendar for all dates. This usage signals an important reality. While the houri began as an Islamic figure, the amplified significance of the houri is due to American and European interpretations of her meaning.

THE LETTER

AFTER MOHAMED ATTA FULFILLED HIS mission by flying American Airlines Flight 11 into the North Tower of the World Trade Center, agents of the Federal Bureau of Investigation found a handwritten Arabic letter in his luggage, left behind at Logan Airport. The bag had not been transferred to his flight to Los Angeles because his earlier Colgan Air flight from Maine had been delayed. He made it onto American Airlines Flight 11, but one of his bags missed the cutoff by two or three minutes. The FBI catalogued the letter as evidence on September 11, 2001, at 4:01 p.m.: "4 page letter. Located outer most pouch of (lower) black bag."

The FBI found two other copies of the letter. One was discovered in the wreckage of United Airlines Flight 93 in Shanksville, Pennsylvania. Another was found in a car registered to Nawaf al-Hazmi and previously owned by Khalid al-Mihdhar, both part of the team that flew American Airlines Flight 77 into the Pentagon. These three letters provided proof that the hijacked planes were part of an organized, unified mission. On September 28, 2001, the Justice Department posted the letter on its website. The Justice Department had been criticized for the way in which it had translated the letter, so it released the original and let other organizations translate the text for the reading public. ABC News posted a partial translation on the same day. *The New York Times* commissioned Capital Communications Group, a Washington-based international consulting firm, to provide a translation. By September 30, it was published in a number of English-language periodicals, and it is the translation that has been most widely circulated.[1]

Five years later, Zacarias Moussaoui became the first person to be charged for the September 11th attacks. During the trial, previously classified data were released. On March 4, 2006, he was sentenced to life in prison without parole. After the trial was completed, the prosecutors posted all 1,202 exhibits presented as evidence at the trial. One of the exhibits was the letter. Identified as "Prosecution Trial Exhibit BS01101," the letter was accompanied by another translation (Figure 1.1).[2]

The letter had been called "Mohamed Atta's letter" or "The Doomsday Letter" or "The Last Night" or "The Spiritual Manual," but we do not know who wrote it. Since the Justice Department has not released all three letters, we cannot compare them. The letter can be found at the National September 11th Museum in New York City and on the Internet. For some people, it seems incredible that Mohamed Atta wrote a letter that detailed the steps of the mission, articulated its rationale, and then left it to be found in a piece of luggage. Others are suspicious because the FBI released only four pages, while Bob Woodward of *The Washington Post* had reported that there were five pages. In an article published on September 28, 2001, one of ten that helped *The Washington Post* win the Pulitzer Prize for National Reporting in 2002, Woodward described a fifth page that was written on standard stenographer paper with the heading "When you enter the plane." The page also

FIGURE 1.1 Four-page handwritten letter in Arabic found in luggage recovered at Logan Airport, Boston, Massachusetts. Exhibit No. BS 01101 in the trial of *United States of America v. Zacarias Moussaoui*.

included a series of prayers or exhortations and some doo-dling that looked like a key.[3] There continues to be confusion about the length of the letter. Most reports follow the FBI and refer to four pages. A few others cite Bob Woodward's mention of five pages and suggest that the FBI may not have been transparent about all three letters.

The letter raises many questions. How were the copies made? How were they distributed? Did every hijacker receive one? Did Atta even write the letter? Or was it fabricated, as the conspiracy theorists suggest? In *The 9/11 Handbook*, Hans Kippenberg reports that one of the masterminds of the attacks, Ramzi Binalshibh, claimed that the letter was written by hijacker Abdulaziz al-Omari, who was part of Mohamed Atta's team.[4] We cannot answer all the questions that the letter raises. What is clear, though, is that the letter offers guidance to the hijackers, procedures for preparing for the attacks, and advice on how to renew their commitment to the mission. It is an odd document that draws on ritual piety, religious exhortation, historical references, and mental conditioning, all the while detailing an intended act of martyrdom whose violent aim was blunt.

This chapter tells the story of American reactions to the letter and how, in the wake of September 11, Americans have used the letter to understand the motivations of the hijackers and the religion of Islam. Americans used the letter's promise of virgins of paradise to signal their revulsion at the hijack-ers. This in turn gave rise to an obscure, yet popular theory that the houris were really "white grapes" and not feminine companions at all. The hijackers would not receive the sexual reward that was assumed to be part of their motivation for the attacks. Since the emergence of the white grape theory, the houri has become a stock joke. The reactions to the letter reveal how news is made, who frames Islamic issues for the media, and how and why certain ideas spread. As Americans tried to make sense of the attacks, they turned to the letter to amplify religious claims about women in paradise and made it central to their account of September 11th. The letter may be forensic evidence for the September 11th attacks, but it also inspires discussion about Islam, terror, and virgins.[5]

THE LAST NIGHT, THE SECOND STEP, THE THIRD PHASE

The letter is an odd assemblage of exhortations and practical guidance, and it reveals how the hijackers envisioned their place in the world and in the eyes of God. The letter was meant to remind, not just to instruct. The practical instructions and recommended prayers in the letter suggest that its objective was to bring the hijackers into the right frame of mind to kill and to kill in a particular way. There are several English translations of the letter, including a useful annotated one.[6] I draw on *The New York Times* version because it was the first full translation that was widely circulated and had the greatest impact in print and online media.

The letter is divided into three sections: "the last night," "the second step," and "the third phase." The first stage of the attack was to begin at night, when the men were to prepare their bodies and minds for the attack. The concern of this first section is that the hijackers might fold if they met with resistance. The aim of the last night was to "renew" the desire to conduct the mission and to prepare the self to execute it. That preparation entailed ritual purity, reflective prayer, and logistical planning. They were to read the Qur'anic suras "al-Tawba" and "Anfal" and to recognize that they will face difficult situations so "tame your soul, purify it, convince it, make it understand, and incite it."[7] The function of these prayers was not only to prepare the soul, but also to condition the self toward the difficulty of the mission: "Pray during the night and be persistent in asking God to give you victory, control, and conquest, and that He may make your task easier and not expose us."[8] The hijackers are also offered religious inspiration for the possibility of victory. In an allusion to the battle of Uhud (625) at which Muslims defeated overwhelming numbers of Meccans, the hijackers are counseled to remember the times when God allows smaller groups to defeat larger forces.

The rest of the first section gives explicit instructions on how to ritualize the preparation. The hijackers were to bless the body, "luggage, clothes, the knife, your personal effects, your ID, passport, and all your papers."[9] They were to check their weapons. "You must make your knife sharp and must not discomfort your animal during the slaughter."[10] Finally, they were to tighten their clothing, their shoes, and make sure their socks fit properly. Then, they were to pray the morning prayer.

The other two sections of the letter, which are not numbered, proceed briskly. The second phase focuses on how to prepare oneself for the actual act of suicide. The hijackers were to go to the airports without fear and with respect for their brothers. They were reminded, "all of their equipment and gates and technology will not prevent, nor harm, by God's will."[11]

When the plane was to take off and "both groups come together,"[12] they were counseled about the right frame of mind during the killing. In particular, they were to remember that their actions were for the sake of God and not for revenge, and they were to muster their strength by thinking of the previous generations, and especially of the prophet Muhammad and his companions. "Then every one of you should prepare to carry out his role in a way that would satisfy God. You should clench your teeth, as the pious early generations did."[13] If their role was to slaughter, then they were to dedicate the slaughter to their fathers quickly so they would not make their victims, identified as "animals," suffer further.[14] They were to remind their brothers that their actions were for God, and they were not to confuse them. And they were to take a bounty of a cup of water, if possible. When the hour approached, they were to welcome death for the sake of God. In the final moments of their lives, they were advised either to be praying or have their last words be the *shahada*, the Muslim affirmation of faith, "There is no God but God, and Muhammad is his messenger."

The letter does not fit into any conventional genre. It does not draw on an existing template, and it is strikingly informal in its tone. While some commentators have pointed out the letter's aim of conditioning the mind,[15] Juan Cole sees the conditioning as drawing upon Sufi or mystical rituals that create a psychological manipulation.[16]

Beyond the conditioning, the meaning and reward of the mission are articulated in four separate passages where there are allusions to what the hijackers could anticipate *after* the mission was complete.

> You should feel complete tranquility, because the time between you and your marriage [in heaven] is very short. Afterwards begins the happy life, where God is satisfied with you, and eternal bliss "in the company of the prophets, the

companions, the martyrs, and the good people, who are all good company." Ask God for his mercy and be optimistic, because [the Prophet], peace be upon him, used to prefer optimism in all his affairs.[17]

This test from Almighty God is to raise your level [levels of heaven] and erase your sins.[18]

Do not seem confused or show signs of nervous tension. Be happy, optimistic, calm because you are heading for a deed that God loves and will accept. It will be the day, God willing, you spend with the women in paradise. Smile in the face of hardship young man/For you are heading toward eternal paradise.[19]

When the confrontation begins, strike like champions who do not want to go back to this world. Shout "Allahu Akbar," because this strikes fear in the hearts of the non-believers. God said: "Strike above the neck, and strike at all their extremities." Know that the gardens of paradise are waiting for you in all their beauty, and the women of paradise are waiting, calling out "Come hither, friend of God." They have dressed in their most beautiful clothing.[20]

The letter draws on the pleasures of paradise twelve times.[21] It mentions the houris twice[22] and the upcoming wedding to the houris once.[23] When the Justice Department posted the letter, it also published the names and pictures of the nineteen hijackers. The identification of the nineteen men was a leading story, but the letter provided the larger context for the headshots. Who were these men? What were they thinking? No matter how long one stared at the nineteen, their photos did not offer much clarity. The letter, however, suggested a message and tone. In news reports, the letter was described as disturbing or shocking. Muslim authorities and Islamic scholars decried the use of Islamic injunctions and prayers for such a murderous act, and US government officials sought to assure the public that the letter was not reflective of mainstream Muslim thought.[24]

What makes the letter especially disturbing is the way that discipline and piety intersect with killing. The ritual practice and focus on the veneration of God read like formulaic spiritual passages, but then the reader is confronted with phrases about sharpening knives. It creates a jolt.[25] Particularly repulsive are the references to the sacrificial killing of the "animals," meaning the passengers and crew of American Airlines Flight 11 (which crashed into the World Trade Center's North Tower), United Airlines Flight 175 (which crashed into the South Tower), American Airlines Flight 77 (which crashed into the Pentagon), and United Airlines Flight 93 (which crashed into a field in Shanksville, Pennsylvania). The dehumanization of the victims reveals the brutality of the hijackers and their vision of innocent people as religious sacrifice.

In addition to readers' immediate shock was another reaction that was expressed in the news stories and which over time became a stock rebuttal to the hijackers. This was the reaction to the letter's promise of the women of paradise.

TERRORISM AND THE HOURI

Even before September 11th, Israeli and American media outlets often highlighted the invocation of virgins associated with Palestinian suicide bombings. While the stories did not necessarily point to the promise of virgins as the motivation for the bombings, articles would often focus on how videos commemorating the martyrs made the connection between the mission and the houri. This created a familiarity with the idea of the virgins as a reward in paradise.

Within the new field of terrorism studies, the virgins gained more recognition. Bruce Hoffman in *Inside Terrorism* focuses on several dramatic instances of the promise of the virgins. He offers the example of a promotion that was aired on Palestinian television. In one scene, a Palestinian couple is caught in an Israeli Defense Force operation, and the woman is killed. When her boyfriend visits her grave, he is also shot dead. He then ascends to heaven where he is greeted by his companion. She is dancing with other female martyrs who are considered the houris in paradise.[26] While this drama accords special status to both men and women, it signals an ambiguity about the women of paradise, and it is unclear whether the houris are transformed martyrs or otherworldly beings.

For some Palestinian theological authorities, the houri constitutes reward. Hoffman cites chief mufti of the Palestinian Authority Police Force, Sheikh Abu Shukheudem, who details the special status of the martyr who feels no pain, is absolved of his deeds, is saved from the terrors of the grave, and will marry "seventy-two beautiful black-eyed women. . . ."[27] According to Hoffman, the promise of the virgins is echoed in other sermons as well as by a "Hamas-affiliated imam," and Sheikh Ismail al-Radwan who in a sermon refers to the "72 black-eyed women."[28] Allusions to the virgins may also be found in sermons, inspirational poems, and martyrdom testimonies of jihadi groups.

There are also references to the houris in texts and poems found in training centers in Afghanistan. *The New York Times* gathered 5,000 documents from abandoned al-Qa'ida and Taliban camps. These documents provide insight into the workings of the camps, from training programs to problems with management. While most of the documents involve the logistics of the training camps, there is evidence of poetry that refers to the promise of the virgins in paradise. This promise is reiterated in poems of the Taliban that emphasize nationalism, valor, honor, and sacrifice. In a poem entitled "Good News," Mawlawi Samiullah Abedzai writes of the value of death through martyrdom and the houris who await the believer.

> *Take Revenge; there are days of uprising.*
> *The world will remain; don't sell your faith in it, brothers;*
> *The houris are waiting for you; these days are coming.*
> *Abedzai requests martyrdom for Allah.*
> *Life in this world is enough; these are days of disaster.*[29]

The use of cosmological imagery on the battlefield illustrates the attempt to articulate the ineffable. We use such language when mundane words fail to signify what we want to express. What links the formulaic mentions of houris in al-Qaʻida, Palestinian, and Taliban writings is not that the women of paradise are such a superlative reward that they justify violent acts. Rather, the invocation of the women becomes the prime way to signify the wondrous realm of paradise, which stands in opposition to the difficulties of earthly battle and life. The houris became the rhetorical way of indicating readiness for violence. Consider the case of twenty-seven-year-old Brooklyn resident and Albanian citizen Agron Hasbajrami, who was arrested in 2011 on charges of providing material support for terrorists and eventually was sentenced to sixteen years in prison for attempting to support terrorism.[30] *The New York Times* reported that he had emailed his contact that "he wanted to 'marry with the girls in Paradise'" to indicate that he was ready to proceed.[31] Authorities are aware of the significance of the mention of the houri as a code.

FRUSTRATION, SEXUALITY, AND TERROR

In his book *Terror in the Mind of God*, Mark Juergensmeyer studies the mindset of religious violence. His book seeks to understand the motivations of people who employ violence due to religious belief. His case studies draw on a range of actors. Islamic militants form one subset, but there are others, such as people who undertake abortion-clinic bombings. In its most expansive argument, the book stresses the importance of religion and incorporating religious reasoning into a world that is being overwhelmingly secularized.

After extended interpretative and qualitative analysis, the book introduces a startling section entitled "Why Guys Throw Bombs," a play on Guy Fawkes's attempt to explode the House of Lords in the Gunpowder Plot of 1605. Juergensmeyer asks why religious violence is predominately "a male occupation."[32] For Juergensmeyer, men employ violence when they face sexual humiliation in a social setting. "Terrorist acts, then, can be forms of symbolic empowerment for men whose traditional sexual roles—their very manhood—is perceived to be at stake."[33] Yet women also partake in religious violence. Robert Pape, in *Dying to Win: The Strategic Logic of Suicide Bombing*, surveys 315 suicide attacks and concludes that 15 percent were perpetrated by women.[34] Juergensmeyer argues, however, that these attacks were driven by secular political ideologies or ethnic separatism, and he does not consider them religious acts. Instead, Juergensmeyer claims that religious terrorists are "bands of rogue males at the margins of respectability" who could be understood through the lens of sexual competence.[35] He connects masculinity and Islamic terrorism:

> Perhaps the easiest aspect to understand is the matter of sexual competence—by which I mean the capacity to have sex, an ability that is limited in traditional societies by moral restrictions and lack of opportunities. There is a certain amount of folklore about men and guns that cannot easily be dismissed—the notion, for instance, that sexual frustration leads to a fascination with phallic-shaped weaponry that explodes in a way that some men are unable to do sexually. As I mentioned earlier, the young bachelor self-martyrs in the Hamas movement enter into their suicide pacts almost as if it were a marriage covenant. They expect that the blasts that kill them will propel them to a bed in heaven where the most delicious acts of sexual consummation will be theirs for the taking. One young man who had committed himself to becoming a suicide bomber said that "when I exploded," and became "God's holy martyr," he was promised a place for himself and his family in paradise, seventy-two virgins, and a cash settlement for his family equivalent to six thousand dollars. It was the virgins that seemed to interest the young man the most.[36]

The problem with this argument is that it does not distinguish rhetoric from motivation. It presents a vision that Muslim men are, in essence, different from other men because of frustrated sexuality. In Juergensmeyer's assessment, Muslim men strike out because, in their gender-delineated societies, access to women is restricted, so they are lured by the promise of sex in the afterlife. Strangely, Marco Polo made the same argument about the eleventh-century Assassins who used the promise of an earthly garden paradise with beautiful women to motivate men to kill prominent political officials. Juergensmeyer's argument has, indeed, medieval roots. By not distinguishing rhetorical frames from political motivation, Juergensmeyer reduces other factors and cannot explain the scale of violence. We learn little about the specific bombers or the planned attacks in theories that invoke limited sexual access. Meanwhile, the image of sex in paradise resonates in American media. The question is not just why Americans focus on the potential of sex in paradise, but how this account became the template for understanding terror motivations and attacks.

THE WHITE GRAPE

How the "white grape" became a form of popular knowledge about the houri reveals print media's perceptions of Islam. The origin of this theory is an unlikely source: a German philological book about the Qur'an that has been described as an "international success story"[37] because it was the first Qur'anic Studies work to be featured in American and European publications.[38] The popularization of the white grape theory did not occur overnight, and the stages of its acceptance in print and new media demonstrate how knowledge about Islam is created and circulated in the twenty-first century.

In 2000, a German scholar writing under the pseudonym Christoph Luxenberg published a dense Qur'anic study entitled *Die syro-aramäische Lesart des Koran: Ein Beitrag zur Entschlüsselung der Koransprache.* Seven years later, in 2007, the book was translated into English and published as *The Syro-Aramaic Reading of the Koran: A Contribution to the Decoding of the Language of the Qur'an.* In the book, Luxenberg offers a bold reading of the Qur'an and in one of its chapters suggests that houris should really be translated as "white grapes." Of all the sections in his book, this was the passage most referenced in the media.

Luxenberg's larger methodological purposes are controversial, and scholars have debated both the value of and the best way to engage with his work. We could ask if houris actually *are* white grapes, but that would involve cosmic knowledge outside the parameters of the earthly world. We could investigate whether the word "houris" should be translated as "white grapes." This exercise is an important one, and a growing body of scholarship offers strong critiques,[39] useful additions,[40] and subtle arguments.[41] Yet the critical question for our purpose is not whether the white grapes theory is correct, but why so many people believe it to be true. From print media to online new media, there is acceptance of the idea that houris are white grapes. This acceptance developed, at first, in reference to Luxenberg's text. The white grape theory thus allows us to trace how true or false claims (depending on your interpretation) are generated and disseminated. This involves tracing how a text travels from scholarship to polemic to popular culture.

Before we contend with Luxenberg's argument, we have to note a significant difference between the Qur'an and the Bible. While the Qur'an and the Bible form the foundation of Islamic and Christian education, respectively, the authorship of the texts is understood differently. Muslims consider the Qur'an to be the literal word of God, delivered to Muhammad via the angel Gabriel. By contrast, some Christians see the Bible as the literal word of God, but the actual text is not considered to emanate directly from God. While both the Bible and the Qur'an are revered by their faith communities, the Qur'an has a singular sanctified status.

Since the nineteenth century, interpreting the Bible has taken a sharp analytical turn. In the educational institutions of Latin Christendom, reading the Bible meant that you glossed passages. You read them aloud, parsed the meaning of individual words and phrases, and contemplated the larger significance of the Bible or its books as God's message. The nineteenth century's embrace of scientific method led to a different way to read and to find meaning. Aside from the need to categorize, there was also the quest for origins. With the focus on textual commentary, scientific method, and historical origins, biblical criticism arose as a field of scholarship. Scholars studied the books of the Bible as textual productions and concluded that there were different authorial strands within the Bible. As biblical criticism developed, it battled against perceptions that the Bible contained holy words to be revered (as opposed to be analyzed), and it established a scholarly standard for reading and understanding religious books. However, the scholarly field stands apart from the full range of Christian beliefs. Consider a Pew Religious Landscapes Survey from 2014 that suggests that nearly one-third of Christian Americans believe that the Bible is the actual word of God to be understood literally.[42]

By contrast, the Muslim belief that the Qur'an is the literal word of God has an inviolability that disallows historical actors.[43] For Muslims, the Qur'an was not written; rather, it was sent by God. There are scholarly schools of thought, however, which set aside the concept of a divine origin and attempt an analytic exercise. Since John Wansborough's *Qur'anic Studies: Sources and Methods of Scriptural Interpretation* (1977), scholars have looked at the echoes and variations of biblical stories in the Qur'an and have attempted to write a history of Islam that is situated in the religious context of Judaism and Christianity. For them, Islam emerges within a religious context informed by different monotheistic sects.

Other scholars have turned to the principles underlying historical analysis and argue that the earliest texts should inform our understanding of Islamic societies, even if these early texts are not in Arabic. They have argued that Aramaic and Syriac texts are important sources for understanding the development of Islamic religious communities. By asserting that historical method requires valuing sources closest to the actual time period, they privilege seventh-century Aramaic and Syriac texts, even if they were not composed in Muslim communities. The initial forays into this kind of historical analysis started with Patricia Crone and Michael Cook's *Hagarism: The Making of the Islamic World* (1977), which suggests that Islam was one sect within the larger Arabic Judaic world. Following cues from Wansborough, Crone, and Cook, scholars challenge the traditional Islamic narrative. In effect, in the field of Qur'anic studies and the early history of Islam, these different methodologies have been used to explain shared resonances with stories from the Hebrew Bible and to employ a kind of biblical criticism of the Qur'an.

Luxenberg's book fits within the larger pattern of drawing on different methods for understanding the Qur'an and its context. Yet Luxenberg goes beyond employing lessons learned from biblical criticism. Instead, he makes the dramatic claim that the Qur'an was not composed in Arabic and suggests that the verses were composed in Aramaic and Syriac, a form of Aramaic spoken by Christian communities in the Middle East. When reading verses, Luxenberg considers whether there could be a Syriac meaning of a word, and then he chooses the most suitable meaning for his interpretation of the verse and the text.

When he comes to the houris, Luxenberg argues that the phrase in Sura 44.54 and 52.20, conventionally translated as "we paired them with dark, wide-eyed maidens," should be read as "we will make you comfortable under white, crystal-clear grapes."[44] To support this meaning, he suggests that the phrase invoking "to marry" or "to pair" (*zawwajnahum*) should be read as the verb signaling "to rest" (*rawwahnahum*). Once he rejects the concept of pairing, he questions how *hur 'in* could be seen as feminine beings. Luxenberg also criticizes the idea of wide eyes. He suggests that reading *'in* as the word for eyes is incorrect because it is not a common plural.

Instead of interpreting the houri as a female companion, as reflected in Islamic tradition, he finds inspiration in the symbolism of the grape in Christian texts. He suggests that the Syriac term can be translated as "white crystal-clear grapes," as suggested by the twentieth-century German scholar Tor Andrae's reading of the *Hymns of Paradise* by Ephrem the Syrian (d. 373). Luxenberg finds other ways to invalidate the conventional idea and meaning of the houri. He makes broad claims that assert that feminine companionship is incompatible with a holy book.[45] One problem that remains for Luxemberg is that the Qur'an also describes young servant boys (*ghilman* and *wildan*) who ensure that believers do not labor in the afterlife. Luxenberg suggests that these terms for male slaves should be read as "iced fruits" instead.

The implications are clear. By reading the Qur'an through a Syriac dictionary, he suggests that the Qur'an is a variation of Syriac texts. For Luxenberg, the Qur'an requires probing linguistic analysis. His reading of the passages about paradise argues that from the beginning, Muslim theologians have misinterpreted the reward of the afterlife. Rather than eternal companionship with maidens and being served by servant boys, believers are to enjoy white grapes and icy fruits.

Luxenberg's approach is not as important as his overall aim. In an attempt to create a more critical analysis of the Qur'an, he disregards the traditional narrative that has been accepted by Muslim scholars for centuries. Luxenberg started with the goal of proving that the Qur'an was a Christian text. Yet the aim of an analysis along the lines of biblical criticism was never quite established.[46] Instead, Luxenberg produced a book with a much more dramatic claim—that the Qur'an is a misunderstood text, and that Muslims have been deceived over the course of centuries. With the aim of elucidating the meaning of the Qur'an, Luxenberg may not have perceived his work as polemical, but his admirers in the media did. It was their political agenda that catapulted Luxenberg's book into the news.

WHITE RAISINS IN THE NEWS

Luxenberg's theory made an impact with the English reading public starting in 2002, even though his book was not translated into English until 2007. The white grape theory did not become popular because Luxenberg's argument was deeply investigated, but because it was compelling. Luxenberg refers to houris as "white grapes"; however, articles that popularized his theory to the English readers sometimes used "white raisins." The mistake is not inconsequential. Grapes are a luxury found in Qur'anic paradise. By contrast, raisins are a dried fruit commodity that emphasizes the absurdity of the houri as reward. In the newspaper articles that popularized the theory, grapes and raisins become fused in a way that they are not for Luxenberg or for the Islamic theological tradition.

Luxenberg's book might have remained in obscurity if it were not for the writer Ibn Warraq's article "Virgins? What Virgins?" which appeared in *The Guardian* newspaper in 2002.[47] The article made an impact in the media cycle, and it was used as the title of his subsequent book of essays *Virgins? What Virgins?* Ibn Warraq puts forward a particular polemic about Islam. His book *Why I Am Not a Muslim* engages the textual tradition in order to challenge conventions about scriptural interpretation, and his larger agenda involves dismissing Islamic religious education and defending the secular culture of the United States and Europe. The website of his foundation, the Institution for the Secularization of Islamic Society, makes the claim that Islamic society has been "held back by an unwillingness" to examine critically its traditions, beliefs, and practices.[48] Ibn Warraq's political stance accompanies his dismissal of standard Islamic beliefs. For example, when referencing the description of paradise in the Qur'an, he undercuts faith in the Qur'an as the word of God and Muhammad's role as a prophet: "Muhammed, or whoever is responsible for the descriptions."[49] This language signals skepticism toward the very basis of Islamic religious and historical narratives.

Ibn Warraq begins his article with a reference to Hamas's attempts to recruit men for suicide missions with the promise of "70 virgins, 70 wives, and everlasting happiness." He goes on to suggest that in the Qur'an there is a tacit endorsement of harming others in the name of martyrdom. He then turns to the opulent descriptions of paradise to represent the cosmic benefits awaiting Muslim males. Instead of noting that all Muslim men are provided heavenly virgins, however, and that martyrdom is not a requirement for receiving them, he reverses the logic. He suggests that all Muslim men have the potential to become jihadi *because* they all receive the same reward. Beyond this discussion of motivation, he displays familiarity with the theological tradition, interspersed with statements about sex ("entirely from the male point of view") and women ("women's sexuality is admitted but seen as something to be feared, repressed, and a work of the devil").[50]

He introduces Luxenberg's text as "the most fascinating book ever written on the language of the Koran, and if proved to be correct in its main thesis, probably the most important book ever written on the Koran."[51] Ibn Warraq does not analyze the work in depth, but he notes Luxenberg's "leaning in"[52] on Ephrem the Syrian. Ibn Warraq ends on a note of heavy sarcasm.

> As Luxenberg's work has only recently been published we must await its scholarly assessment before we can pass any judgments. But if his analysis is correct then suicide bombers, or rather prospective martyrs, would do well to abandon their culture of death, and instead concentrate on getting laid 72 times in this world, unless of course they would really prefer chilled or white raisins, according to their taste, in the next.[53]

What is fascinating about Ibn Warraq's extended review is that it does not consider whether Luxenberg is correct or not. Instead, it mocks the perversity of the jihadi who has the brutality to be able to kill, but not the intelligence to evaluate the rewards that have been promised to him. Ibn Warraq does not expound on Luxemberg's other seventy-five examples that deal with faith or the name of the Qur'an itself. Instead, he chooses the example that the reader would identify as perverse and crude. Were it not for Ibn Warraq's review in *The Guardian*, Luxenberg might not have been known by the English-speaking world. It was this review that propelled the white grape theory beyond the world of scholarship.

Four months later, Alexander Stille followed with a front-page *New York Times* article entitled "Scholars Are Quietly Offering New Theories of the Koran." In a balanced and nuanced article, Stille referred to the larger question of meaning in the Qur'an by discussing Ibn Warraq's and Luxenberg's texts and interviewing some Islamic scholars. The article raises the issue of the politics underlying scriptural interpretation. While Stille did not choose sides, he brought more attention to Luxenberg's argument, and he linked the white grape theory to the question of religious authority in Islamic regions.[54]

Two notable developments followed. *Newsweek*'s international edition (July 23, 2003) published Stefan Theil's "Challenging the Qur'an."[55] Theil focused on the lack of "critical study of God's undiluted word" that could bring about more modern Muslim societies. At the end of his article, Theil invoked the historical role of biblical criticism, in breaking "the church's grip on power—and in developing a modern, secular society."[56] Theil's article invoked the houris in the introduction, but also mentioned other arguments in Luxenberg's book (Theil calls them "bombshells"), such as the passages that suggest veiling for women is wrong and that the Qur'an is, in effect, a Christian liturgical document.

The article had political repercussions. On July 24, Pakistan's Information Minister Sheikh Rashid Ahmed ordered customs officials to confiscate the international edition of the magazine, and two days later announced that the article was banned on the grounds that it was insulting to Islam and would incite religious violence.[57] Bangladesh soon followed, with Bangladeshi information minister Tariqul Islam banning the magazine for "confusing and objectionable" contents.[58] Soon after, Reporters Without Borders called on the governments of Pakistan and Bangladesh to lift the ban. Meanwhile, *Newsweek*'s stringer in Peshawar fled to safety.[59]

Interestingly, the bans were implemented in Muslim-majority South Asian countries. The Egyptian ambassador to Pakistan solicited the Grand Imam of al-Azhar, al-Sharif Dr. Mohammad Sayed Tantawy, to address the issue. In "The Origins of the Qur'an," Tantawy attempted to refute Luxenberg's arguments about the development of the Qur'an by referring to the Qur'anic verses. The self-referential argument is clear for someone who sees the Qur'an as the word of God. It does not address the argument if you do not accept that premise.

After discussing veiling and how the Qur'an does not encourage women to be terrorists, Tantawy returns to the charge of houris as the motivation for Muslim terrorism:

> "Houris" mentioned in the original version of the Qur'an means "lustrous wide-eyed virgins" and not raisins and fruits. However, Atta's assumption that they will be married

off to 72 of them is not based on any grounds whatsoever. Besides, it must be made clear that suicide bombers do not blow themselves up for the sake of sexual reward in the afterlife. They have a worldly cause, be it misguided, namely that of freeing their families and countries from occupation, oppression, and injustice.[60]

The idea of the houris as white grapes or raisins gained more attention when it was discussed in an op-ed by *New York Times* columnist Nicholas Kristof in 2004. In "Martyrs, Virgins and Grapes," Kristof, like Ibn Warraq, begins with a reference to suicide bomber Mohamed Atta.[61] Alluding to the "beautifully written, but often obscure" Qur'an,[62] Kristof says that there is "growing evidence" that there may be Syriac or Aramaic words in the Qur'an. Kristof's use of the word "written" suggests that he either does not understand how Muslims believe the Qur'an was transmitted or chooses to ignore it. Kristof states that houris are "white" or "white grapes" in Aramaic and uses this translation to suggest that Islam must encourage the tradition of interpretation in order to defeat Muslim fundamentalism. "The history of the rise and fall of great powers over the last 3,000 years underscores that only when people are able to debate issues freely—when religious taboos fade—can intellectual inquiry lead to scientific discovery, economic revolution, and powerful new civilizations."[63] Kristof ends his op-ed with the statement that the world has a stake in seeing the Islamic world "get on its feet again," and that a rebirth of Islamic societies should begin with "future terrorist recruits" being promised a "plateful of grapes."[64]

Kristof penned another houri-inspired column five years later. Entitled "Islam, Virgins and Grapes," it used the example of the white grape theory in a discussion of a conference on Qur'anic scriptural interpretation that was held at the University of Notre Dame. The conference brought together scholars of the Qur'an who wanted to explore Islamic narratives. Attendees included Christoph Luxenberg and Nasr Hamid Abu Zayd, an Egyptian scholar whom the Egyptian courts forcibly divorced from his wife because of his philosophical approach to studying the Qur'an. For Kristof, the conference held the key to achieving freedom and lack of extremism in Islamic societies: "If the Islamic world is going to enjoy a revival, if fundamentalists are to be tamed, if women are to be employed more productively, then moderate interpretations of the Koran will have to gain ascendancy."[65] What is vital for Kristof is not a raisin or a grape or a feminine companion, but the freedom to exercise the same kind of analytic tools employed in biblical criticism.

The op-eds were syndicated and reprinted in newspapers across the nation.[66] After their appearance, there seemed to be a greater awareness of the white grape theory in print media and on the Internet. In effect, Ibn Warraq's article had set the template for how to understand the houris, Qur'anic interpretation, and the causes of terrorism. In linking the white grape theory with the current state of Muslim societies, Kristof lends greater prominence to the houri. The enhanced visibility of the white grape theory gave rise to a developing industry of Internet polemics and satires about Islam.

THE VIRGINAL COMEDY

The houri has become a joke. Cartoons, parodies, and Internet stories all draw on the promise of females in paradise to

ridicule Islam or to dismiss the motivations of suicide bombers. The comedy can have different tones and agendas. It can
be absurdist and celebratory, dark and pornographic, mock-
ing and dismissive. Yet, in each of these different registers,
the joke depends on the Muslim fool who believes that a virgin is waiting for him in heaven.

Some jokes about houris depend on the dissonance
between the promise of otherworldly companionship and
the reality of worldly sexuality. The specificity of the number seventy-two only adds to the absurdity. Comedian Steve
Martin offers a parody in which each of the seventy-two virgins voices her own feelings about her function. The piece
ridicules American popular culture more than anything else.
It begins: "Virgin No. 1: Yuck, Virgin No. 2: Ick, Virgin No.
3: Ew." Other statements include "Virgin No. 5: Do you like
cats? I have fourteen!" "Virgin No. 43: In the spirit of full
disclosure, I'm a single mom; Virgin No. 44: You like my
breasts? They were my graduation gift."[67]

Most of the references to the houri depict Muslims as
sexually deviant. This follows a polemic introduced in the
medieval era according to which Muslim heaven had a sexual, material nature that suited the carnal, base nature of
Muslim men, and Muhammad in particular. The target of
this critique was the religion of Islam, but it depended on
assumptions about the true nature of heavenly reward. For
authors in Latin Christendom, heaven was about closeness
to God, and any reminders of bodily functions or earthly
pleasures were repulsive. The resonance of this medieval
argument can be seen today on Internet sites that detail the
Islamic afterworld with fascination and disgust. For example, in "The Islamic Heaven: A Pornographic Brothel" the

Islamic paradise is depicted as a place where women spend an eternity as sex slaves.[68] There are also works that promulgate Luxenberg's theory, such as Norbert Pressburg's *What the Modern Martyr Should Know: Seventy-Two Grapes and Not a Single Virgin: The New Picture of Islam* (2011), which is based on a German publication entitled *Good Bye Mohamed* (2009).

In many jokes, the Muslim suicide bomber is a stock figure who thinks he will be receiving a reward, but discovers he has been tricked only after he kills himself and approaches the gates of heaven or hell. In one cartoon, a suicide bomber is escorted by the Devil to the entrance of hell in an elevator. The banner inside reads "Welcome Osama." The suicide bomber looks perplexed and scared, his eyes bulging and his finger under his lip, as the Devil reads "And on the 72nd level of Hell, we've got 72 suicide bombers who you promised would have 72 virgins each."[69] Some of the jokes involve women, as in the case of "Jihadi Jokesters: Waging Holy War for All the Hot Ukrainian Ladies." Alongside revealing shots of women, the jihadis are counseled: "The field hospital in Ukraine: You don't have to blow yourself up, the virgins are already here."[70]

In a blog post entitled "Another idiot" or "A real incident in Pakistan," we see a man wearing a suicide vest over his shalvar kameez. The caption reads, "A Taliban suicide bomber stopped and searched by police was found with a metal shield around his penis. Asked about the purpose of this protection, his response was: 'I want to keep my penis intact after the explosion, so as not to have sexual problems once I get my 72 virgins in heaven!'"[71]

In a news spoof, a potential female Taliban suicide bomber loathes the idea of seventy-two virgins in paradise. She runs away into the Islamabad Railway Station when she considers that the seventy-two virgins in paradise may actually be seventy-two virgin men. In this joke, what is a reward for men is a punishment for women. The piece ends with a punchline: "As she was taken into custody, Khalida Akhtar also reportedly told officers that she would have gladly sacrificed herself for higher causes if she could trade those 72 virgins for two experienced guys, a masseuse, a butler, and a chef."[72] Here the joke is a variant of the stock figure of the Muslim female who does not realize that she is oppressed by her own society.

The most controversial lampoon involving houris was an editorial cartoon designed by Jens Julius for the Danish *Jyllands-Posten* contest in 2005. This contest asked cartoonists to illustrate prophet Muhammad, as a challenge to the Muslim belief that he must not be depicted. The series of cartoons was meant to inflame, and it led to violence and worldwide protests. In one of the cartoons, a line of suicide bombers approaches the puffy clouds of heaven. Each man is burned, with smoldering bits emanating from his body. At the left of the frame, smoke suggests a long line of suicide bombers stretching into the distance. A figure identified as Muhammad (his name is written in the upper left corner of the frame) calls out to them, with arms thrown up into the air, "Stop Stop we have run out of virgins!" This joke replicates Latin Christendom's position that only Muslims could believe in something as preposterous as a material heaven, and only the most base would harm self and others for a sexual reward.

WHAT DOES MOHAMED ATTA RECEIVE?

The commentary, discussion, and jokes about the houris are one way that Americans have responded to the September 11th attacks. The question "What does Mohamed Atta receive?" has become a counterpoint to the promise of the houris found in the letter, and it has been used as the basis of a wholescale dismissal of Islam and its scriptural traditions. By focusing on the houri, news media emphasize the point that Muslims are sexually driven and lack understanding of their own texts. The secularism of Europeans and Americans is held out as a superior model for religion and society.

Beyond the question of what Mohamed Atta receives—a virgin or a grape—is the image that the houri presents as symbol, motivation, and metaphor. In Avi Perry's thriller *72 Virgins: Countdown to Terror Attack on US Soil*, the houri symbolizes the rewards of paradise for terrorism, and the association with violence is reinforced by the pathological figure of Abu Musa, who fantasizes about the seventy-two virgins.[73] He is a psychopath who turns on his German Muslim girlfriend Hilga and murders her.[74] Other invocations of the houri are strategic. *Seventy-two Virgins*, which British politician Boris Johnson wrote as a comedy, names the houris in the title but does not even refer to them in the book.

Within these allusions to the houri is an underlying question: What kind of person kills another in such a violent spectacle? Martin Amis, who wrote a fictionalized account of Mohamed Atta in the "Last Days of Mohamed Atta," offers his own insight:

Ah yes the virgins: six dozen of them in heaven—half a gross. Mohamed with his two degrees in architecture, his excellent English, his excellent German: Mohamed Atta did not believe in the virgins, did not believe in the Garden. How could he believe in such an implausibly and dauntingly, priapic paradise. He was an apostate: that's what he was. He didn't expect paradise. What he expected was oblivion. And strange to say, he would find neither.[75]

This bleak, nihilistic vision contradicts the story of the white grape, which makes the suicide bomber the idiot, the Muslim the illiterate simpleton, and the houri the sexualized reward that cannot be true. The houri is not just an arcane philological argument, an Internet meme, or a literary device. Instead, the houri has become a popular symbol that conveys a negative perception of Islam in a post–September 11th world.

The story about the letter, then, is neither a story about Islam nor about one Muslim's twisted interpretation of it. It is a story of how we read, how we assimilate knowledge, and what we choose to believe and argue. It is a story that reflects the storytellers—the scholars, the journalists, the polemicists, the cartoonists, the novelists, and the bloggers—more than it reflects the thoughts and motivations of Muslim men and women. And like most stories, this story is far more complicated than we allow it to be. After all, the fascination with the houri began centuries earlier.

THE WORD

LONG BEFORE IT BECAME ASSOCIATED with suicide bombers, the houri was an idea that captivated French and English writers. Reading about Islam or traveling in Ottoman territories, such writers encountered references to the houri and incorporated her feminine promise into their own literary imaginings. They transformed the Arabic *hur al-'in* and coined the word "houri" as their own. They made use of the houri as a myth, idea, and inspiration, and they introduced Islamic conceptions of feminine purity into discussions about women and their nature. For medieval Muslim commentators on the Qur'an, the houri was understood as a heavenly being, a promise, and a metaphor. For the early modern French and English, however, the houri was a woman, and she was a woman of the Muslim East whose beauty and purity came to represent the exemplary woman.[1]

The term "houri" entered French in the seventeenth century and English in the eighteenth century. Medieval texts had already presented the vision of an Islamic paradise where men could enjoy sex. In the thirteenth century, Macro Polo repeated the story of the Assassins and their false paradise of beautiful women, and in the fourteenth century, Sir John Mandeville's *Travels* contrasted Prester John's ideal kingdom with an Islamic heaven supplied with perpetual virgins.[2] Starting in the fifteenth century, these virgins were given names—*horhin* and *hora* in the anti-Islamic polemic *Confusión o confutación de la secta Mahomética*. By the seventeenth century, the French traveler du Loir had introduced the word "houri" in his discussion of Turkish men's treatment of women. The introduction of the word was associated with anti-Islamic polemics, French and English travels, and concern for the welfare of Muslim, especially Turkish, women. Once the term "houri" was introduced to the French and English reading public, it was used to describe beautiful females in the Ottoman Empire. Eventually, English women would be praised as even "handsomer than one of the houris."[3]

The discovery of the houri offered a way for French, English, and Spanish writers to frame their doubts about Islam as a religion and Turks as a people. The writers' concerns were centered on how Muslim men treated women and on the envisioned roles of women in the ultimate realm of paradise. Even while sixteenth-, seventeenth-, and eighteenth-century writers argued for better treatment of real women on earth, and criticized the promise of sexualized women in paradise, the term "houri" began to represent their own idealized form of the feminine. These dichotomous functions of the houri, as a source of criticism of Islam and a universal model of feminine beauty, demonstrate Europeans' conflicting views of Islam.

THE MUSLIM EAST AND ITS *HORA* AND *HORHIN*

Before houris entered the English imagination, the English had variously incorporated Saracens, Moors, and Turks into their worldview. The Saracen was the Greek and Latin name for inhabitants of the Syrian and Arabian deserts and was used in Christian theological texts to designate Arab Muslims. The Moors were the Spanish or North Africans whose skin color and appearance marked them as different from Christians. Moors may have been Muslim, but their religion was secondary to their geographic context. By contrast, the Turk was neither a person from a distinct civilization (such as Arabia) nor of a distinct type (of Spain and North Africa). Turks were associated with imperial power and were linked with the Balkans and Anatolia. People were understood through their different regions of origin: Spanish, North African, Arabian, Iranian, and Ottoman.

I will use the terms "Saracen," "Turk," and "Moor" to reflect the language of the sources. Each of these words was associated with the idea of a civilization east of Europe, and each of these places was also understood as an alternative to Christian kingdoms. I also use the expression "the Muslim East," which, although it may not have been used by late medieval and early modern writers, it evokes what they admired and feared.

References to the territories of the Muslim East were found in Latin traditions and Old French romances such as the late eleventh-century *Chanson de Roland*, a chanson de geste that narrates the Battle of Roncevaux in 778 between the French and the Muslim king Marsilla.[4] Offering a standard representation of Saracens, this romance circulated in a multilingual England from the twelfth to early fourteenth century.[5] As early as the 1330s, Saracen characters appeared in fifteen out of forty-four items in *The Auchinleck Manuscript*, a pre-Chaucerian text that includes hagiographic legends, religious narrative and instruction, poems of satire and complaint, and humorous tales and debates.[6]

The notion of a sensual paradise that promised celestial sex had long troubled theologians of Latin Christendom, who were offended by the material rewards of the Islamic afterworld. The discomfort with sexuality in paradise is plainly manifested in an anti-Islamic polemic from the sixteenth century. Juan Andrés (d. 1515) was a Spanish Muslim jurist who converted to Christianity. His text *Confusión o confutación de la secta Mahomética y del Alcorán* (1515) offered an influential primer on Islam. It was translated into Italian (1537), French (1574), Dutch (1580), Latin (1594), German (1598), and English (1652).[7] The text offers a critique of Islam and includes extensive treatment of the virgins of paradise called *horhin* or *hora*.

Chapter nine, dedicated to paradise, mentions chaste virgins "which God hath created in paradise, and they are called Horhin, and in the singular number Hora."[8] Andrés describes their garments, their beauty, and their jewelry. The virgin embraces "the Moore, and the Moore her," and they continue for fifty years "taking all manner of pleasure that a man can have with a woman."[9] Andrés emphasizes that God is said to approve of their actions and rewards them with his presence. "And after they shall have thus taken their pleasure God shall say, O my servants, now ye have eaten and drank, and are clothed, dressed, and adorned with jewels, and have taken your pleasure in my Paradise and glory, I will now shew you my glorious face."[10]

Juan Andrés writes:[11]

> But tell me, O Moore, what will the women who shall be
> at this feast, say and doe, when they shall see themselves

comfortless, and when they shall see their husbands they had
in this world, sporting with and embracing their Virgins. . . .
I say, that the womens glory will be turned into punishment,
and sorrow, especially when each of the men shall take his
Virgin, and shall go away with her to his Mansion or fortress, and the women shall be left alone and comfortless like
widdowes.[12]

Here the complaint about the sensual heaven is that it leaves
wives abandoned, and forces them into an effective widow-
hood. The mention of the *hora* and *horhin* is significant, but
remains within the context of theological concepts. It is not
until we encounter more imperial French and English ambi-
tions that the houris are reconsidered as reflecting deplored
or exalted differences of the Muslim East.

Since the publication of Edward Said's *Orientalism* in
1978, it has been generally accepted that English and French
representations of the Muslim East were driven by European
self-projections and fantasies. Influenced by the colonial
paradigm, medievalists too have engaged with the question of how the Muslim East is represented. But the image
of the Saracen, Moor, and Turk is pre-colonial, and its basis
was not projected fantasy, but real-world contact. Before
Saracens, Moors, and Turks put in their appearance in plays,
poems, and travel literature, the English had actual contacts
with Muslims. These pre-colonial contacts were marked not
by imperial domination, but by trade and diplomacy that
"undid Eurocentric confidence."[13]

The British exchange with Turks was substantial and
eclipsed those with other non-Christian groups. Nabil
Matar offers a useful perspective on early English contacts with Turks. In the Elizabethan period, there may have

been between eighty and one hundred Portuguese Jews in England, who would have been identified as Marranos. There would have been even fewer Amerindians, who were considered "de-Indianized" because they were on their way to being civilized through conversion to Christianity. Matar notes that, by contrast, Turks and Moors traded in English and Welsh ports, stood trial in English courts, and eminent ambassadors and emissaries impressed London "with their charm, cuisine, and 'Araby' horses."[14] Playwrights of the time wrote numerous plays in which Turks and Moors figured, but Turks were not just figures in Anglo-Saxon stories or Elizabethan plays. They were real people whom Britons were able to encounter in their streets and in their towns. Beyond maritime exchange and trade, there were meetings between Britons and Turks at the highest levels of court; trade relations with Safavid Persia, Mughal India, and the Ottoman court began under the reign of Elizabeth I (r. 1558–1603). Elizabeth herself had a personal correspondence with the *valide sultan* or queen mother Safiye (d. 1619), who encouraged Elizabeth to trade with her son Mehmed III (r. 1595–1603). The two queens exchanged letters intended to support Anglo-Ottoman trade and presented each other with gifts. Elizabeth sent her own portrait, a coach, jewelry, and cosmetics. Safiye sent a suite of Turkish costumes to the English queen who appreciated intricate textiles.[15] For the British, the Turks were the most emulated foreigners.

If Turks were familiar in the sixteenth century, they were nevertheless depicted as foreign and strange. As Matar masterfully demonstrates, the discourse of English superiority and Moorish and Turkish infidelity preceded colonial enterprises. By the end of the seventeenth century, the English had relations with Muslims while both accepting the reality of and rejecting the validity of Islamic religion. Yet there was a developing opposition to Islam. While other groups such as Jews and Eastern Christians were tolerated, Muslims did not fit into the same schema. Other groups were in a position of weakness, and Muslims remained powerful in the face of English and Christian imperialism. Matar notes that Jews, Eastern Christians, French Protestants, and English and Irish Catholics had never "sunk British ships, captured and enslaved British mariners or threatened the economic welfare of the realm."[16]

Matar further argues that initially Amerindians were understood through the lens of the infidel. Once the power of the Moroccan sultans diminished, Turks and Moors were understood within the same rhetorical frames. This conflation amounted to a "representation of a representation."[17] Britons perceived the Amerindians as infidels and demonized them as engaging in heathenish practices such as sodomy. The colonists' defeat of the Amerindians gave rise to a new paradigm for demonizing a group of people. Simply put, the English recognized Turkish power, but writers had difficulty placing the Ottomans within an English worldview. English writers borrowed from the earlier characterizations of infidel practices such as sodomy, and began to demonize Turks as a nation.

It is within this larger context of power that the image of the Turk appears. Beginning in the Elizabethan era and throughout the Enlightenment, the Turk offered the image of a depraved character. To "turn Turk" or to convert was the greatest betrayal of a new Christian economic imperialism where diplomacy and trade brought England and the Ottoman Empire into close contact.[18] In Elizabethan drama, the Turk was a threatening villain. Pubs, inns, and coffeehouses often had signage showing a Turk's head with a turban and scimitar.[19] This common imagery of the Turk combined fear and aspiration for imperial British power.

TRAVEL WRITING

Starting in the seventeenth century, travel writing about the Ottoman Empire and Iran became an established genre. Now representation of the Muslim East was no longer dependent on Turks and Moors in England; travel literature offered the larger context of the Muslim East through eyewitness accounts. The writing often foregrounded what was remarkable about a particular locale, people, or tradition. The genre was both outward-looking and inward-looking. By exploring the world outside England and France, writers and readers satisfied their curiosity about foreign lands and peoples, and by way of contrast, they were also able to comment on what they saw as the strengths and failings of their own societies.

In the eighteenth century, the English made gains in the Americas, West Indies, Ireland, India, Guyana, and sub-Saharan Africa. In the seventeenth century, before these territorial gains, the English already longed for empire. Travel writing developed "English proto-nationalism" and began to provide themes that would dominate later characterizations of the Middle East.[20] While the Ottoman Empire was still seen as "sophisticated, civilized, urbane, orderly, and austere,"[21] in the abstract the Muslim East was understood as a realm of "corruption, constraint, slavery, mystery, peculiar sexual practices, slothfulness, decadence."[22] Sometimes comparisons between different regions helped the English make sense of their world, and descriptions of women in foreign societies were part of a discourse about freedom.[23] The Ottoman beauty was restrained, veiled, with skin of polished ivory, whereas Irish women were coarse, unruly, unbounded, and dirty.[24]

The hunger for reading about the Muslim East was reflected in many print runs. Henry Blount's *Voyage to the Levant* went through eight reprints between 1636 and 1671.[25] Richard Knolles's *Generall Historie of the Turks* went through seven editions between 1603 and 1701.[26] George Sandys's *A Relation of a Journey Begun An: Dom: 1610* was a bestseller that was reprinted many times and offered an account of Sandys's travel through France, Italy, the eastern Mediterranean, Venice, Istanbul, Alexandria, Cairo, Jerusalem, and Malta. Such books were read not only to understand the Ottoman Empire, which was seen as the other imperial heir to the Romans, but also to formulate British policy.[27]

As Saree Makdisi argues, there was no dominant racial and cultural identity in England around 1800. The struggle to understand the world was taking place alongside the articulation of an English identity. As an English, white identity emerged, Africans, Arabs, and Scottish Highlanders were disparaged.[28]

Seventeenth-century French travel writing portrayed the Ottoman Empire as threatening. The Persians were seen as more mannered and civilized[29] than the menacing Turks. By the late seventeenth century, there was in travel writing a fully developed portrayal of Islam and regional practices.[30] Muslims were depicted with certain dominant characteristics. In particular, lust (*luxure*) and coarseness (*paillardise*) were "considered essential features of Muslim identity."[31] For the writers, these perceived traits offered proof that Islam was false. Its lascivious nature could be detected in the pleasures of paradise.[32]

Passages from the travel writer du Loir are striking. Du Loir praised the honesty of the Turk and the sound reason of the Ottoman court.[33] It is not surprising that travel writing, with its focus on the interior landscape and encounters with women, would be the genre that gave the term "houri" to French and English audiences. Du Loir named the houri and understood her function as a feminine model of Islam.

In fact, du Loir makes an argument similar to that of Juan Andrés, that Turkish men show little regard for Turkish women. The difference between Juan Andrés and du Loir is the source of their authority and the object of their critique. Juan Andrés used theological texts to criticize Islam as a faith. Du Loir used observation to criticize Turkish men. It is in the context of du Loir's world of travel, trade, and ideas that the houri was introduced to the wider French and English reading public.

What little we know of du Loir comes from his fascinating letters, *Les Voyages du Sieur du Loir* (1654).[34] He left from Marseille in November 1639, visited Malta, Smyra, and Constantinople, where he lived from January 1640 to March 1641. He returned through Greece and Venice. *Les Voyages* comprises ten letters he wrote to officials describing the lands he visited. In his writings, he also offers transliterations of Arabic and Ottoman texts. The genre of the voyage combines instruction and *belles choses*; knowledge and aesthetics were fused. As Michael Harrigan observes, the guiding principle of the genre was that "what should instruct should also be pleasing."[35]

In the sixth letter to Monsieur Le Pailleur, written in Constantinople on August 5, 1640, du Loir begins by remarking that the Turks are not as coarse and brutal as many have imagined. Instead, they have gentle manners. Whereas the Greeks who live in the same climate are perfidious and vain, the Turks are sincere and modest.[36] After discussing Turkish women's visits to baths, he describes Turkish women, their marriage ceremonies, their musical instruments, and their dances.[37] Du Loir notes that all children are considered legitimate, irrespective of their mother's station, and that men still have obligations after a marriage is dissolved.[38] He praises Turkish women for their strengths, sweetness, and beauty,[39] and criticizes Turkish men for treating women with great indignity. Men leave them in ignorance, only to pray to God, and do not let them enter mosques. For du Loir what is more incredible is that "they do not even want them to enter their paradise where they hope to be with others whom they call Houris and they believe they are in the world only as reproductive vessels, and their only purpose is for their pleasure."[40] It was through this passage that the word "Houris" entered the French language in 1654. The French Academy admitted the term in the fourth edition of their dictionary in 1762 and officially recognized the women of paradise who "contribute to the pleasures" of Mahomet's elect.[41]

The term "houri" entered the French language at a time when the French were fascinated by the idea of a Muslim East and were reading translations of Arabic literature. To give some perspective, the word "seraglio" entered English in 1581 and "harem" in 1634. Between 1704 and 1777, Antoine Galland published the French translation of *1001 Nights*. Montesquieu's *Persian Letters*, with its descriptions of bathhouses, was published in 1721. However, the focus on the *voyage* offered a different kind of knowledge to French readers. Du Loir did not criticize Islam as a religion as much as he complained about the nature of Turkish men. The central problem, for du Loir, was that the Turkish men did not properly value their beautiful, charming women. In this du Loir anticipates eighteenth-century concerns about Muslim women. Whereas the seraglio or the harem became a site that illustrated Oriental despotism in the seventeenth century, during the eighteenth century, the focus was not just on the space and its significance, but on the treatment of its women.[42]

The most famous example that melds the harem with the image of the houri may be found in the letters of Lady Mary Montagu (d. 1772), who accompanied her husband Edward Wortley Montagu when he was posted as the British ambassador to the Ottoman Empire in 1717. Her letters, published after her death in 1763, are notable for their attention to women; Montagu had access to women's areas that male writers did not.[43] She was able to offer a detailed view of women's lives in the Turkish court. Her readers tended to ignore her deist and freethinking philosophy, and focus on her encounters with Turkish women in the *hammam*, or bathhouse.[44] Her account of women's interior lives was read in the context of tales of the seraglio that explored political and familial values.[45]

Montagu does not explicitly mention houris, but she draws upon the aesthetics of the houri in her descriptions of Turkish women. Fair Fatima is depicted in terms of the "harmony of her features," "the exact proportion of her body," "that lovely bloom of complexion," and "the unutterable enchantment of her smile."[46] Fatima's eyes, houri-like, are large and striking: "But her eyes!—large and black, with all the soft languishment of the blue!"[47] Fatima is clad in exquisite clothing.

> She was dressed in a caftan of gold brocade, flowered with
> silver, very well fitted to her shape, and shewing to admiration
> the beauty of her bosom, only shaded by the thin gauze
> of her shift. Her drawers were pale pink, her waistcoat green
> and silver, her slippers white satin, finely embroidered: her
> lovely arms adorned with bracelets of diamonds, and her
> broad girdle set round with diamonds.[48]

Referring to Fatima's twenty maids as "ancient nymphs," Montagu remarks that she "could not help thinking, I had been some time in Mahomet's paradise."[49]

Montagu tries to rebut the view, found in English writings, that Muslim women were considered to be soulless, allowing Muslim men to justify their sexual slavery. While Montagu rejects this idea, she also offers a caveat:

> 'Tis true, they say, that are not of so elevated a kind, and
> therefore must not hope to be admitted into the paradise
> appointed for the men, who are to be entertained by celestial
> beauties. But there is a place of happiness destined for
> souls of the inferior order, where all good women are to be
> in eternal bliss.[50]

The unnamed celestial beings are the houris. Montagu invokes paradise in explicit and implicit ways. Not only does she refer to the paradise of the houris, but she is influenced by the aesthetics of the houris in her descriptions of Turkish women.

It was in the genre of travel writing that English and French readers first encountered real Muslim females. Unlike earlier plays and theological texts, the female was not the daughter of the tyrant or a wife of Muhammad. Rather, she was a real woman and part of the social fabric. The women about whom Lady Montagu wrote were not in the public space, but they nonetheless offered new access to the social world of the Ottoman Empire. Lady Montagu sought to entertain and enliven, and to report the beauty and sophistication of the women, but she also reinforced the vision of the odalisque, the female slave or concubine confined in the harem. Ultimately, however, she depicted a different kind of harem. This was a harem that was free, generous, spirited, and offering true companionship, although it remained a confined courtly urban space. Lady Montagu did not have the same kind of access to women with different material realities. As the image of these exquisite women became more prominent in the European artistic tradition, Montagu reinforced, consciously or not, feminine aesthetics that were based on the houris of Islamic paradise.

In travelers' accounts, we encounter the first detailed introduction to the Muslim East as a place of lived experience. As the writers strove to characterize local customs, readers were able to glimpse the lives of actual women. The earlier representations of Saracens, Turks, and Moors were centered on male power and paternalistic tyranny. It is not until travel literature that we find the intimate view of the bathhouse, of the sultan's domestic quarters. It is in these interiors that readers are introduced to the Muslim East through its women.

FIGURE 2.1 *The Great Odalisque* (*La Grand Odalisque*), 1819. Jean-Auguste-Dominque Ingres (1780–1867). Oil on canvas, 91 × 162 cm.RF 1158. Photo: Thierry Le Mage. © RMN-Grand Palais / Art Resource, NY.

The descriptions of interior life inspired fascination with the image of the Muslim woman in the harem or seraglio. Jean-Auguste-Dominique Ingres (d. 1867) had already painted *The Great Odalisque* in 1814 (Figure 2.1), but we know from his notebooks that he read a French translation of Montagu's letters between 1815 and 1817.[51] In 1862, at the age of eighty-two, he returned to the images in the letters to paint the *hammam* scene depicted in *The Turkish Bath* (Figure 2.2).[52] The painting, an exercise in depicting the female nude, shows life within the confines of the bath. Women are free of clothing and of the outside world as they provide companionship to each other. Some are languid, others play music, yet others dance. The scene is of a closed, inside world. The sense of seclusion is reinforced by the painting's aperture. We look into the bath, and we see the beauties within.

FIGURE 2.2 *The Turkish Bath*, 1862. Jean-Auguste-Dominque Ingres (1780–1867). Oil on wood, 110 × 110 cm; diam. 108 cm.RF 1934. Photo: Gérard Blot. © RMN-Grand Palais / Art Resource, NY.

FEMININE BEAUTY

This fascination with the closed-off world of the harem was accompanied by a celebration of the houri as a model of feminine beauty. The first developed mention of the houri in English is in Horace Walpole's letters. Walpole (d. 1797), the fourth Earl of Oxford, was the author of *The Castle of Otranto* (1765), a romance that shaped the gothic genre. His letters commented on the personalities and manners of his age. In 1743 Walpole presented the Earl of Lincoln with a parody of a Persian letter, ostensibly sent by "Thamas Kouli Kan Schah

Nadir" to the Earl. In the letter, the Earl is teased as being "highly favoured among women." The fictitious shah promises to send him fifty beautiful maidens from Persia, fifty from Georgia, fifty from Circassia, and three thousand black eunuchs. He concludes the letter with this wish:

> Adieu! Happy young man! May thy days be as long as thy manhood, and may thy manhood continue more piercing than Zufager, that sword of Hali which had two points: and when thou art full of years, may Azrael the angel of death conduct thee to those fields of light, where the favourites of the Prophet taste eternal joys in the arms of the beautiful houris![53]

Aside from the mention of houris in this parody, Walpole also referred to the beauty of houris in speaking of lovely English women. In 1745, he wrote that Lady Granville, who had come late to a party, was "dressed like Imoinda, and handsomer than one of the houris."[54] Imoinda is the beauty in Aphra Behn's (d. 1689) novel *Oroonoko: or the Royal Slave*, the story of an African prince who is enslaved, and then reunited with his love Imoinda on a slave plantation in South America. The novel ends with Oroonoko killing Imoinda and their unborn child and exacting revenge on those who have stolen his freedom and happiness. (Walpole has here conflated two locales, by mentioning houris and Imoinda in the same sentence.) Walpole also wrote on one occasion that his nieces "looked as well as the houris."[55] In 1780, Walpole writes in another letter that "in Mahomet's paradise every true believer will fling his handkerchief to one of the houris in preference to all the rest."[56]

Samuel Johnson (d. 1784), the renowned English critic and lexicographer, displayed English ideas about women and Islam in his play *Irene: A Tragedy* (1749).[57] The play tells the story of a Greek woman captured by Sultan

Mahomet during the conquest of Constantinople in 1453. The plotline is based on one of the stories in Knolles's *Historie of the Turkes* in which the sultan is so enchanted with the captive Irene that he ignores his royal duties. Johnson shifts the focus of the drama to Irene when the sultan offers her the opportunity to be his queen if she converts to Islam. Eventually, she is killed in a palace intrigue.

The play contains a reference to houris: "Suspend thy Passage to the Seats of Bliss, Nor wish for Houris in Irene's arms."[58] The play's epilogue may have been written by Johnson or William Yonge, Walpole's secretary of war.[59] It provides a clear articulation of English ideas about women, power, and Islam. Here Johnson (or Yonge) offers a woman's rejoinder to the practice of polygamy.

> *Marry a Turk! A haughty, tyrant king,*
> *Who thinks us women born to dress and sing*
> *To please his fancy—see no other man—*
> *Let him persuade me to it—if he can:*
> *Besides, he has fifty wives; and who can bear*
> *To have the fiftieth part her paltry share?*
> *'Tis true, the fellow's handsome, straight and tall;*
> *But how the devil should he please us all?*
> *My swain is little—true—but be it known,*
> *My pride's to have that little all my own.*
> *Men will be ever to their errors blind,*
> *Where woman's not allow'd to speak her mind;*
> *I swear this eastern pageantry is nonsense,*
> *And for one man—one wife's enough in conscience.*

In vain proud man usurps what's woman's due;
For us alone, they honour's paths pursue;
Inspir'd by us, they glory's heights ascend;
Woman the source, the object, and the end.
Though wealth, and power, and glory they receive,
These all are trifles, to what we can give.
For us the statesman labours, hero fights,
Bears toilsome days, and wakes long tedious nights;
And when blest peace has silenc'd war's alarms,
Receives his full reward in beauty's arms.[60]

The promise of polygamy is ridiculed by the female narrator, who recognizes women in general as "the source, the object, and the end." The play was performed for twelve nights on Drury Lane in 1749. While Johnson received a sum for the performance, he considered it a failure.

In many ways, the widening world of the seventeenth and eighteenth centuries is reminiscent of the globalization of the late twentieth century. Perceptions of Islam were initially determined by anti-Islamic polemics; through travel, these perceptions expanded to consider the lived experience of Muslim societies. In the world that consumed travel writing, the houris were an idea that marked Islamic beliefs as unjust to Muslim women, but also as idealized for Christian women. The houri may have been one of the bases on which writers attacked Islamic beliefs, but she also became one of the metaphors used to signal extraordinary beauty.

While no writer cited in this chapter defended the idea of the houri as a sexualized companion for Muslim men in paradise, all were taken by the term as it evoked the ideal female. From that point onward, houris began to escape the bounds of the Muslim East and become a new way to characterize the Christian lady of beauty. The term "houri" entered French writing in the seventeenth century and developed in English writing in the eighteenth century, but it was in the following century that the term would transcend its Islamic origins entirely.

THE ROMANCE

THE MORNING AFTER JANE EYRE agrees to marry Mr. Rochester, he takes her to Milcote to buy new dresses and to visit the jewelers. Rochester is the indulgent lover who wants to adorn Jane in brightly colored fabrics—rich amethyst silk and superb pink satin. Reserved, modest, principled, Protestant Jane prefers a sober black satin and pearl-grey silk and refuses to enjoy the shopping spree and all it suggests.[1] Yet, as Rochester's child's governess and bride-to-be, Jane is forced to accept his authority. On the ride home, he seeks her gaze and wants to hold her hand. Jane refuses to play the lover's game:

> I thought his smile was such as a sultan might, in a blissful and fond moment, bestow on a slave his gold and gems had enriched: I crushed his hand, which was ever hunting mine, vigorously, and thrust it back to him red with the passionate pressure.
>
> "You need not look in that way," I said; "if you do, I'll wear nothing but my old Lowood frocks to the end of the chapter. I'll be married in this lilac gingham: you may make a dressing-gown for yourself out of the pearl-grey silk, and an infinite series of waistcoats out of the black satin."
>
> He chuckled; he rubbed his hands. "Oh, it is rich to see and hear her!" he exclaimed. "Is she original? Is she piquant?

I would not exchange this one little English girl for the Grand Turk's whole seraglio, gazelle-eyes, houri forms, and all!"

The Eastern allusion bit me again. "I'll not stand you an inch in the stead of a seraglio," I said; "so don't consider me an equivalent for one. If you have a fancy for anything in that line, away with you, sir, to the bazaars of Stamboul without delay, and lay out in extensive slave-purchases some of that spare cash you seem at a loss to spend satisfactorily here."

"And what will you do, Jane, while I am bargaining for so many tons of flesh and such an assortment of black eyes?"[2]

When Charlotte Brontë published Jane Eyre in 1847, her readers were well acquainted with a literary and artistic world that represented the Ottoman Empire through images of harems, odalisques, sultans, and slaves. As Joyce Zonana has astutely argued, readers would have automatically seen that the Bluebeard-like story of *Jane Eyre* had parallels with the sultan-harem narrative in which a sultan entraps helpless beauties.[3] Rochester was behaving like an indulgent, authoritative Ottoman sultan. Jane, the quiet, rebellious girl, would have been consigned to "harem" life as a concubine in a bigamous marriage. Brontë opens the novel with Jane sitting "cross-legged like a Turk" and continues with references to Rochester as a sultan.[4] Beyond these descriptors, the novel exposes the power of men over the fates of women. Rochester locks up his first wife Bertha and tries to entrap Jane as a second wife. The feared abusive sultan who imprisons women is actually an English gentleman.

Jane Eyre reflects the entrenched perceptions that the success of the Turks was due to the absolute despotism of the sultan and, by extension, the tyranny of Turkish men over their wives. Jane's exchange with Rochester is about the possibility of a Turkish-style slavery existing within an English home. As a governess, Jane is an elevated servant, after all, and her marriage to Rochester could in a sense formalize her domestic slavery. When Jane lashes out about the slave markets of Istanbul, she resists the implication of Rochester's purchases. She refuses to feel enslaved. She is wary of relinquishing her autonomy to a husband. Rochester, by contrast, sees Jane as the beautiful prize, better than the sultan's harems and slave markets of the Muslim East. Rochester's flirtation and flattery as a lover and his promise as a future husband are represented by the phrase "houri forms, and all!" When calling to mind the houris, Rochester is not referring to subjected women. He is invoking a specific image of feminine beauty.

Superficially, Rochester's reference to the houri suggests that he is an overbearing master who would enjoy a harem of powerless beauties. But if we understand the houri, as the English and French did, as also a universal model of feminine beauty, then Rochester is seen to be a lover praising the spiritual and physical beauty of his future bride. The irony is that Rochester is like a sultan in his desire for a multiple marriage. Brontë did not just draw on the image of the oriental despot; she also reflected the nineteenth-century understanding of feminine models of beauty as purity.

References to houris can be found in nineteenth-century English poems, travel accounts, novels, monthly magazines, and engravings. The houri appears in celebrated literary works such as *Don Juan*, *Ivanhoe*, *Jane Eyre*, *The Island of Doctor Moreau*, and in lesser-known texts, like *The Algerine Captive* and *Star of Love*. In this literature, the houri is simultaneously a tenet of Islam, a universal model, a standard of beauty, and an image of frivolity. The houri that emerged in English literature used Islamic beliefs to shape conceptions of feminine Christian virtue. This chapter traces the emergence of this nineteenth-century houri and demonstrates how the houri became a central metaphor for feminine ethics and beauty. English writers took the houri and made her their own. They created a distinct houri that reinforced the oriental sultan-slave paradigm, presented images of wonder, and offered a contested model for feminine ethics.

The houri of Islamic theological texts was not a woman as much as a feminine spiritual being. In nineteenth-century English literature, the houri becomes a woman, an oppressed woman, and ultimately, a Christian woman. What started as an Islamic figure transformed into a universal Christian ideal.

BYRON AND THE ORIENTAL TALE

By the early nineteenth century, the houri was a conventional metaphor in the genre of the oriental tale. This popular genre did not depend on travel to the Muslim East or even translations of Arabic and Persian works. However, the texts engaged with the idea of the Muslim East and questioned associated social and political values.

The work that inaugurated the form of the oriental tale was William Beckford's *History of the Caliph Vathek* (which was translated into English from the French in 1786). In the story, the grandson of Harun al-Rashid was an oriental despot who is "much addicted to women."[5] His fifth palace, known as the "Retreat of Joy, or the Dangerous," held "young females as beautiful as the Houris and not less seducing, who never failed to receive, with caresses, all whom the Caliph allowed to approach them."[6] Unlike earlier allegorical works like Montesquieu's *Persian Letters* (1721), Voltaire's *Zadig*

(1749), and Samuel Johnson's *Rasselas* (1759), *History of the Caliph Vathek* presented a world of "intense personal fantasy and gratification."[7] Whereas the earlier works had used the Muslim East as an allegory, in the Romantic works, the writer's self was projected within the Muslim landscape. *The History of the Caliph Vathek* also provided a line of demarcation between the eighteenth century's oriental tale and the nineteenth century's romance.[8] The oriental tale went on to develop into a genre that included Walter Savage Landor's *Gebir* (1798), Southey's *Thalaba* (1801), Thomas Moore's *Lalla Rookh* (1817), Byron's *Turkish Tales* (1813–1816), and Julia Sophia Pardoe's *Romance of the Harem* (1839).

In the oriental tale, women likened to houris were often beautiful daughters. In "The Slippers: A Turkish Tale" (1805), we read of Bakarak, who was "one of the richest merchants in Bagdad . . . yet he had a treasure in his possession still more desirable than his ivory or his pearls; it was the enchanting Zelica, his only child, who, scarcely fifteen, and blooming like a Houri of the Paradise. . . ."[9] In "Wealth, Wisdom, and Virtue: An Eastern Tale" (1805), the narrator casts his eyes on a Muslim's daughter: "she was beautiful as a full moon; charming as one of the Houri's—It was Fatima, the daughter of Hassan: I burned for her."[10]

It was due to the poet Byron that the term took on a more expansive, Romantic meaning in which the encounter with beauty had its own form of sanctity. George Gordon, the sixth Lord Byron (d. 1824), had read about the Ottoman Empire and was influenced by Lady Montagu's accounts of her travels. His journeys to Greece, the Balkans, Spain, and Anatolia were reflected in his poems and letters, and his writings were perceived as authentic because of his travels. Yet he still projected his persona onto his interpretation of the Muslim East.

As Edward Said cautions, the actual Orient "provoked a writer to his vision; it very rarely guided it."[11] Lord Byron's East was limited to the Near East, the East of the Balkans, and Turks. He did not venture into Arab, Iranian, Egyptian, or North African regions. His experiences, for the most part, were Mediterranean and drew upon the image of the fearful Turk who oppressed Greeks and hapless, pure women. In many of his poems that involve Turks, houris provide a recurrent image of beauty, purity, and restrained sexuality.

Byron's references to the houri appear as early as his first published work, which made him famous. In *Childe Harold's Pilgrimage* (1812), Byron introduces Childe Harold as the Romantic hero who finds himself though travel and adventure. In the poem, we read of houris who are likened to Spanish women:

> *Match me, those houris, whom ye scarce allow*
> *To taste the gale lest Love should ride the wind*
> *With Spain's dark-glancing daughters—deign to know*
> *There your wise Prophet's paradise we find,*
> *His black-eyed maids in Heaven, angelically kind.*[12]

In the final line, Byron shows his familiarity with Islamic tradition. Yet the houris in the poem are akin to Spanish women with their dark eyes. The Spanish are an earthly proxy for Muslim beauty. Furthermore, while houris may be pure, they still have latent desire in Byron's vision.

In another series of poems categorized as the "Turkish Tales," Byron provides his own interpretations of the oriental tale. These poems include *The Giaour* (1813), *The Bride of Abydos* (1813), *The Corsair* (1814), *Lara* (1814), and *The*

Siege of Corinth (1816). In three of the poems, Byron uses allusions to the houris to evoke the oriental landscape. In *The Bride of Abydos*, he rhapsodizes: "But soft as harp that Houri string/His long entrancing note!"[13] When Giaffir hears his daughter Zuleika, he exclaims: "But hark!—I hear Zuleika's voice,/Like Houris' hymn it meets mine ear."[14] When Selim contemplates his love for Zuleika, Byron asks: "Oh! who so dear with him could dwell?/What houri soothe his half so well?"[15] In *The Siege of Corinth*, we find the phrase "Secure in paradise to be/By Houris loved immortally."[16]

In two other poems, *The Giaour* (1813) and *Don Juan* (1819), the houri offers a more developed image. In *The Giaour*, houris are presented as the ideal of beauty. The term "giaour" is said to be a derogatory Turkish term for Christians, and the poem tells the story of a Christian man who loves the beautiful Leila, who is owned by Sultan Hassan. When the sultan learns that Leila returns the giaour's affections, he has her drowned. The giaour is then driven to exact revenge. He kills Hassan and then enters a monastery. While Leila's beauty may be like that of an otherworldly houri, she is trapped by worldly male tyranny.

Byron not only extols Leila's beauty, but focuses on her gaze and her large, dark eyes.

> *Her eye's dark charm 't were vain to tell,*
> *But gaze on that of the Gazelle,*
> *It will assist thy fancy well;*
> *As large, as languishingly dark,*
> *But Soul beam'd forth in every spark*
> *That darted from beneath the lid,*
> *Bright as the jewel of Giamschid.*[17]

The poem continues to refer to paradise and its entryway of the bridge Sirat. It depicts a paradise of houris: "With Paradise within my view,/And all his Houris beckoning through."[18]

Byron turns to a description of Leila, depicted as a Circassian beauty elevated like a paradisiacal houri who is fair and pure. Beyond the houri-like description of Leila, there are other houris "at the Prophet's gate."[19] "They come—their kerchiefs green they wave,/And welcome with a kiss the brave!"[20]

In *The Giaour*, then, Byron introduces two themes concerning the houri. The first is the houri as the unparalleled beauty. The second is the houri as a class of women who await their designated believer in paradise.

In *Don Juan*, Byron develops the image of the houri as sexual reward in paradise. In Canto eight, the Russians battle the Turks. They win when they kill the Turkish khan and his five sons at the Battle of Ismaʿil, a Turkish fortress on the Danube. Byron attributes their eagerness in battle, even against difficult odds, to the promise of the houri.

> *The eldest was a true and tameless Tatar,*
> *As great a scorner of the Nazarene*
> *As ever Mahomet pick'd out for a martyr,*
> *Who only saw the black eyed girls in green,*
> *Who make the beds of those who won't take quarter*
> *On earth in Paradise; and when once seen,*
> *Those houris, like all other pretty creatures,*
> *Do just whate'er they please, by dint of features.*[21]

The houri is not just an ethereal beauty without wishes and desires. In the following passage, the houri desires a young man.

And what they pleased to do with the young khan
In heaven, I know not, nor pretend to guess;
But doubtless they prefer a fine young Man
To tough old Heroes, and can do no less.
And that's the cause, no doubt, why, if we scan
A Field of battle's ghastly wilderness,
For one rough, weather-beaten, veteran body,
You'll find ten thousand handsome coxcombs
bloody.[22]

For Byron, the affect the houri has on the khan is visceral. He rushes into battle, forgetting his own four brides.

Thus the young khan, with houris in his sight,
Thought not upon the charms of four young brides,
But bravely rush'd on his first heavenly night;
In short, howe'er our better faith derides,
These black-eyed Virgins make the Moslems fight,
As though there were one heaven, and none besides—
Whereas, if all be true we hear of heaven
And hell, there must at least be six or seven.[23]

In the most dramatic verse, Byron depicts the khan's imaginings of paradise before his death.

So fully flash'd the phantom on his eyes,
That when the very lance was in his heart
He shouted, "Allah!" and saw Paradise
With all its veil of mystery drawn apart,
And bright Eternity without disguise
On his soul, like a ceaseless sunrise, dart:—
With prophets, houris, angels, saints—descried
In one voluptuous blaze,—and then he died.[24]

The canto presents an extended reflection on the nature of battle and death. For the khan, the death has an apocalyptic dimension when the veil of mystery will finally be lifted. The battle, then, is what will allow him to reach the eternal state. Within the "voluptuous Blaze" is the allure and promise of the houri in the next life. We could consider these verses as projections of European fantasies that are dependent on the exercise of political and intellectual power, as Edward Said argues.[25] Or we could consider the texts as providing an ironic critique of eighteenth-century Romanticism, as Andrew Warren suggests.[26] What is interesting is how the houri enters the scene as motivation and standard.

After Byron's "Turkish Tales," oriental tales proliferated, sometimes influenced by Byronic language. Some collections drew upon *1,001 Nights* or Persian stories, while other authors developed new works replete with the visual imagery of the Muslim East. Often, the stories were serialized in monthly magazines. This genre, sometimes distinctly written for gentlemen or ladies, offers a useful record of how the works of well-known authors circulated and provided a model for other less celebrated writers. The stories often feature a despot, sometimes a sultan or sometimes Muhammad, who entraps others with his perversity. The houri often figures as a reference that establishes the oriental setting.

A houri appears in "The Talisman of Oromanes, or the Merchant Abudah" in *The Tales of the Genii*, published first in the late 1700s and frequently reprinted in the nineteenth century:

> At these words, with grace ineffable, she advanced to the transported Merchant; who, with thrilling joy, received from her ivory hands the rich, sparkling draught, and sucked it in

with mad delight. The Houri immediately disappeared, and Abudah, falling senseless on the chest, resigned himself to sleep, and to a second adventure.[27]

Here the houri is a magical genie, and there is no distinction between this fantastic figure and the Islamic heavenly being.

Other publications show the direct influence of Byron. In "A Visit to Jerusalem by An American" (1837), the story combines the genre of voyage with Byron's oriental images, including the houri:

> By some mischance in the shock of fight, a dark, furious-looking fellow was thrown, "dashed thundering to the earth," where he lay in his fanciful costume, the stern reality of Byron's beautiful image, "fallen Hassan lies, his unclosed eye yet lowering on his enemy." The turban torn from his shaven head, floated away with the breeze, exhibiting to the defiling gaze of Christian dogs, the long raven lock cherished for the Houris in Paradise; while his face, discolored with rage and dust, his garments rent, and the wild steed plunging riderless over the plain, breathed forth the poetry of an Oriental discomfiture.[28]

The invocation of Byron's Hassan of *The Giaour* demonstrates the poet's continued influence on the oriental tale. The text is replete with literary conventions that emphasize the adventure and exoticism of the Middle East: turbans torn, rage and dust, and houris in paradise.

While Byron, like Lady Montagu, claimed an authenticity due to his travels, it was his representation of the sensual East that made him such a celebrated figure. As first depicted in *Childe Harold*, developed through his "Turkish Tales," and expressed in the ultimate form of *Don Juan*, Byron creates an

East populated with women who seem like houris on earth, developing the image of the houri who is so beautiful and alluring that she inspires men to battle and death.

Byron's poems also exerted an influence on literature intended for women. *Les Dames de Byron*, sometimes titled *The Gallery of Byron Beauties: Ideal Pictures of the Principal Female Characters in Lord Byron's Poems*, was a collection of excerpts of Byron's poems in which he describes heroines. First published in London in 1836, the earliest American edition was published by R. Martin in New York in 1848. In the collection, the context of the poems is set aside. Instead, each heroine is accompanied by an engraving that celebrates her beauty. Among them are found Leila of *The Giaour* and Zuleika of *The Bride of Abydos*. In her engraving, Leila exemplifies feminine grace as she pensively gazes into the distance (Figure 3.1). Her wide and dark eyes contrast with the pearl diadem that crowns her head. While her nobility is signaled through her jewels, dress, and manner, the opening in her tunic reflects a sweet sensuality. Similarly, Zuleika (Figure 3.2), by her youth and expression, projects an innocent sweetness.

Other illustrations in *The Gallery of Byron Beauties* present Muslim women interacting with infant children[29] or fleeing in fear.[30] These other Muslim figures can hardly be distinguished from the Christian Marion or Inez of *Childe Harold* or Generva of the Minor Poems.[31] When we look at the engravings, religious and regional identity are not important to the identity of the women. Instead, it is their beauty that is meant to capture the viewer's eye.

Byron's beauties may have played a significant role in the evolution of the "houri" into a descriptor for American females. By focusing on feminine grace and beauty as

FIGURE 3.1 *Leila, Gallery of Byron Beauties: Ideal Pictures of the Principal Female Characters in Lord Byron's Poems,* 1867.B825B99 F7 1867, Rare Book & Manuscript Library, Columbia University in the City of New York.

FIGURE 3.2 *Zuleikha, Gallery of Byron Beauties: Ideal Pictures of the Principal Female Characters in Lord Byron's Poems*, 1867.B825B99 F7 1867, Rare Book & Manuscript Library, Columbia University in the City of New York.

opposed to religious markers or narrative context, Byron elevated the houri to a figure of universal aspiration for ladies. Byron did not construct the houri as a literary form, but he made it prominent by associating it with a larger vision of what it meant to be strong, beautiful, and virtuous. His legacy within American monthly magazines and published books about heroines was the realization that the virtues of Byron's ladies could also be American virtues.

SENSUAL PARADISE

The sensuality of Islamic paradise was noted as both strange and threatening. In Latin Christendom, Christian theologians were disturbed by the idea of a sensual Islamic afterworld. The *Book of John Mandeville* from the mid-fourteenth century discusses how every man will have twenty-four virginal wives with whom to have intercourse.[32] Christians used the literal interpretation of the Qur'an to argue that Islam was irrational, with its arbitrary laws and pursuits of pleasure.[33] While Saracens were respected for learning, they were also seen as inferior because they were unable to recognize the universal rationality of Christianity.[34] That rationality privileged the spirit over the letter and the soul's fulfillment over the body's needs. Latin Christendom's theologians saw sex as a taint, and the idea of a material sensual paradise was abominable.

The contrast between a spiritual Christian heaven and a material Islamic paradise are on display in Royall Tyler's (d. 1826) novel, *The Algerine Captive or the Life and Adventures of Doctor Updike Underhill: Six Years a Prisoner among the Algerines* (1792). The book was one of the first popular novels to be published in the newly founded United States and also circulated in Europe.

In the first part of the narrative, Dr. Underhill discusses his upbringing as a gentleman in New England. In the second part of the narrative, Dr. Underhill is held captive in Algiers. The captivity narrative allows him to compare the United States with the differing culture, religion, slave system, and political formation of the Barbary States. In one illuminating episode, a Muslim theologian, identified as the "artful priest" or "mullah," questions Dr. Underhill about his religious beliefs.[35] The mullah challenges Underhill for adopting his parents' beliefs without giving them significant thought, and he goes on to argue for the superiority of Islam.

After a spirited exchange about the role of violence in Islamic and Christian histories, Dr. Underhill falls silent when the mullah points out that when a slave converts to Islam, Muslims "immediately knock off his fetters and receive him as a brother. . . . We leave it to the Christians of the West Indies, and Christians of your southern plantations, to baptize the unfortunate African into your faith, and then use your brother Christians as brutes of the desert."[36] At this point, Dr. Underhill pivots to his next accusation:

Author. But you hold a sensual paradise.
Mollah. So the doctors of your church tell you; but a sensual heaven is no more imputable to us than to you. When the Most Holy condescends to reveal himself to man in human language, it must be in terms commensurate with our conception. The enjoyment of the houri, those immortal virgins who will attend the beatified believer, the splendid pavilions of the heavens, are all but types of significations of holy joys too sublime for man in flesh to conceive of. In your Bible, I read, your prophet refers to the time when he should drink

new wine in his father's kingdom. Now would it be candid in me to hastily brand the heaven of your prophet as sensual, and to represent your faithful in bliss as a club of wine-bibbers?

For the theologically sophisticated, the sensuality of the images of paradise was understood as a reflection of the ineffable nature of God's bounty. However, the popular idea of virgins as literal reward was far more commonly evoked. The conversation reflects the tension in Christian and Islamic theologies regarding the difference between literal and metaphorical rewards.

Dr. Underhill's conception of a sensual Islamic paradise was often depicted in mid-nineteenth-century visual arts, in which the houri emerges as a celestial odalisque. In the lithographs and engravings of French artists Nicolas Eustache Maurin (d. 1850) and Jean-Pierre-Marie Jazet (d. 1871), the houri appears as a central figure of Islamic paradise.

Maurin's series about Islamic paradise comprises six lithographs, each drawing on the sensual nature of paradise. The titles include *Le songe* (*The Dream*), *L'odorat* (*The Smell*), *L'ouïe* (*The Hearing*), *La vue* (*The Sight*), *Le gout* (*The Taste*), and *Le toucher* (*The Touch*). *The Touch* (ca. 1840) shows a lover with his beloved (Figure 3.3). We see a fair beauty arched back on a cushion, in her lover's arms. Both are clad in silk garments. His has an embossed floral pattern, and hers is striated. With her fair skin and hair, she calls forth the image of a Circassian beauty. With pearls on her wrists, rings on her fingers, a gold choker on her neck, and bejeweled clasps on her slightly open caftan, we see her delicate beauty and a hint of the nakedness

FIGURE 3.3 *The Touch* (*Le toucher*), ca. 1840. Nicolas-Eustache Maurin (1799–1850). Recueil. Oeuvre des Maurin. Bibliothèque nationale de France.

underneath. As the lovers embrace, cherubs look on. In *The Dream* (ca. 1840), the lover dreams of paradise; a fair-headed houri caresses him while three others look on and another plays the harp (Figure 3.4). The sensuality of the paradisiacal scene is amplified by the opulence of the sleeping chamber with its silk cushions, brocade draperies, and just-smoked shisha.

In Jazet's engraving of paradise (1859), there is a garden scene that shows houris and men enjoying the splendor around them (Figure 3.5). At the center of the composition is a houri in a dancing pose. Two other dancers are behind her. One holds cymbals. Another is dancing with her veil. On the right, a man is looking upward, flanked by two fair-haired houris. One is holding a book, while the other is gently

FIGURE 3.4 *The Dream* (*Le songe*), ca. 1840. Nicolas-Eustache Maurin (1799–1850). Recueil. Oeuvre des Maurin. Bibliothèque nationale de France.

caressing the man's back. In the left corner of the engraving, a dark-haired houri is talking with a man who is smoking shisha. A group of men behind them are enjoying the dancers, as two other houris prepare to serve a platter of fruit and a flask of wine. In the background, small groups of men gather and enjoy each other's company in a garden with a mosque in the distance. The scene depicts the perceived pleasures of paradise. There is music, dance, food, libation, and community in a verdant setting.

As the English, French, and Americans engaged with the Ottoman Empire in the nineteenth century, they developed a cultural vocabulary that was influenced by concern for real Muslim women and fascination with ethereal houris. The oriental tale was a site of fantasy. Writers, painters, and

FIGURE 3.5 *Islamic Paradise* (*Le paradis de Mahomet*), 1859. Jean-Pierre-Marie Jazet (1788–1871). Recueil. Oeuvre des Jazet. Bibliothèque nationale de France.

poets envisioned a Muslim East symbolized by the beauty of its women.

FEMININE MARVELS

As the houri came to represent feminine beauty, her attributes began to exemplify the idealized woman, irrespective of religion or nationality. Her beauty spoke of the marvelous East, but transcended the association with Muslims as people or Islam as a religion. Sir Walter Scott's *Ivanhoe* (1820), an oriental tale set in medieval England, offers a useful example. In the novel, it is not a Muslim, but rather the Jewish Rebecca who is identified as the houri.

In the first allusion to the houri, the Templar Brian de Bois Guilbert says that the beauty of Lady Rowena eclipses that of the women he saw during the Crusades: ". . . and if the purity of her complexion, and the majestic, yet soft expression of a mild blue eye, do not chase from your memory the black-tressed girls of Palestine, ay, or the houris of old Mahound's paradise, I am an infidel, and no true son of the Church." De Bois Guilbert's problem is that he is in love with the beautiful Rebecca, who soon faces charges of sorcery. The image of the houri here takes on a wider significance. She is a marvel whose beauty tempts men to transgress religious lines. Prince John examines Rebecca and asks her father: "What is she, Isaac? Thy wife or thy daughter, that Eastern houri that thou lockest under thy arm?"[37] The question has a sexual charge. The description of Rebecca is redolent of houri-like characteristics:

> Her form was exquisitely symmetrical, and was shown to advantage by a sort of Eastern dress, which she wore according to the fashion of the females of her nation. Her turban of yellow silk suited well the darkness of her complexion. The brilliancy of her eyes, the superb arch of her eyebrows, her well-formed aquiline nose, her teeth as white as pearl, and the profusion of her sable tresses, which, each arranged in its own little spiral of twisted curls, fell down upon as much of a lovely neck and bosom as a simarre of the richest Persian silk, exhibiting flowers in their natural colours embossed upon a purple ground, permitted to be visible—all these constituted a combination of loveliness, which yielded not to the most beautiful maidens who surrounded her.[38]

Rebecca is a houri, but a Jewish houri. She is marked as Eastern due to her dress, which is characteristic of Jewish women. Her beauty troubles Brian de Bois Guibert, who does not want to fall in love with her but cannot help himself. This Jewish houri invites the crossing of boundaries in a religiously delineated society.

The association with the houri also extends to Christian women in Romantic literature. Keats writes of his love to Fanny Brawne in letter dated March 1, 1820:

> My dearest Fanny—The power of your benediction is of not so weak a nature as to pass from the ring in four-and-twenty hours—it is like a sacred Chalice once consecrated and ever consecrate. I shall kiss your name and mine where your Lips have been. Lips! Why should a poor prisoner as I am talk about such things? Thank God, though, I hold them the dearest pleasures in the universe, I have a consolation independent of them in the certainty of your affection. I could write a song in the style of Tom Moore's Pathetic about Memory if that would be any relief to me. No—'t would not. I will be as obstinate as a Robin. I will not sing in a cage. Health is my expected heaven and you are the Houri—this world I believe is both singular and plural—if only plural, never mind—you are a thousand of them. Ever your affectionately my dearest J.K.[39]

In Mary Wollstonecraft Shelley's *Falkner a Novel* (1837), the narrator sees a girl:

> ... my attention was attracted, riveted by the vision of a lovely girl, who had glided in from another room, and stood near us, radiant in youth and beauty. She was indeed supremely lovely—exuberant in all the charms of girlhood—and her beauty was enhanced by the very contrast to the pale lady by whom she stood—a houri she seemed, standing by a disembodied spirit—black, soft, large eyes, overpowering in their lustre, and yet no more so from the soul that dwelt within—a cherub look—a fairy form, with a complexion and shape that

spoke of health and joy. What could it mean? Who could she be? And who was she who knew my name? It was an enigma; but one full of promise to me, who had so long been exiled from the charities of life; and who, "as the hart panteth for the water brooks," panted for love.[40]

In Shelly's passage, the girl is like a houri in her radiance and beauty and gliding movement. Her ethereal beauty is enhanced by the comparison with her older companion. In the Romantic genre, houris figure is many different ways. They are linked with Islamic despotism, Eastern exoticism, and Christian, Muslim, and Jewish feminine beauty.

These images are oriental projections, but they are projections that were based on theological ambiguities. No matter their intentions, the writers relied on a houri that transcended Islamic meanings. Whether the writer's agenda concerned the self or family or society, the use of the houri had its own set of implications for English and American women.

FEMININE MODELS

The metaphor of the houri in American literature was applied in contested ways. The houri is not just a marvel, but a way of thinking about how American women should or should not behave.

In "The Life, Adventures, and Opinions of David Theo Hines of South Carolina, Master of Arts and Sometimes Doctor of Medicine" (1840), a woman in Kentucky is said to be "as beautiful as a houri."[41] More striking than the idea of a Kentucky houri is that the houri became part of the debate on feminine ethics and beauty. "Female Beauty of the

Mind" (1837) puts forward an argument about the nature of feminine beauty that would resonate with Jane Eyre and her appreciation of simple frocks:

> Yet, it gives us pain to see, that the thoughts of ladies too much centre upon beauty, ornament, dress and showy accomplishments, after the order of things, which once gave them so much importance, has forever passed away. It was natural that they should think, converse, and care for nothing but these things, when they constituted their only hold upon consideration. It is humiliating to see them thinking of little but fashions and dress, now that they are in possession of other and far higher and surer claims upon homage and admiration. Who is there, who in the sanctuary of his hidden thoughts, would balance a moment in formatting a partnership for life, between a flaunty belle, though robed in the finest silks of Persia, and tinted ever so brightly with native or apothecary's vermilion, and a plain young lady, neat, modest, intelligent, instructed, with a full mind and regulated heart? Who would hesitate between the beauty, fairer than the fabled houri, who could talk of nothing but the fashions and the weather; and the woman, who, without beauty, was wise and good and true, and compared with the other, as the rose to the piony?[42]

The houri here is beautiful and frivolous, not simple and true. This idea of modest feminine beauty accords with plain Jane who sees herself as strong and principled and unwilling to be swayed by frivolity. At the other end of the scale, we find the celebration of a feminine vision in the poem the "Star of Love" (1840).[43] The poem by R. H. appeared in the *Ladies' Companion*, a magazine that typically presented ladies with a variety of offerings, including musical scores, engravings of picturesque scenes and the season's fashions, original stories and poems, monthly serials, essays on ladies' issues such as motherhood and children, and cultural pieces addressing such topics as Mozart's *Don Giovanni* or translations of Voltaire's *Zadig*. In the poem and the accompanying engraving, the "Star of Love" was a woman whose beauty is celebrated.

> *Beauty and soul in wreath divine,*
> *Are twined around thy forehead's shrine,*
> *While sweetest thoughts and sunny smiles,*
> *Gleam out 'midst love's ambrosial wiles,*
> *Like twin stars on the crest of night,*
> *Thin eyes are flashing lustrous light,*
> *And on thy lips of crimson hue,*
> *Thy breath dissolves in balmy dew,*
> *Just as the night's tears on the rose,*
> *Melt when the gates of morn unclose.*
> *Houri of Fancy's fairest dream,*
> *So sweetly does thine image beam,*
> *As if some angel with his wing,*
> *Had waked thy young heart's slumbering,*
> *From visions clothed in glory's light,*
> *In realms of Paradise all bright,*
> *That doubly strong thy claims should prove,*
> *Young beauty to—the Star of Love!*[44]

The poem goes on to emphasize the Star of Love's virginal innocence: "That soon thy youthful heart shall twine/In rosy links at Hymen's shrine."[45] The accompanying engraving (Figure 3.6) shows a voluptuous young woman with dark curls gazing at the reader. In the composition, she is both sensual and pure.

FIGURE 3.6 *Star of Love, The Ladies' Companion*, October 1840, Vol. 13. Opp. p. 261. Engraving.General Research Division, The New York Public Library, Astor, Lenox, and Tilden Foundations.

When it comes to feminine models, the ladies' magazines suggest a wider debate on what constituted feminine beauty. The "houri forms" of Jane Eyre recalled the larger question of what it meant to be a good and beautiful woman. Was it to be principled, austere, and simple? Or was it to embrace the aesthetics of fineness, with its elegant features, fabrics, and manners? This was the debate between Jane Eyre and Rochester. The houri offered a solution, representing a beautiful woman adorned with luxury who was nonetheless pure in essence.

THE AMERICAN HOURI

Americans inherited multiple polemics about Islam and fantasies about Muslim women. In one polemic, the woman is a slave, just as all men are slaves to the despot Muhammad. In another polemic, the houris are transcendental beings who show the possibility of the feminine sublime. When it comes to the houri, Islamic tropes inspired as much as they repulsed. In the eighteenth century, writers had used the houri to express discomfort with oriental despotism and the closed world of the harem. In the nineteenth century, writers gave shape to and were influenced by the Romantic movement and saw the houri as something else. The houri was both a representation of the wonders of the Muslim East and a representation of the possibility of a Romantic, Christian femininity. The houri was transformed from a female inhabitant of the Muslim paradise into a superlative feminine beauty who could be found within Muslim, Jewish, and Christian communities and could reside in the capitals of Istanbul, Paris, London, or Boston. The Americanized houri offered a new image for thinking about women and their ethical and aesthetic functions within a rapidly modernizing and economically growing society.

The houri as both the older oriental and the newer feminine heroine can be found in Ameen Rihani's *The Book of Khalid* (1911). Considered the first Arab-American novel, *The Book of Khalid* mingles English and Arabic literary conventions within the framework of an American immigrant tale.[46] At the end of the first section, Khalid considers himself to be a dervish and visits what he calls the "house of metaphysics."[47] This is actually a brothel, where Khalid consorts with the mistress, whom he identifies as "the Medium."[48] In the context of the liaison between Khalid and the Medium, Rihani makes these observations about sexuality from the Arab and American perspective: "We believe, however, that the pruriency of the Orientals, like the prudery of the Occidentals, is in fact only an appearance. On both sides there is a display of what might be called verbal virtue and verbal vice. And on both sides, the exaggerations are configured in a harmless pose."[49] It is notable that in the book, Rihani spells the term as "huris" as opposed to "houris." This suggests that he was transliterating from the Arabic, rather than drawing on the English literary tradition. Nonetheless, his introduction of the houris shows that they were a recognizable product of the romance of the Muslim East.

In a post–September 11th world, we have forgotten the history of the houri in English literature. While the writers of these texts recognized their differences with Islam, they also endorsed the universal standard of beauty exemplified by the houri. In some ways, the post-9/11 media resemble the Romantics. They are both worldly in their understanding of global connections, but limited by their scant knowledge about Muslim societies. They are concerned about freedom and reform, but they reduce a theological metaphor into the representation of a real woman. For contemporary media, however, the judgment about the houri results in a condemnation of Muslim society. By contrast, for the Romantics, the houri was the possibility of a universal femininity that transcended earthly concerns. Within the many meanings of this nineteenth-century houri—slave, adornment, youth, oriental daughter—was a model of woman that writers used as a standard, and debated as a type.

A REWARD

THE TERM *HUR* FIRST APPEARED in the Qur'an, in the context of banquet scenes that represented life in paradise. The Qur'an speaks of the inevitability of the Last Judgment and the need to submit to God by heeding Muhammad's message. The individual's choice leads either to reward in heaven or punishment in hell. The Fire (*al-nar*), or hell (*jahannam*), is ready for those who ignore Muhammad's message and disregard the command to live on a "straight path," or *al-sirat al-mustaqim*. The Garden (*al-janna*) is the reward for those who convert and maintain an ethical and spiritual standard.[1]

This ultimate reward and punishment are conveyed in "swift glimpses" of what life would look, feel, and smell like in the everlasting future.[2] Scenes of punishment contrast with scenes of splendor. Qur'anic verses say that to deny the Last Judgment and the creation of God has stark consequences. Denying God's power results in an eternity in the most terrifying of places. Hell is filled with molten liquid, beings that inflict pain, and the inability to stop one's own body from punishing itself. Life in hell is its own dark, lonely, contained terror. If the terror is described in evocative language, then its paradisiacal opposite is even more so.

The Qur'anic paradise is not just a beatific vision of resting in the favor of God. Paradise is its own reward. It is replete with the luxuries of the natural world, such as gold, silver, saffron, and musk. Its textiles are the finest silks, brocades, and carpets. In the Garden, believers are renewed. Their form is at the height of beauty. There are no feelings of ill will or jealousy, no bodily pollutions. It is in this setting of cosmic perfection that the *hur* appear. Sometimes referred to as *hur*, other times as *hur'in*, these figures are described in terms of spiritual and sexual purity. While other rewards are identified by and understood as being transformations of earthly things, the term *hur* is not used as an analogy to earthly companionship. Verses mention silk (22.23, 35.33), fine brocade (18.31, 76.21, 44.53), carpets lined with brocade (55.54), and bracelets of gold and pearls (22.23, 35.33). In paradise, these luxuries are part of a cosmic perfection. But even wonders of paradise are based on earthly luxuries. Verses mention wine mixed with camphor (76.5) that runs through the fabled fountain *salsabil* (76.18), a marvel that invokes the sense of smell. While *salsabil* is a feature of paradise, it is the earthly products of wine and camphor that are identified as flowing there.

The Qur'an does not draw on a preexisting earthly object or being when it mentions the *hur*. In the banquet scenes in the Qur'anic verses on paradise, *wildan* and *ghilman* are male youths whose function is to pour drink from silver vessels. These two terms were used for earthly slave boys, especially as cupbearers in drinking establishments. In the Qur'an the *wildan* and *ghilman*, who serve drinks, are contrasted with the *hur*, who are not given any particular task but are interpreted as companions.

The *hur* and *wildan* and *ghilman* are not to be seen as transformed humans. There is no indication that they ever lived and died on earth or that they committed to Islam by pronouncing the *shahada*, or creed, "There is no God but God, and Muhammad is his Messenger." Instead, they are heavenly beings designed for believers in a perfected cosmic realm. These beings appear only sporadically, but they maintain a presence. *Hur* are mentioned explicitly in four verses (44.54, 52.20, 55.72, 56.22) and implicitly in six others (37.48–49, 38.52, 55.56, 56.35–37, 55.70, 78.33). In three other verses they may be alluded to in the context of the idea of pure companionship of paradise (2.25, 4.57, 3.15). The *hur* and the male servants, *wildan mukhallahun* (56.17, 76.19) and *ghilman* (52.24), are linked in suras that place the *hur* in a banquet setting (56.22, 52.20–24). The male servants are also described through metaphors about pearls (56.23, 76.19).

These passing allusions in the rich, poetic, and evocative Qur'anic verses have given rise to centuries of questions, speculations, and imaginings of the *hur*. From the earliest collections of traditions in the tenth century, we have records of Muslim men and women questioning the meaning of the *hur* as feminine beings of paradise. What are they? What are their attributes? Will I receive one (or two or seventy or seventy thousand)? Will they be better than earthly wives?

Viewed as a heavenly reward, the *hur* posed a challenge to Muslim theologians. Commentators drew upon etymologies to explain the meaning of the term. They linked *hur* with the root *h-w-r*, which connotes whiteness, and *'in* with the word for "eye." On this interpretation, *hur* are female companions with remarkable eyes, in which the white or sclerotic part of the eye is set off by a large intensely black pupil, resembling the eyes of a cow or gazelle. The eyes and the gaze became the defining characteristic of the *hur* in commentaries, hadiths or traditions of the prophet Muhammad, and later dictionaries.

Along the way, theologians speculated about her skin color and her confusing relationship with earthly wives.

Hadiths record ever more elaborate traditions of the houri's skin, scent, and even spit. As a more formalized set of descriptions developed, writers imbued her with greater love for the male believer. While her relation to earthly wives was never settled, she effectively replaced an earlier vision of paradise where the reward was everlasting life among ancestors and progeny, wives and children. Instead, eschatological manuals from the ninth century onward began to depict a remarkably solitary Garden. Gone was the social life that characterized earlier visions of the Garden. In its place was the interaction of the male believer and his perfectly created houri.

Muslims came to understand the ambiguous reward of the houri through different genres that culminated in the interpretation of a pure, virginal female companion. In relating the interpretative choices that led theologians, storytellers, and poets to promote the idea of the houri as the prime female companion of paradise, the beauty of the houri shifted through the centuries from a social meaning rooted in spiritual purity to an individual vision intimating heavenly sexuality.

At the heart of the mystery of the houri and her prominence in the landscape of Islamic paradise is the meaning of beauty in Islamic traditions. Beauty is not just pretty and pleasurable, but pure and affirming. Just as Islamic paradise collapses the division between the material and spiritual world by proposing a spiritual afterworld that is made with luxuries so pure that they are transformative, so the houri is beautiful both to the senses and to the spirit. This combining of spiritual and material, of senses and soul, is the reward of paradise, where houris act as both the culmination of the landscape and the most visible female being. More than any other reward of paradise, the houri embodies the linkage of aesthetic and ethical perfection and the possibility of spiritual and physical companionship. The houri is a singular being in a reconfigured cosmic world that is the true reward for righteousness on earth.

THE GARDEN AND THE FIRE

The Garden and the Fire are central tenets in Islamic history. In the Qur'an, believers are reminded that they will be judged, and the consequences for their actions will be paid in the time after death. The polemic includes verses about the Last Judgment, accountability for individual actions, and salvation made possible through harkening to Muhammad's message and submitting to the will of God through conversion to Islam. This message is suffused throughout the Qur'an, appearing in verses that describe paradise and in other verses that remind believers that there are consequences for their actions.

There is also mention of the Garden and the Fire in historical texts. In Ibn Ishaq's (d. 768) *Sirat Rasul Allah*, the first chronological record of the life of Muhammad (ca. 570–632), which was edited by Ibn Hisham (d. 833 or 828), there is a story about a Jew who prophesies the coming of the prophet. This Jew spoke of a prophet whose message would reveal the reality of the resurrection, the reckoning, the scales, and the Garden and the Fire. The response to his vision was incredulous: "Good gracious man! Do you think that such things could be that men can be raised from the dead to a place where there is a Garden [*al-janna*] and a Fire [*al-nar*] in which they will be recompensed for their deeds?"³ The story is instructive. Not only does the Jew foretell the arrival of Muhammad and the coming of Islam, but he identifies the new faith through its doctrine of the afterlife and its promise of two places yet to be experienced—the Garden and the Fire.

The Garden is a reward in and of itself since it offers glorious gardens near the throne of God. Within the Garden are also specific rewards for believers. Righteous Muslims are promised a life and an afterworld with a resplendent landscape, transformed bodies, luxury goods, and a servant class to attend to their needs. The description of Islamic paradise is remarkable for the specificity of its details about everyday domestic life. Believers will live in pavilions or tents of hollowed pearls and enjoy sumptuary goods. Reclining on silk carpets, they will wear brocade and fine silk. They drink from silver and gold vessels, and they smell of camphor and musk. Each scene of paradise offers a different luxury that is designed to please. Within this paradise, there is no taint, just pleasure in a cosmically pure realm.

The Garden is ultimately a sensory reward. While it may be a reward for righteousness on earth, it is described through the framework of amplified human senses. The elect can see shade for as far as a camel rider can ride in 100 years. They can smell the fragrance of saffron from the soil and musk from fountains. They can taste any fruit or flesh of their desire. And they can feel the most exquisite silks and brocades on their bodies. The sensory afterlife allows believers to enjoy the luxuries of the world with their renewed bodies, and the sensory realm is also devoid of any taint or temptation. Wine is enjoyed, but will not intoxicate. Sexual opportunity is ample, but will not be sullied by bodily fluids. And there is no labor. The Garden is the realm of rest, socialization, and enjoyment; it is not a place for work, labor, and the weariness of life. To perfect the leisure of paradise, within the perfected Garden, there is a class of beings who are designed to facilitate the ease and leisure of paradise.

LABOR

Part of the reward of the Garden is that whatever the believer wishes becomes manifest. If a believer wants to eat a meal of flesh or fowl (52.22, 56.21), it simply appears. When a believer wants to drink something pleasurable like wine that does not intoxicate (37.47, 52.23), it is poured forth from a clear-flowing fountain (37.45). The Garden immediately and invisibly fulfills the believer's desires. Labor is for life, and the Garden is, in part, a reward for that earthly physical and spiritual labor. The existence of a labor force within the Garden enhances the luxurious nature of the banquet. It reminds believers that the afterworld is a transformed world. The *wildan* and *ghilman* have specific functions in paradise. They are an essential labor force that ensures the smooth running of the banquet and meets believers' expectations of a good life. They are so numerous that they can be scattered throughout. Their function as laborers is essential, and also provides a useful way to understand the houri's comparable function of providing companionship.

Three Qur'anic verses characterize the *wildan mukhalladun* and *ghilman* as young (56.17) and pure as a pearl (76.19, 52.24). Two verses emphasize their everlasting youth. "Round them will serve youths of perpetual freshness" (56.17, 76.19). In other verses that do not mention the male youths explicitly, believers recline and enjoy each other's company as youths serve them (56.17–19, 52.23–25, 76.13–19). The youth are connected with the non-intoxicating drink (56.18–19) or the drink from the fountain *salsabil* (76.17–18).

Both *wildan* and *ghilman* are associated with pearls. "If though seest them, Thou wouldst think them scattered pearls" (76.19). The use of the word "pearl" suggests that the verses are not just depicting earthly servants, but a transformed slave class. Just as people and objects assume their purest forms, even servants will have the spiritual value of being pure. The luxury of the servant frees the believer from the rigors of life, but also provides a spectacle of beauty that has the expansive quality of being "scattered" about. The luminous quality of the servant boys is expressed through the pearl, which had associations of status in the late antique world[4] and of sanctified purity that linked hanging pearls with heavenly Jerusalem.[5]

Qur'anic commentators debated how time affected the youth. They argued that the supratemporal aspects of the Garden extended to the youth: they could not die or even age.[6] One question that consumed commentators was the meaning of "scattered" or "well-guarded like pearls" (*lu'lu'an manthuran*). Al-Tabari (d. 923), al-Qurtubi (d. 1273), Ibn Kathir (d. 1373), al-Mahalli (d. 1459), and al-Suyuti (d. 1505) suggest that *manthuran* or "scattered" indicates that there are so many youth that they are throughout the Garden.[7] They interpreted *maknun* or "well-guarded" as the inside of the pearl, which they argued was the most protected and beautiful.[8] The commentators seem to have shared a vision of the infinite expanse, luxury, and purity of the Garden. For them, the servant boys were understood in terms of beauty and accessibility.

Some commentators attempted to place the males within an earthly framework. Al-Zamakhshari (d. 1144), al-Tabarsi (d. 1153), and al-Qurtubi questioned whether the slave boys might be children of Muslims who died young or non-Muslims who were categorized as *kuffar* (unbelievers) or *mushrikun* (polytheists).[9] With this line of inquiry, these commentators signal that the hierarchy of the earthly world is replicated in the Garden, where non-Muslims or children serve believers. The two potential choices have different ontologies, but result in the same station. Either the boys are potential Muslims who did not live long enough to make active choices about their faith, or the boys rank lower in the religious hierarchy, but are still able to be part of a resplendent world. The stratification of earthly life, then, still operates in the imagining of the future world.

Arabic poetry is another source for thinking about the servant boys. Like the terms for luxurious materials and objects, the terms for the youth derive from earthly matters, in this case the practice of slavery. *Ghilman* was the Arabic term used for male slaves, and the Qur'anic *wildan* and *ghilman* show commonalities with the *saqi* or young boy who, in the Arabic poetic tradition, was a cupbearer in drinking houses. Whereas Qur'anic commentators sought to understand the hierarchy of those who are served and those who serve, early Abbasid poets developed wine poetry or *khamriyya* that celebrated the beauty of the cupbearers and sometimes made explicit connections to the *wildan* and *ghilman* of the Garden. The famed poet Abu Nuwas (d. ca. 813–815) tells of a romance between the poet and his young male lover.

I have a lad who is like the beautiful lads of Paradise
And his eyes are big and beautiful

> *His face is as the moon in its full perfection*
> *And you think he is mysteriously struck by a magician*
> *Because he is so tender and pretty*
> *We spent three nights together as if we were in Paradise*
> *Doing nothing but making love and pleasure.*[10]

The poem compares the cupbearers to the youth of paradise and depicts them as sexual companions. This dimension is present in some Arabic poetry, but it does not appear in the Qur'an, commentaries, or eschatological literature. Poetry draws upon metaphor and does not have to fit into the domain of theology.

COMPANIONSHIP

Imaginative speculation about the houris is more expansive than the verses that name them. In the Qur'an, the houris are named explicitly four times. In three instances, they are designated as *hur'in*. In the remaining one, they are named just *hur*. The term is not explained. None of the verses employs *hur al-'in* (with the definite article *al*), which is the most common usage in later Arabic texts.

While the naming is not consistent, there are two things that link the verses and their surrounding language. The first is the theme of companionship. In 44.54 and 52.20, houris are introduced with the phrase "*zawwajnahum bi-hur 'in.*" If we accept the conventional translation, the phrase indicates pairing or coupling with the *hur'in*: "we shall pair them with *hur'in.*" The houri is thus presented as a companion in paradise, paired with the believer. The gender of the companion is not developed in the verse. Qur'anic verses do not use a feminine pronoun for the houri, and some contemporary interpreters have questioned whether the houri is, in fact, female.

While Qur'anic commentators were certain about the gender of the houri as female, they were uncertain about her station. If the houri is the object of the verb "to couple," then what kind of companion is she? Commentators questioned the relationship between houris and wives and asked which is better: the houri or the wife? In this debate, the wife generally fares better than the houri because she is an active Muslim who has converted and lived life according to the religious code. The question has significance because it invokes the linkages between the earthly and otherworldly worlds, and attempts to place women within that continuum. Yet commentators were generally less concerned with issues about wives, marriage, slavery, and concubines. As a result, their explication of verses is stripped of modern notions of race and gender. What comes across, instead, is that irrespective of station, the houri is seen in the capacity of an awarded companion.

Aside from the nature of companionship, the four verses also evince the characteristic of purity. Houris are designated, like the *wildan mukhalladun,* as "pearls well-guarded" or *lu'lu' maknun* (56.22–23). In another verse, the houri is described as being *maqsurat,* or "restrained" (55.72). As a reward that is also a being, these verses suggest that spiritual purity and modest comportment constitute the houri's formation. The mention of pearls also links her with the *wildan mukhalladun* as a transformed being designed for the Garden.

There are other verses that may implicitly refer to the houri. Some invoke companions who are "restraining in their glances," or *qasirat al-tarf* (37.48, 38.52, 55.56). Three verses that invoke the houri as restrained are in the same sura. We learn first of companions "restraining in their glances" (55.56), then of companions *khairat hisan*, or "good and beautiful" (55.70), and then arrive at the explicit mention of *hur maqsurat fi al-khiyam*, or "houris restrained in their pavilions" (55.72). This contextual frame suggests that all references to companions can be interpreted as the houri. Other verses mention *kawaʿib atraban*, or "companions of an equal age" (78.33) or "restraining glances of equal age" (38.52) or just "of an equal age" (56.35–37). Here companionship is associated with a particular stage of life. While houris are not explicitly invoked in these verses, the reward of companionship is affirmed.

If companionship is a standard theme within paradise, then so is purity. In addition to explicit descriptions of the houri as a "pearl well-guarded," there is also reference to companions of a purity "like gems and small pearls whom no man or jinn before them has touched" (55.56, 55.74). This purity is reinforced by the word *abkaran*, or "virginal" (56.35–37). In these verses, purity is cast as being untouched by men and jinn. Here virginity, as well as proprietary honor, is intimated. The reference to jinn is striking because it suggests that jinn, as God's creations, also have access to companions. In this sense, jinn are not just beings who create mischief on earth and inhabit an intermediate space; they also have access to the time and space after the Last Judgment. This verse suggests a role for jinn which is not fully developed in eschatological literature. It could be argued that the inclusion of jinn here is to emphasize the absolute purity of the companions who are untouched by any creation and in any realm. The term *abkaran* is often used to describe the houris as virgins.

Here we have a term that explicitly signals the sexual status of the houri. Yet it would be a mistake to view the purity of the houri as only sexual. The verses invoking pearls also suggest sanctity. The implicit verses that concern companionship, then, refer to both types of purity. The companions are pure because they are ontologically designed to be pure, and they are also untouched by any class of being.

The idea of the houri that develops from the explicit and implicit verses is of a companion sanctified and untouched by experience. Three verses complicate the neatness of assuming that all references to companions point to the houri. Found within three suras from the later Medinan period whose verses were dominated by social legislation rather than evocation of the afterlife, there is reference to paradise as containing *azwaj mutahhara* or "companions pure" (2.25, 3.15, 4.57). The phrase draws on the word for spouses, *azwaj*. The noun for "spouse" stems from the verb "to couple or join." It is difficult to determine the constitution of these pure companions.

In explicating the four explicit verses, Qur'anic commentators devoted their attention to the meaning of the term *hur'in*, and they focused on the size and appearance of the houris' eyes. For al-Tabari and al-Qurtubi, the houri was fair like the color of an eggshell.[11] For al-Tabari, al-Qurtubi, al-Mahalli, and al-Suyuti, her eyes displayed an intense contrast between white and black which makes her gaze like one of a cow or gazelle.[12] The commentaries convey the idea that the companions epitomize beauty with their wide eyes and fair complexions.[13]

Some commentators also reflected upon the status and station of the companions and questioned whether they were like the women on earth. The answer depends on how companionship is configured. While commentators suggest that the males will be wed to the *hur*, it is unclear whether the *hur* are fulfilling their function as reward or replacing earthly social relations. The relationship between *hur* and wives is ambiguous. This ambiguity is brought into high relief when al-Qurtubi reports debates about which is better, women or the *hur*.[14]

Contextual analysis helps understand the houri's functions. The *hur* are part of the resplendence of the Garden and also are in apposition to the *wildan* and *ghilman*. In this sense, the *hur* can be seen as feminine companions and the *wildan* and *ghilman* are male companions. They constitute a pair of rewards with somewhat different functions.

For the commentators, the *hur* are a reward that does not complicate the social dynamics of a believer's life. After all, life in paradise is supposed to be whatever the believer desires. Individual fulfillment is meant to be a reward for a pure life on earth. The configuration of the social relationships is less important than the way that the believer is rewarded. The question does arise whether houris are wives or compete with wives. But the two belong to different ontological categories. Houris are reward. Unlike slaves, they do not have protections or social networks. Wives are companions who will be purified. They do not have to be concerned with troublesome feelings like jealousy. The two, in effect, exist in different registers of meaning. Ultimately, the contrast of white and black and the size of the eyes are what characterize the *hur*. With the rise of the medieval Arabic dictionary, we see how the definition of the houri was set. In al-Razi's thirteenth-century dictionary *Mukhtar al-Sihah*, the *hur* are given an entry and framed with the Arabic definite article *al* to form the noun *al-hur fi al-ʿin*. The definition identifies the *hur* as women with an intense contrast between the white and black of their eyes. Their alluring black eyes are like those of a gazelle or cow. The entry further clarifies that they are not of *bani adam*, or humanity.

It is worth stepping back from the developed understanding of the houri to ask why medieval theologians considered her a reward. With her cow or gazelle-like restrained glances, she communicates modestly with the direction of her gaze. This signaling is made all the more dramatic by the striking contrast of the white of her eye and the darkness of her pupil.[15] She is aware of her station as one of the many rewards of paradise, and she is designed to fulfill her purpose as a companion.

A SENSUAL BEING

While houris are introduced in the Qur'an and are explained through Qur'anic commentaries, they are further developed in the hadiths. Hadith collections are an important repository of religious tradition because they offer a record of the questions that Muhammad was asked and the stories the community transmitted in the early generations after his death. Hadith exhibit the ways in which Muslims imagined the rewards of paradise. In the hadith, houris magnify the wonders of the Garden and appear as sensual beings as their bodies, adornment, and comportment are described.

The status of the houri as companion is ambiguous in the Qur'an, but in the hadiths the houri is an active female who walks, talks, and beckons to the believer. Unlike earthly women, houris are cosmologically composed. They do not have resurrected bodies that are purified. Rather, they are literally made up of the materials of the Garden. Houris are, in effect, an embodied landscape. From knee to toe, they are made of saffron, from knee to breast, they are musk, breast to neck, they are amber, and neck to head, they are camphor.[16] Their hair is raw silk. Their flesh is so fair that you can see the marrow in their bone just as one could see wine through a crystal glass.[17] Because the houri is composed of luxurious materials, even her spit smells more pleasant than anything in the world.[18] These traditions about the marvelous nature of the houri can be found in hadith collections, eschatological manuals, and Qur'anic commentaries. The houri is adorned with luxurious materials and objects. With one glimpse, the believer can see jewels and fine brocade. With one breath, the believer can smell the scent of saffron and musk. With one touch, the believer can feel silk. The houri is not silent. She sings out to the believer in a melodious voice.

In the hadith traditions, the houri is understood not just in terms of companionship, but also of ownership. She is designated for the male believer and awaits him. As a sensual reward, she is also an active being. She glides through the landscape, and her scent wafts through the air. She speaks in her melodious voice to the believer, expressing her love. She dazzles with the luxurious nature of her body and dress. All of these traditions are framed within the descriptions of the Garden, which are equally opulent. The evocative Qur'anic vision of paradise as a social community that contains purified luxuries gives way to a developed paradise where family relations disappear and life is defined by and detailed through luxurious objects.

Houris play a central role in the narrative drama of the Garden. As a setting, the Garden is a place of amplification, but also of stillness.[19] Scenes of the Garden can also be static.

Its depictions of perfection are so driven by the description of material goods that it is difficult to show action, movement, or even conversation. While the Garden can be a realm of sensory overload, it encompasses little narrative drama. An exception is the houri, who is one of the few active figures in the Garden. The houri is not just the most visible female in the Garden, but the most visible being of the Garden. In one tradition, male believers greet each other in the Friday market where the houris glide through the landscape, amazing the believers with their beauty and their scent.[20] Wives and children do not occupy the same public space or point of focus. In fact, no particular believer or servant functions as a focal point as does the houri.

If hadiths develop the sensuality of the houri, it is in eschatological manuals that they are given central roles in tours of paradise. Eschatological manuals draw on traditions and offer readers a narrative about paradise. In these manuals, houris are not just part of the heavenly landscape, they are also active companions who introduce the believer to his new home. In Ibn Habib's (d. 853) *Kitab wasf al-firdaws*, the houri greets the believer with an explicit promise written on her chest: "You are my love, I am your love, my eyes are only for you and my soul leads to you."[21] In the narrative setting, the houri plays a pivotal role in welcoming the believer to the Garden. The believer is introduced to the wonders of paradise by his houri.

In the mystical narrative of al-Muhasibi's (d. 857) *Kitab al-Tawahhum*, the houri welcomes the believer to his palace. As the believer enters, he sees his attendants and marvels at the palace itself. He makes his way through the grounds and enters an inner chamber where the houri is sitting on the bed. In this scene, the houri acts as a realization of the believer's placement in the Garden, and she complements his soul as he begins to comprehend his nearness to God. In the mystical journey, the houri offers an important signpost for the believer's movement into paradise, into his palace, and into his domain. It is also notable that her appearance is in an interior chamber and on the bed. She has been waiting in repose for him as he has earned his place in the Garden.[22]

By the time of the more developed text attributed to al-Qadi, *Daqa'iq al-akhbar fi dhikr al-janna wa-l-nar*, the houri has such standing that she holds a court of her own. She has been transformed from sensual companion to a kind of queen. Her court is filled with its own retinue. The houri has her own servant girls (*al-jariya*), and even their beauty rivals earthly standards.[23] The believer looks at the girls wondering if they are his houris, only to discover that they are mere servants to his intended companion.

Hadith collections and manuals take the promise of the houri and amplify the descriptions and the contextual drama so that she becomes the reigning female in paradise. In these narratives, the houri is not just a static reward. In the dazzling descriptions of her beauty and her court, the afterlife as a family setting erodes. Instead, the Garden is represented as not just a place for all of the believer's desires, but a particular desire to have companionship with a purified woman in a cosmologically magnificent realm. In these narratives, houris transcend their functions as labor or companions or descriptions within the landscape of the Garden. They are not mentioned in groups: 2, 70, 72, or 70,000. Such numbers do not appear in the Qur'an, but in theological texts, to signal the concept of infinite reward. The eschatological manuals develop the houri as a character who plays a pivotal role in introducing the believer to his new realm. As the Garden's prime sensual being, she is a culminating reward.

Yet questioning the nature of companionship does not just involve the houris. In an interesting series of traditions, Ibn Habib records traditions that show a woman questioning which husband she would receive in paradise if she married twice in life (the answer is the first one).[24] Another woman asks if it is possible for her to marry her dead fiancé (the answer is yes, if she does not marry another).[25] The sources show that women, too, pondered the nature of companionship in paradise.

A SACRED WEDDING

While Qur'anic verses and hadiths reflect the expectation of the houri as reward, other genres show that the houri functioned as an aspiration. In these stories, which extol heroic fighting or piety during frontier battles, the houri plays an intriguing role as nurse or wife who appears to the wounded believer as he is dying. In these stories the houri is not just a reward, but a focal point during the process of dying. Her appearance signals the beginning of cosmic time as the dying believer moves from the state of earthly living, determined by a contract with God, into another state of immortal life introduced by the sacred wedding with the houri.

The earliest and most evocative of such stories may be found in the *Sirat Rasul Allah*. Houris offer consolation during the Battle of Uhud (625), when Muslims fought against the Meccans against overwhelming odds. This is the same battle that was invoked in the letter of Mohamed

Atta described in Chapter 1. In one instance, the prophet Muhammad sees two houris wiping the brow of a fighter who is dying on the battlefield, and he turns away, affording privacy to the moving scene of death. When questioned why he turned away from the dying man, he reveals his vision that the man was with his "two wives from the houris."[26] An accompanying tradition records that "'Abdullah b. Abu Najih told me that he was told that, when a martyr is slain, his two wives from the dark-eyed houris pet him, wiping the dust off his face, saying all the while: 'May God put dust on the face of the man who put dust on your face, and slay him who slew you.'"[27] The houris traverse the realms of time and space, and elevate the battlefield to a kind of sacred space. In these stories, houris are cosmic companions who tend to the wounded as they undergo the painful and terrifying process of dying.

In another place in *Sirat Rasul Allah*, the fighter 'Ubayda b. al-Harith recites a poem.

> *A battle will tell the Meccans about us:*
> *It will make distant men give heed,*
> *When 'Utba died and Shayba after him,*
> *And 'Utba's eldest son had no cause to be pleased with it.*
> *You may cut off his leg, yet I am a Muslim.*
> *I hope in exchange for a life near to Allah*
> *With Houris fashioned like the most beautiful statues*
> *With the highest heaven for those who mount there.*
> *I have bought it with the life of which I have tasted the best*
> *And which I have tried until I lost even my next of kin.*[28]

In the first instance, the houris constitute a female presence on the battlefield that accords special status to the man who will soon be considered a martyr. In the second instance, they are cited as rewards and characterized in terms of their beauty. Likened to beautiful statues, they embody the superlative nature of paradise and the reward for those who fight like lions. These mentions of houris demonstrate that in historical traditions, houris were connected with reward for dying in battle. In the *Sirat Rasul Allah*, houris are active cosmic females crossing from the afterworld into the earthly world, from the infinity of paradise to finite earthly time. They are rewards in the next, immortal life, and they usher the male believer from earthly time to cosmological life, from dying to eternal living.

In the following two centuries, in texts that enumerate the merits of jihad, the reward of the houri is depicted as a sacred wedding for those who die in battle. These texts or *fada'il al-jihad* form a genre that discusses types of jihad, battle traditions, and rituals of piety, with the objective of preparing fighters for martyrdom. In this larger categorizing and counseling acts of jihad, houris are occasionally mentioned. For example, in Ibn al-Mubarak's (d. 736 or 797) *Kitab al-Jihad*, there are 262 traditions about jihad, of which 13 relate to the houris.[29] In Ibn Abi Zaminayn's (d. 1009) *Qudwat al-Ghazi*, there are five allusions to a wedding night with the houris for the men who are soon to be martyred. In Ibn al-Nahhas's (d. 1411) compendium of jihad traditions *Mashari' al-ashwaq* mentions of the houri appear as well.

The terminology of the houri is not always the same. Sometimes, the stories refer to *al-hur al-'in* with definite articles for both *hur* and their eyes, unlike the Qur'anic usage.[30] Other times, they refer to a "woman from the people of the Garden"[31] or sometimes "your wives from the *hur al-'in*."[32] Given the question in the Qur'anic commentaries that contrasts the wives and the houris, the use of "*hur*" and "wives" for the houris suggests an ambivalence between the houri as a singular cosmic being and as an earthly replacement. In fact, according to Maher Jarrar, it is in the genre of *fada'il al-jihad* that the sacred wedding to the houris first gains popularity.[33] This marriage is different from earthly marriage. In Islamic legal tradition, marriage is a legal contract between man and wife. The marriage to the houris has a different framework. Unlike an earthly marriage, the marriage to the houri is a fulfillment, a sacred promise of the Garden.

In this genre, as in the stories in the *Sirat Rasul Allah*, Muslim men who die in battle do not have to enter the Garden to encounter the houri, but can meet her on the battlefield at the moment of death. Ibn al-Mubarak's early collection includes stories that link the battlefield with visions of paradise, in the form of the houris who descend to the battlefield to wipe the dust from the fighters' brows.[34] One notable strand in the collection involves traditions surrounding the Umayyad dynasty's (661–750) campaigns along the Byzantine frontier. In one example, commander Yazid bin Shajara extols the creations of God and refers to the gates of heaven, the gates of paradise, the gates of hell, and *al-hur al-'in*.[35] In another tradition from Byzantine territory, a man recalls walking in a garden or vineyard, noticing grapes, and then a residence. He enters his new domain, and sees a woman on a throne or a bedstead of gold. He casts his eyes down. Then he sees the end of the garden. The scene is repeated as he sees another woman and casts his eyes down again. She says, "I see you, and you have seen your wife from the *hur al-'in*, and the man was overjoyed."[36] Fighters meet their designated houris in other traditions as well. Sometimes the houri speaks to them and tells them, "I am your own wife."[37] In one tradition, the fighter's companion confirms the houri's status.[38] One tradition even identifies the houri designated as the fighter's wife as ʿAina, a figure who appears in the hadith as the head of all the houris.[39]

The promise of the houri is also a motive for conversion. In one story, a man converts to Islam so he can be allocated the two wives from paradise.[40] In another story, a Christian man boasts that he ate pork, drank wine, and consorted with his wife. Two men came and washed his belly, and the man saw two wives of the houris who were not jealous of each other. He eventually converts to Islam.[41] In yet another story, we again see a man convert to Islam because of the promise of two wives in paradise.[42] In these stories, meeting the houri is a transformative experience. Her beauty is so spectacular that Christians convert after seeing or learning about the promise of the houri. Traditions recount that they are overwhelmed or mad with joy when they learn of their reward.[43]

In *Kitab Qudwat al-Ghazi*, there are five traditions that suggest that the houri was invoked in other frontier wars, including Umayyad campaigns in Sicily.[44] The traditions also expand the tours of paradise, amplifying the descriptions of gems, green silk, clothes, and the houri al-ʿAina.[45] A full narrative is developed in one tradition in which the palace not only is filled with opulent goods, but also contains *ghilman* who pass through the palace complex.[46]

By the time of Ibn al-Nahhas's *Mashariʿ al-ashwaq*, there is repetition of earlier traditions from Ibn al-Mubarak and explications of references to houris in the Qurʾanic verses in suras Rahman (55) and al-Waqiʿa (56). There is a remarkable section regarding the temptations of the world and all the reasons that a person can be held back from going on jihad.

These reasons include fearing death or attachment to family or pride in lifestyle. Each reason is brought forward and debated, and the afterworld always emerges as superior to the earthly world.

In one passage, Ibn al-Nahhas makes a distinction between a man's love for his wife and the promise of the houri. While the text can be seen as dismissive of the wife, its larger purpose is to emphasize the superiority of the afterlife to this earthly life. In earthly life, bodily pollution and material desire taint the wife. She menstruates, she has to bathe, she requires grooming, and she desires things. She makes demands and is not always grateful. By contrast, the houri is beautiful like a gem, and even her spit would beautify the world. Ibn al-Nahhas reflects on the cosmic wonders of the houri and the possibility of encountering her. Yet the text goes on to praise the wife's beauty, which will be even more transformative.[47] In effect, men will have both houris and wives in the Garden, and they are both cosmologically purer and more beautiful than the women of this world.

While the descriptions of the afterlife evoke a full earthly life with the promise of sexuality, they are cast within the framework of opulence and beauty. In these texts, there is no suggestion that every believer is awarded a houri in the Garden. Instead, it is the dying warrior who is granted a vision of the houri on the battlefield. What is striking in these collections is how contemplating the houri as cosmic bride develops emotional states. Men are overcome with joy and even go mad upon catching a glimpse of the houri. Even Christians who enjoy the pleasures of pork and wine are compelled to convert when they understand the nature of the houri and the possibility of a sacred wedding.

In this genre, the houri is an aspiration and a rhetorical motivation. She represents the wonders of paradise and the special station reserved for those who are able to enter the realm of the Garden through battle and martyrdom. The stories about the sacred wedding with the houris are not prominent throughout the text. Most of the traditions in the *fada'il al-jihad* genre involve how to prepare for death, with a focus on the requisite piety and preparation to meet God. Significantly, the texts recast the nature of reward. While theological literature promises houris for all men, the jihad literature elevates fighters, who are able to see or meet their houri *before* entering the Garden. Even within the genre, however, the sacred wedding was a smaller reward than attaining God's favor after struggling on the path of God with full piety in the heart. The virtuous could look forward to otherworldly rewards that were linked to the presence of God.[48]

ENTERTAINMENT

While the reward of the houri began as a theological doctrine, the houri's function may not have been limited to religious edification. The figure of the houri may have inspired earthly female companions. The earliest intimation of the houri as an entertainer is in the hadith collections where the houris are said to have melodious voices. The houri is one of the sole characters in the Garden who vocalizes thoughts and feelings. It is in this respect that the houri resembles the earthly singing slave girl.

The Garden is mostly depicted in terms of the sense perceptions: sight, taste, smell, and touch. This may be a function of the limits of language. How are we to understand paradise, which is outside the realm of human experience? The ineffable nature of eschatological time lends itself to sensory metaphors. The Garden uses material objects to involve the senses of sight, smell, and taste. Qur'anic verses mention gold, silver, camphor, amber, drink, and food. In all these descriptions, what is missing is sound. While believers call out to each other or socialize, there are few conversations. While we know that believers can feast on any food of their desire, there is no soundscape in paradise. There are no birds singing or animals calling. In the stillness of the Garden, there is a silence. The one exception that can be found in the eschatological traditions is the houri and her melodious voice that calls out: "We live forever and never pass away, we are affluent and never austere, we are content and never discontent. Blessed are those who belong to us and to whom we belong."[49] This suggests a message that is sonorous, but not necessarily a song. It is not expressed through a musical instrument, but the most beautiful of voices.

The houri's voice is vital to her role as the prime, active female of the Garden. While wives do speak out in order to praise their husband's beauty,[50] the houri speaks directly to the believer about her purpose. If *wildan* and *ghilman* correspond to the earthly slave boy or cupbearer, then does the houri resemble the concubine or singing slave girl? If we interpret the houri's purity as exclusive sexual access, then she looks like a heavenly concubine. However, the focus on her beauty and the fact that she has a voice in the Garden suggests that it may be more accurate to view her as a singing companion whose art transcends the earthly world.

The most developed text about the singing slave girl was by al-Jahiz (d. 868). In *Risalat al-qiyan*, he presents the quandary of the slave girl. She was beautiful, yet she could lead men astray by distracting them from their families and responsibilities. The possible connection between the *hur* and the *qiyan*, or singing slave girls, is intriguing. Both serve men by providing entertainment and companionship, and both were praised for their physical beauty and melodious voices. However, the *qiyan* needed male admirers because they were the prime means of income, network, and social mobility. The *qiyan* are tainted in the sense that they are accused of scheming and clouding men's judgment.[51] By contrast, houris have a purity that is reflected in their exquisite substance. They are the ultimate companions because they are cosmically beautiful in a realm that transforms human bodies and temperaments. Companionship with the houri cannot cloud judgment. It can only confirm that pure female companionship is a reward for the righteous male. The houri is akin to the non-intoxicating wine of paradise. Just as intoxicating drink—forbidden in earthly life—is enjoyed without taint in the cosmic perfection of paradise, so a melodious female is enjoyed there without the taint of earthly schemes.

The pursuit or achievement of beauty does connect the houri and the *qiyan*. In fact, adornment associated with the houri may have been adopted by slave girls, who wore ornaments and inscribed poetry on their hands, feet, and forehead. Ibn al-Washsha' (d. 936) mentions how *qiyan* adorned their bodies with poetry inscribed with musk and amber.[52] They decorated themselves like houris on earth.

Servants in the Garden are characterized by their function and their aesthetic appeal. Like the servants on earth, their purpose is to provide services so that believers do not have to labor. Yet they are distinct from earthly laborers in that they reflect the resplendent nature of the Garden's landscape. The *wildan* and *ghilman* are not just useful. They are beautiful on the inside and agelessly pure to the inner core. They are shimmering points of utility that make the Garden more beautiful. The houris are not just companions, but they are beautiful in composition and pure in essence. They are both beings and objects. They are the ultimate refinement of feminine beauty and the part of the Garden's landscape that moves, interacts, and speaks. Ultimately both of these types of cosmic servants share characteristics with earthly models associated with the banquet. The *wildan* and *ghilman* recall the *saqin*, and the houri the *qiyan*. Yet the *wildan* and *ghilman* cannot be reduced to slaves or the houri to concubines. Because the Garden links ethical consequence with aesthetic expectations, the servants are far more than laborers. They are beautiful beings who are an essential part of the rewards that make up the Garden. They also reflect the future transformation of the believer and the world. In effect, they affirm the majesty of God.

Entertainment that evokes the houri appears in illustrated manuscripts such as Mir Haydar's fifteenth century volume, which is written in the Uighur script. The illustrated manuscript includes sixty-one miniature paintings of Muhammad's ascension and night journey to the heavens (*al-isra' wa-l mi'raj*) in which Muslims believe the angel Gabriel escorted Muhammad through the levels of the Fire and the Garden. In the manuscript, houris appear with flowering trees as part of the landscape of paradise.[53] Sometimes, houris are invoked in a different capacity. In some manuscripts of al-Qazwini's (d. 1283) compendium of marvels, *Kitab 'aja'ib al-makhluqat wa ghara'ib al-mawjudat*, winged tree dwellers of Java or the Pacific islands are described as houris.[54] Here the houri is not a being of paradise, but an unfamiliar creature in an unknown realm.

The houri also serves another entertainment function, and that is as a parody of the literal rewards of paradise. Since September 11th, we have seen jokes in print and online media about the empty promises of heavenly virgins. Yet the skeptical attitude was also in evidence in an earlier time. Persian mathematician and poet Omar Khayyam (d. 1131) is said to have remarked:

> *They say houris make the gardens of Paradise delicious,*
> *I say that the juice of the vine is delicious,*
> *Take this cash and reject that credit*
> *The sound of a distant drum, brother, is sweet.*[55]

Khayyam prefers wine to the reward of the houri that can only be enjoyed in another realm. These verses urge the reader to embrace life here and now rather than hope for the future reward of cosmic perfection. That abstract reward is too distant and too uncertain for Khayyam and his pursuit of earthly pleasures.

The houri, then, was an ambiguous figure in paradise that was first mentioned in the Qur'an and developed in theological literature. Yet the function of the houri was not rigidly set. She represented beauty in the Qur'an, a divine nurse tending to the dying in early historical accounts, the proof of the majesty of God's creations in eschatological manuals, and a purified companion who could inspire courage in traditions about jihad.

Omar Khayyam's verse suggests a different interpretation. Believers who require a reward make a miscalculation by valuing the future over the present. It is an astute observation that reflects the function of the houri. Indeed, contemporary discussion about the houri not only involves how she shapes Muslim ethics or behavior, but also engages with interpretation to define her meaning and place in the twenty-first century.

THE PROMISE

VISIONS OF THE AFTERLIFE ARE ineffable. Eschatological literature often uses the genre of the tour of the afterworld as a way to frame cosmic fears and desires that cannot be easily articulated. In the twenty-first century, digital media offer dynamic ways to visualize these tours. On the Internet, there are constructed digital Islamic afterworlds where houris are a topic of popular preaching. These afterworlds vary in their focus and details, and their productions can range from carefully designed to informally assembled. They present another space in which to consider the afterlife and its relevance to Muslims, and they offer the opportunity to engage Muslim viewers internationally. Through subtitles and translations, the online videos extend beyond local communities and regions. They can reach anyone who has the means to access the Internet.

The online lectures and tours of paradise do not just constitute religious instruction in a diluted form. Instead, they present a twenty-first-century exhortation that is meant to reform Muslims and to impress upon them that the consequences of their actions on earth will be reflected in the afterworld. While the videos differ, they all share a concern about modernity, a focus on the salvation of humanity, and a desire for cosmic order.[1] In the videos, houris are a reward that reveals the limitations of this world and the promise of a future after death.

This chapter surveys online sites through different genres, languages, and platforms to present eschatological material about the houri in reformist lectures, jihadi videos, *a cappella* songs, and Syrian civil war clips that were accessed between January and August 2015. In contrast to the materials considered thus far, the digital media are not fixed, but are mutable, repetitive, and difficult to assess. Sometimes a site generates traffic in the first few months, and then sits all but unvisited for years afterward. Other times, a site is popular, disappears, and reappears in another form. Over the past decade, the numbers and format of videos have changed frequently. Determining authorship and reception can be vexing.

A snapshot of eight months of digital discourse shows the range and movement of the online world. Sites often shift. Others are taken down. Terrorist attacks can result in the deletion of websites. After the attack on the Bataclan Concert Hall in Paris in November 2015, some French reformist websites discussed in this chapter could no longer be found. Recent policy shifts by Internet companies such as YouTube, Facebook, Twitter, and Google also result in the deletion of sites. Another notable example is that, since November 2017, YouTube has been taking down the videos of Anwar al-Awlaqi, whose work will be examined here.[2]

The videos considered in this chapter may seem random or idiosyncratic, but they are connected. Aside from the fact that the clips all draw on traditions of the houri, they also are linked through tags about the houri, virgins, and paradise in Islam. When you watch one video, particularly on YouTube, other related videos appear in the right vertical column. If you type "paradise," "heaven," "apocalypse," or "hereafter" and "Islam" or "Muslim" into Google and YouTube, you will find websites and blogs developed to provide religious instruction and, on YouTube, clips that can reach a wide audience through subtitles in English, French, and Turkish, among other languages. These clips allow a sampling of material on Islamic paradise, and they constitute a forum for computer-literate Muslims. The Hajj may be the ultimate gathering for Muslims worldwide, but the Internet offers another space where Muslims of different regions and languages can share their feelings about what it means to be Muslim in the twenty-first century.

The dynamic online sites are populated by different Muslim constituencies whose aim is to reform Islam. Chapter 6 will turn to Muslims who are exploring questions of gender inequality. This chapter focuses on preachers who spread their message beyond their local constituencies and on jihadis who seek to sway Muslims toward violent struggle. Aside from influencing believers through argument, both mainstream Sunni and jihadi videos seek to induce feelings. Charles Hirshkind reports that YouTube clips are praised as *mu'aththir* if they are able to be "effective, affecting, moving, emotional, impassionate, stirring, exciting."[3] If a production is *mu'aththir*, it is able to influence viewers' emotional states. Hirshkind identifies this "pious affect" as "an emerging media practice"[4] that constitutes an Islamic devotional exercise.[5] The use of vocalization or *nashid* in the videos can produce cathartic experiences that reinforce ideology[6] or encourage personal bonds within online forums.[7] In these online paradises, the houri is part of a promise of an alternative world that can be *felt* before it is experienced at the end of time. In addressing viewers' feelings and creating virtual symbols and rituals, the online productions draw upon the houri to justify the need to reform behavior or to incite violent struggle. The online world is becoming a forum for an interconnected, virtual global Islam.

ESCHATOLOGICAL MANUALS

Before online videos, there were print manuals. Houris appear in eschatological material printed in Cairo, Beirut, and Damascus in the 1990s. These pamphlets, manuals, and books constitute a significant moment in the intersection of print revolution and expanding theological authority. Jean-Pierre Filiu and David Cook have both noted how Arabic books on the Islamic apocalypse proliferated in the 1990s and have continued into the twenty-first century with topics like September 11th and America's role in the Middle East.[8] Some of the manuals are inexpensive imprints of classical works, such as selections from al-Ghazali's (d. 1111) *Ihya' 'ulum al-din*, which presents the traditional Sunni view on faith and paradise. Other manuals are written by contemporary authors and have not been vetted by theological authorities. While the reprints of canonical texts continue to elevate the theologians of earlier centuries and their standing in Islamic learning, the popular manuals claim a religious authority that has not been conferred by scholarly consensus.

I started collecting the manuals in Syria and Jordan in the late 1990s and the early 2000s. The booksellers outside the Umayyad mosque in Damascus had the largest selection and most interesting volumes. Their tables were piled with titles on topics like faith, prayer, veiling, and Muslim parenting. Several of the booksellers divided their merchandise by category.[9] On one side were books about faith, women's issues, and children's guides. On the other side were eschatological literature and sex-education books for male readers. The gender divide was clear.

The eschatological manuals enumerate the stages of the apocalypse. They discuss the signs of the final hour and how Muslims could determine if the end of time was coming near. While their texts are drawn from the Qur'an and hadiths, their covers offer powerful visual representations of the terrors of the grave, apocalypse, and the hell-fire. For example, *The Lesser and Greater Signs of the Hour* shows the image of the one-eyed Dajjal, an anti-Christ figure, the twins Gog and Magog, and other signs of the end of time (Figure 5.1).[10]

The *Women of the People of Fire* evokes the terror of the realm with a picture of a woman screaming within the engulfing flames (Figure 5.2).[11]

While not as numerous, there are also covers that depict the idealized world of the Garden. *Women of the People of the Garden* shows a veiled woman looking out over a landscape of flowers, lush greenery, and waterfalls alongside a bounty of apples (Figure 5.3).[12]

The graphics may seem simplistic, but their iconography recalls the wonders of paradise. Their simple layout suggests that the world is, in effect, just as two-dimensional; the real reward is in another fuller, more complete promised realm. What is fascinating is that the covers also offer a template for depicting paradise in online videos.

FIGURE 5.1 *Lesser and Greater Signs of the Hour*. Cover, *'Alamat al-sa'a al-sughra wa-l-kubra*.

FIGURE 5.2 *Women of the People of the Fire. Cover, Nisa' min ahl al-nar.*

FIGURE 5.3 *Women of the People of the Garden.* Cover, *Nisa' min ahl al-janna*

TOURS OF PARADISE

While paradise can only be visited after death, online lectures often take listeners on a "tour" of the magnificent realm. The lectures blend verses from the Qur'an with prophetic tradition, Qur'anic commentary, and personal insight. Often, the purpose of the tours is to reform Muslims so they will be more likely to enter paradise. The strategy is to focus first on the rewards of paradise and then to show how the earthly counterpart is tainted, corrupted, or not worth succumbing to temptation. Some of the tours are grounded on argument, while others seek to evoke pathos. These objectives are not mutually exclusive, but they draw on different methods. The videos often use reasoning and humor to explain the Qur'anic promise of the houri through temptations in modern life, whereas the ones that seek to develop religious affect depend on music and images to encourage meditation on injustices perpetrated against Muslims. What is striking about the videos is how they seek to reach a Muslim audience in Europe and the Americas.

The online tours present the speaker as a male authority figure. (I have found no videos of women offering tours of paradise.) One French video offers a good example of how the speaker, through Qur'anic commentary, animates the discussion of paradise. In "A travel in Paradise!," Rachid Abou Houdeyfa (d. 2019), an imam in Brest, France, discusses the promise of paradise while sitting in front of a swimming pool. In the clip, he is speaking French with English subtitles, which expands the possible audience.

> As we all know, my dear brothers and sisters, in this life we are attracted by plenty of pleasures: swimming pools, palm trees, beautiful cars, money, and so forth. Such as the swimming pool and the palm tree behind me can attract anyone!

That is quite natural! My dear brothers and sisters! But in order to avoid falling excessively in those delights while forgetting the afterlife, the believer has to remember what Allah (Glorious and Exalted is He) has prepared for the virtuous ones in paradise.[13]

He then focuses on the meeting of fathers, mothers, and children in the afterlife. For him, paradise is a wonderful realm where there are streams of wine and milk. It is a place where the family can be reunited, and there are "no worries, no stress, no jealously, no resentment, only satisfaction and tranquility."[14] There is a visual argument on offer in the video through the setting with its cool waters, breezes, and swaying palm trees: What we see appears like an earthly paradise, but we are reminded that it is a pale version of paradise at the end of time.

There are two different versions of Ahmed Ali's "The Final Abode." In the first, longer version, the camera focuses on the speaker.[15] In the second, shorter clip, the camera shows an abstract image of paradise while there is a chant in the background. Interestingly, online comments from viewers dismiss the effectiveness of the "background music" and ask that it be removed from the video entirely.[16]

Ahmed Ali is based in the United Kingdom, and his lectures offer an elaborate tour of paradise. In his telling, the houri reveals the true reward for both men and women. In introducing the houri, he weaves together Qur'anic recitations, hadith, and personal commentary. His informal tone is compelling.

There will be *hur al-'in* sitting on her throne. This is the Queen! And when he . . . when he looks at her, when he looks at her, she is so beautiful, so beautiful . . . in the *akhira* [hereafter], this is real. . . . He won't know what's hit him.

You know a woman so beautiful, can it be? He will look at her for forty years, forty years, you know, he won't know what's hit him. He will, you know, his eyes, you know, he'll think he's in a coma. He will look one direction, and I am assuming his mouth will be open [laughter]. What's this? What's this?[17]

After extolling the beauty of the houri, he addresses the men:

Now this is when I want my sisters just to put their headphones on, cause this part . . . is only for the men. Now you are thinking—you know what—how beautiful can she be? You know, come on—how beautiful can a woman be? Yeh, you know what? You have to look up to the maker. . . . You know when Allah makes something, then believe me, he can make something. And these *hur al 'ins* are so beautiful, so beautiful that Rasul Allah *'alayhi as-salam* once said. . . . You know just her fingertip, if it was ever to become visible in this *dunya* [earth], you know the *nur*, the light, the gleam, call it what you want, of her fingertip, it's so bright, it is so beautiful, that, that would overpower the light of the sun and moon put together. This is just her fingertip. You need to get there to believe it, don't you guys. . . . It's going to get better, believe me, don't be disappointed.[18]

His explanation relates prophetic traditions to earthly realities. For example, "The sweet smell coming from her hair would fill the entire *dunya* with a sweet smell. Better than Head and Shoulders or your Timotei. I mean this is what you call shampoo."[19] Comments like these evoke daily life, engage the audience, and elicit laughter.

Afterward, he addresses whether women on earth, or *dunya*, are better than women in paradise.

The women of the *dunya* will be more superior than the *hur al-'in*. . . . So now she's got the answer that she was looking for, by the grace of Allah, it saved many heart attacks today [laughter], many heart attacks. You know—from this my sisters need to learn [to] look how, how much regard Allah has for them, how much regard Allah has for them that even women, when before Rasul Allah came, what was a woman? You know in the entire world, even in Western world, they were still debating whether she was a human being, they were still debating whether she was a human being, and in the land of Arabia, they were burying them alive. And this is when Allah's Messenger declared . . . Just as men have rights, the women have also rights. And he elevated their ranks in the *dunya*. . . . He didn't let them down in the *akhira* [hereafter]. . . That even in the *akhira*, in spite of this great creation of Allah . . . these servants of Allah will be far superior to this creation of Allah *subhanahu wa-ta'ala*. Even in *al-janna*, Allah has elevated them. . . .[20]

The reason that women are superior is because of their righteousness. Ali goes on to argue, based on hadith, that there are specific ways in which the women of earth will have a higher rank in the afterlife than the houris.

So now that she's got the answer she was looking for, she wanted to hear more. As women like to do, they love it when you tell them how beautiful they are, and so you should. That's the least that you can do. . . . How will they be more superior? How is it that the women of *al-janna* are more superior to the women in paradise. . . . Because of their fasting, because of their worshipping and prostrating before Allah, because of their reciting the Qur'an, because of their giving their *zakat* [alms-giving] and *sadaqah* [charity]. It is a result of this, they are far superior to the women of paradise.[21]

So even if the men receive houris in the afterlife, the wives from the earthly world will be superior to the heavenly beings because they are Muslims in substance. They are people who have submitted to the will of God and have chosen to live a righteous life, so their value exceeds a mere reward.

While there are several tours of paradise online, the most comprehensive is by Anwar al-Awlaqi. As part of a multivolume series entitled "The Hereafter Books," the lectures present Muslims with what will happen to them from the time of their death to the entry into the afterworld. The twenty-two lectures address the stages of the soul from earthly life to the apocalypse to judgment to the hereafter.

Killed by a US drone strike in Yemen in 2011, al-Awlaqi was a leader of al-Qa'ida in the Arabian Peninsula. Through his online lectures and publication of *Inspire* magazine, he influenced people to attack Americans. Among those he influenced were Major Nidal Malik Hasan, who killed thirteen and wounded thirty-two at Fort Hood, Texas, in November 2009; Umar Farouk Abdulmutallab, who attempted to blow up an airliner bound for Detroit in December 2010;[22] and Faisal Shahzad, who attempted to detonate a car bomb in Times Square in New York City in May 2010. Even after al-Awlaqi's death, his online lectures continued to provide inspiration to individuals like Tamerlan and Dzhokhar Tsarnaev, who set off two bombs at the Boston Marathon, killing three people and injuring 300 others in 2013,[23] and Saïd and Chérif Kouachi, who claimed that their deadly attack on the offices of the French satirical publication *Charlie Hebdo* in 2015 was ordered and financed by al-Qa'ida in Yemen.[24]

Al-Awlaqi's lectures did not offer overt encouragement to violence, and in fact, he would state explicitly that the lecture was not meant to inspire violence. He suggested, however, that classical texts could offer a template for living a present life, and in effect historical example became "a kind of code."[25] The lectures show how mainstream material can be used as an entry to jihadi polemic, leading to the more radicalized lectures that appear in YouTube in the vertical column to the right. By reviewing the comments left by viewers, we can see which groups are using the site. For example, there were many comments that disapproved of the background vocalization in Ahmed Ali's video, which suggests that its audience was not interested in the affective element common in jihadi productions.[26]

In his lectures, al-Awlaqi discusses various features of paradise in an engaging, informal fashion. The series begins with the "Torment of the Grave" and continues through the "Apocalypse"; the traditions about paradise are found in the last three sections: "Tour of Jannah Paradise," "Socialization in Paradise," and "People of Paradise." In these three sections, he explains the logic of paradise as a perfected realm of salvation that is preferable to earthly life. He interprets the verses with real-world metaphors. He refers to the believer's "real estate" in paradise and to the various structures as "your property."[27] He supports his interpretation by splicing Qurʾanic recitations into the tour.

For al-Awlaqi, life in paradise is discovering one's true self in one's true place. He says that upon entering paradise, "You will know your house. . . . Your heart is attached to your house."[28] This house and the surrounding landscape of paradise do not have typical architecture, he says, because they are not confined by earthly limitations. Everything resembles earth, yet it is different. "Such is the promise of Allah, and never does Allah fail in his promise."[29]

Upon entering through the gates of the Garden, the first thing that the believer sees is "your wife in *janna*" and her stunning beauty:

> He is walking up and he goes next to his palace and then suddenly he just cannot move, and he sees his wife. Whether it is his wife from *janna* or his wife from *dunya*, he will just see her face and freeze in his tracks. And he will just sit there contemplating at her beauty. Beauty, that is, we are uncapable of describing in worldly terms. Allah *subhanahu wa-ta'ala* says about them . . . companions of equal age and Allah says . . . we have created their companions of special creation and made them virgin pure and undefiled, beloved by nature, equal in age. Their beauty is so much that it is said by one of the scholars who wrote about *janna*, that this man will stand there and stare at her for forty years just contemplating at her beauty. And these women of *janna* are not beautiful because they were voted in by a panel of men at the beauty contest. They are beautiful because Allah *subhanahu wa-ta'ala* said they are beautiful, and it is enough for us to know that Allah *subhanahu wa-ta'ala* says they are beautiful.[30]

Al-Awlaqi emphasizes the special creation and supports his descriptions by citing traditions about the marrow showing through the houri's skin and clothes. Al-Awlaqi admits that even he cannot understand how this is possible, but trusts God because the wonders of paradise are only approximated in earthly life.[31]

Toward the end of the lecture, al-Awlaqi addresses the question of what happens when a woman marries more than one husband. He takes on the inequity of reward in the Garden suggested by the fact that the houris are specifically for men.

So sometimes our sisters felt left out. And the husbands are having all this fun, he's marrying all of these women. I was able to keep guard on him very well in *al-dunya*, and did it, and have him not get married on me. But there he goes to *al-janna*, and he has all these women with him. So what's the deal with that?[32]

After acknowledging what is perceived to be an inconsistency between earthly life and otherworldly promise for women, Al-Awlaqi counsels women on why the granting of houris will not make them feel badly.

Dear Sisters, first of all, let's get it straight that in *janna*, you will have no bad feelings, first of all, nobody will have any bad feelings. . . . Allah *subhanahu wa-ta'ala*, we have taken out of their hearts any bad feelings. So there's not going to be any jealousy, no pain, no suffering, no despair, nothing of this in *al-janna*.[33]

In paradise the self is transformed, so that there can be no sense of ill will or jealousy. Further, he suggests that men and women have different natures: Men's needs are different from women's.

No. 2. Allah *subhanahu wa-ta'ala* knows his creation. He knows what men want, and he knows what women want, and Allah will give everyone what will make them happy. Allah *subhanahu wa-ta'ala* knows that men want to have a lot of wives, that's a fact, and anybody who's saying otherwise is not really telling his wives the truth. This is the fact of the matter, this is how men are created. And Allah *subhanahu wa-ta'ala* will give them what they want. Everyone in *al-janna* will have at least two wives.

And women, they have certain desires and needs and all
of these desires and needs will be fulfilled in *al-janna* and
more.[34]

Al-Awlaqi tries to suggest that women are incapable of having more than one male. At this point, he briefly loses his
consistently smooth delivery as he describes the difference in
rewards for men and women.

> So there shouldn't be any bad feelings, that, how come? Also
> from a psychological point of view, a woman would never
> desire to have more than one husband. See, so, even the psy-
> chological makeup of females is different than males. . . . So
> don't worry that your husbands will have *hur al-'in*. You will
> be very very happy in *al-janna*.[35]

It is worth noting his discomfort with respect to the equality
of rewards for men and women. When it comes to women,
he can only reiterate that paradise is the transformed realm
where women will receive what they desire. The promise of
the houri, for al-Awlaqi, is a promise for men.

VIRTUAL JIHAD

The idea of jihad has a multifaceted history that includes both
the ethics of striving to better oneself and the motivation for
battle. The jihad of terror attacks, suicide bombers, and online
executions is a twentieth- and twenty-first-century phe-
nomenon. After 1969, hostage-taking, murders, and threats
could be witnessed on television and in homes around the
world.[36] Terror, which had been a tool of statecraft and of

resistance, became a public act because millions of viewers could witness.

Terror attacks reach a huge audience on television and the Internet. The National September 11 Memorial & Museum estimates that nearly two billion people, one-third of the world's population, witnessed the attacks on the World Trade Center towers through the Internet, television, or radio.[37] The reach is extraordinary, but it also requires media to frame the story and narrate the events. By selecting a channel or website, we can elect to witness footage of the attacks and commentary on them. This form of participation in experiencing the terror act is new, and it vastly increases the visibility and impact of the attacks.

Twenty-first-century jihad is ultimately a new media spectacle. When we see a beheading video, we bear witness to an act of cruelty against the victim, but we also fulfill the aims of the terror groups by bearing witness to the violence. Jihad on the Internet is an immediate and intimate communicative act. We glide along, surfing sites developed by unknown authors. Consider the killings of Daniel Pearl, Nicholas Berg, James Foley, Steven Sotloff, and Moaz al-Kasasbeh, all of which were uploaded to the Internet. The terror act can be viewed in the privacy of our homes, on our screens, and on our smartphones.

The online tours of paradise present eschatological material in order to reform religious behavior. Jihadi clips intend to develop the feeling for jihad. The "pious affect"[38] in these videos has a meditative quality that suggests the creation of an online affirmation ritual.[39] The jihadi videos are more concerned with this meditation than establishing a particular authority figure. Often, they offer a meaningful image or a series of images, accompanied by vocalizations in the background. One can identify a jihadi video, then, not just by the subject material, but also by the way in which the material is presented. Philipp Holtmann suggests that this virtual realm creates an alternate leadership where symbols gradually introduce viewers to groups that seek to provoke virtual and actual violence.[40]

Take, for example, a clip from al-Awlaqi discussing an excerpt of *Mashari' al-ashwaq* by Ibn al-Nahhas, mentioned in Chapter 4. The text addresses the nature of jihad and was popularized by the Egyptian Sayyid al-Qutb (d. 1966) who advocated for jihad as a form of Islamic political practice. While al-Awlaqi mentions in the beginning that the purpose of the course is to study the text, not to support violence, he provides a translation of the text that expounds on how to go on jihad. In the section about the *hur al-'in*, he discusses the difference between the *hur al-'in* and earthly wives and the problems with earthly wives. This video is a good example of what Holtmann calls "media jihad," which offers a "separate sphere with its own logic and mechanisms."[41] In the clip there are accompanying images, beginning with the silhouette of a rider with a black flag on a horse. All three motifs of horse, rider, and black standard are contemporary symbols of jihad battling forces of injustice. The image conveys the jihadi polemic that the battle with the horse and rider unites the past and present.[42] The visual argument suggests that the cosmic battle began with the campaigns of Muhammad and will end when the black banners of the East appear to announce the apocalypse.[43]

The beginning of the video claims that earthly women are corrupted, demonstrating the point with images such as a Neanderthal-like woman beating a man and a bride in a white dress and stiletto heels kicking her groom. The second part of the video, which presents the promise of the houri, shows an idealized coupling and landscape: a close-up of stylized blue eyes, colorful birds, planets, a bouquet of flowers, and two swans in an idyllic landscape. The following transcription of the audio notes the corresponding images:

> If you cannot go to jihad because you are attached to your beautiful wife, then even if you were to assume that your wife is the best woman in the whole world and that she is the most beautiful woman in the whole world. Now didn't she start out as a lowly droplet and [image of cartoon of woman clubbing man] would end as a decomposed body? And in between her birth and death, she never ceased carrying stool in her gut. Her menstrual period keeps you away from her for a good portion of her life. Her disobedience is more than her obedience. If she does not wash, she would smell horrible. If she doesn't comb, her hair becomes ruffled. The older she gets, the more ugly she becomes [image of bride kicking husband]. Pleasing her is not easy. And her love costs you a lot. You are always trying to impress her, and nothing is ever enough. She only loves you when you give her what she wants. And if you don't, she would soon leave you and find someone else. As if she is telling you, if you want me, spend on me. In general, you cannot enjoy her without enduring pain and suffering.[44]

By contrast, the *hur* are pure and beautiful and inspire wonder. Al-Awlaqi questions why anyone would not want to meet them.

> It is amazing how such a woman is keeping you away from the women of paradise. In the name of Allah, the blood of the *shahid* [martyr] does not dry before he meets his wife in paradise. She is beautiful with big lustrous eyes [image

of woman's blue eyes]. A virgin as if she is an emerald. She has loved no one and will love no one but you. She was created for you [image of two colorful birds] and only you. If her finger appears, it would overshadow the moon. If her bracelet appears in the dark night, it would mean no darkness in the universe. If her wrist appears, it would take away the mind of every sane human being. If she appears between the heaven and earth [image of planets in the horizon of a fantastic landscape], the distance between them would be filled by her scent. And if she spits in the oceans of the world, the saltwater would turn fresh. The more you look at her, the more beautiful she becomes. The more time you spend with her, the more you love her [image of a bouquet of flowers]. Does it make any sense to learn about such a woman and not try to meet her? What about when you learn you will not be married to one but seventy of the *hur* [image of two swans in an idyllic landscape].[45]

The choice, then, is whether to be limited by short-sighted earthly loyalties or to embrace the inevitability of death and enjoy the rewards that can be gained. The images suggest their own argument: the earthly wife wears her husband down (as illustrated by the images of women beating their husbands); the houri is the true partner. She complements his soul, a relationship illustrated by two colorful green birds. This is not a random choice, since an often-cited hadith states that martyrs will be as green birds.[46] This cosmic coupling of martyr and houri will take place in the perfect world with an idyllic landscape.

Keep in mind that leaving your wife behind is inevitable. You will die and so would she. And *insha'allah* you will be reunited in paradise, and then you will find her to be even more beautiful than the *hur* [image of open blue sky with flowers with a field of flowers in the foreground]. When that happens, you will find her free of all of the contaminations of this worldly life. Wake up before it's too late. Free yourself from the prison [image of a martyr draped with a green flag] of this world and pray to Allah to grant you martyrdom. Don't let anything stand between you and this great reward.[47] Abu Huraira narrates that the Messenger of Allah says that the *shahid* feels the pain of death just like one of you would feel the pain of an insect.[48]

The lecture makes the argument that jihad is the right course for those who will be awarded in paradise with houris and rewarded even further by seeing their spouses transformed into their pure selves. The images strengthen the argument by suggesting that earthly wives are not worth the difficulty, while the women of paradise can be achieved through battle.[49] Like Ahmed Ali's lecture, al-Awlaqi's text goes on to suggest that the earthly wives will be transformed in paradise. Nonetheless, the message is clear: Why remain with your wife on earth, when you will receive bounties of houris, and enjoy your wife in a more purified form in paradise?

NASHID AS MOTIVATION

If terrorism is a media production, then it has a script, a score, and even a soundtrack. The online videos not only draw on visual imagery to suggest the superiority of paradise and the houris but also are accompanied by *nashid*s (*a cappella* songs) that rouse the spirit for jihad. For those Muslims who interpret the ban on music strictly, the *nashid*s are an accepted form of vocalization, because they are not accompanied by musical instruments. Hirshkind suggests that it is human voice that brings one close to God, and Islam presents an acoustically mediated piety that guides the visual aesthetics.[50] The image may put forward the argument about houris, but it is the vocalization that offers the opportunity to meditate on the possibilities of jihad. Tilman Seidensticker suggests that these kinds of songs have been "composed, sung, and recorded" since Afghans fought the Soviets.[51]

There are *nashids* about a range of Islamic precepts, but jihadi *nashids* gained visibility as a recruitment tool on the Internet. *Nashids* may offer a way to bond before ideological connections begin to take place.[52] They are a critical, affective form of recruitment. Often, the *nashids* are illustrated by pictures of well-known al-Qa'ida leaders, Islamic State symbols, or al-Shahab operations with English or French subtitles.[53] *Nashids* have become the soundtrack of jihad[54] especially because the Islamic State's song "Dawlat al-Islam Qamat" ["My Ummah, Dawn has appeared"] has accompanied jihadi video productions. The Islamic State *nashid* can be categorized as a battle hymn, but it departs from older models.[55] While the older *nashids* envisioned a small group fighting an overwhelming force, the new Islamic State *nashids* demonstrate power and confidence.[56]

A search of the Internet will yield Arabic, Turkish, and Urdu *nashids*.[57] Many songs have multiple postings with differing visual imagery. While some of the videos purport to show scenes from Iraq or Syria, many more are accompanied by static images. A lion for strength, a beautiful mountain scene for inspiration, or a dirty, hungry child clasping a bunch of bruised grapes to inspire anger.[58] In some of the most inventive videos, the footage is borrowed from Hollywood movies. A video playing the *nashid* "Bi Jihadina," sung by Syrian Abu Mazin and interpreted by Saudi singer Abu ʿAli, shows the battle scene between Saladin and the Crusaders from the movie *Kingdom of Heaven.*[59]

In some respects, the choice of visual imagery is strategic. If the video shows gratuitous violence, it can be flagged for removal. (Although they can quickly be uploaded on different sites or by using different tags.)[60] The still images and the Hollywood scenes, then, do not lead to censorship. Moreover, the calendar-like images first popularized by the apocalyptic manuals express a particular aesthetic. The seemingly trite images of rainbows, houses on lakes, and waterfalls offer a ritualistic, meditative opportunity. For example, one *nashid* is illustrated by the figure of a woman in the distance at the end of a platform in the clouds.[61]

A *nashid* frequently posted on the Internet is "Hur al-ʿin Tunadini." The English text in the *nashid* contrasts a young man's wish to go on jihad with the wishes of his mother:

> *The Hoor al-ʿin are calling me so let go of me*
> *mother, let go*
> *Don't cry mother, you can't stop me from this path*
>
> *O mother, my way has become clear*
> *And my heart if happily treading its path*
> *a blazing war and jihad*
> *and blood which flow for honor.*

This *nashid* is used in various video compilations. There is one with images of a tank and soldiers making their way through a ruined urban landscape.[62] There is another video, with English and Arabic text, of an impoverished child holding a bunch of spoiled grapes.[63] The earthly bunch of grapes contrasts with the promise of the grapes in the Garden. The same *nashid* is also found in YouTube clips uploaded by rebel groups in Syria. In one, a Free Syrian Army brigade shows their willingness to fight the Assad regime.[64] In another clip, a young man with a beautiful voice sings a *nashid* about houris. At the end of the song, while his fellow fighters praise him, he shyly looks into the camera.[65]

The online *nashid*s about houris show a dynamic and flexible medium that uses the houris as a symbol of the promised realms of paradise. While some videos stress the message of an ongoing crusade, others show footage of fighters in the Syrian civil war.

AL-HUR AL-'IN AS REJOINDER

The houri is a potent and important symbol for the promise of salvation in online productions, but she is not much encountered outside discussions of religious motivation. The reach of the jihadi videos is hard to gauge. As of August 2015, Houdefya had about 1,000 hits, Ahmed Ali anywhere from 25,000 to 64,000 hits, Anwar al-Awlaqi's "Hereafter Series" 142,000 hits, and the young Syrian man singing a *nashid* 88,000 hits. We do not know who watches the videos, how many times they watch them (my own research has elevated the numbers, for sure), or what they think of them. However, there are nearly two billion Muslims worldwide. The jihadi videos may gain the attention of American and European media, but in reality they pertain only to small, though visible, subgroups of reformist Muslims and jihadi propagandists.

One way to gauge the reception of the houri by a more mainstream audience is through director Najdat Ismail Anzour's 2005 Ramadan television serial *al-Hur al-'in*. The series garnered media attention because of the plotline of suicide car bombings taking place within a compound in Saudi Arabia. The residential compound was for families from other nations, and the women in these families struggle within restricted Saudi society. The series condemns terrorism, Saudi society, and the treatment of foreign Arabs and women. It shows "terrorists perverting Islam and censures Saudi Arabia's religious custodianship."[66] Christa Salamandra notes that Syrian directors had once shied away from overtly religious material, but started to address the topics in order to dramatize their own vision of Islamic society.[67] Anzour explained his purpose.

> And Islam is implicated, considered a religion of terrorism. We have tried, as far as we were able—we're not religious or committed, we're secularists. But at the same time, we see that this is affecting our society. Drama is very useful in this, because it clarifies things. Drama does not solve problems, but it can shed light on matters like this phenomenon, and can begin to get into details . . . not in a didactic way, but in a dramatic way, one that is pleasing, close to the people.[68]

Outside the video productions of reformists and jihadis, the houris are not widely considered. In the world outside the carefully constructed tours of paradise, houris are a metaphor belonging to the past. That is not to say that they are not significant, but their current significance has everything to do with women's rights and little to do with justifications for religious violence.

THE QUESTION

HOURIS ARE FEMININE HEAVENLY BEINGS and not actual women, but writers have often used the figure of the houri as a way to reflect upon the meaning and status of real Muslim women. The tendency to conflate a feminine model belonging to paradise and the societal expectations of earthly women creates odd misperceptions. Writers evaluate earthly Muslim women by comparison to idealized, unattainable feminine attributes. At the same time, other writers use heavenly houris to identify the mistreatment of earthly Muslim women. If the houri presents a standard for the disadvantage of earthly women, the reverse is also true: the forms of companionship between Muslim men and women shape how houris are understood. While the meaning of the houri has never been clear, it has been affected by societal forms of companionship.

The previous chapters have presented discussions *about* Muslim women, but traditional sources also record questions *from* Muslim women. There are questions in Ibn Habib's *Kitab wasf al-firdaws* from women who seek to understand which husband or fiancé will be theirs in the afterlife. In this chapter, we turn to twenty-first-century texts and their line of questioning. In English and Arabic texts, online videos, and YouTube video channels, we encounter two kinds of discussions about the houri. The first seeks to understand the nature of the houri and responds to the leading questions in earlier eschatological manuals, "Do men receive *hur al-ʿin* in paradise?" and "What are the characteristics of the *hur al-ʿin*?" These sites usually present a list of classical sources. Sometimes they provide commentary about wide eyes or the contrast between white and black, and they often contain traditions about the marrow of the bone that is visible due to their fair skin. The second discussion about equality gives rise to the more consequential question: if men receive houris in paradise, what do women receive? The question does not merely concern what women receive. Rather, it asks whether what women receive is equal to men's reward of the houri.

The difference between the questions of the ninth century (which husband will I eternally receive?) and the twenty-first century (what do women receive?) is significant. The earlier inquiry was limited to married women and their desired reward. If a woman had more than one husband during her life, or desired to be with her fiancé after her death, this posed a problem. The question did not concern unmarried women or generalized rewards for women. There was no expectation of a distinct reward for women that did not extend to men, which was understandable in its societal framework. Paradise may be an amplified realm,[1] but it is a realm that is still comprehensible in the terms of earthly experience. In the classical texts, we do not see questioning as to whether women enjoy paradise in the same way that men do. Indeed, the texts suggest that all believers enjoy paradise as a realm, and men as a subset of believers enjoy the specific reward of the houri. Today, however, there is the assumption that men and women ought to have similar or at least parallel rewards.

If men and women are equal, their rewards should reflect that equality.

There is a range of answers to the question of what women receive in paradise, and each answer suggests a different understanding about how women and men relate to each other. This final chapter examines how contemporary Muslims, in English and Arabic print and new media, answer the question about women's rewards. Whether the answers suggest an inherent misogyny in Islam or posit the permissibility of male houris for women, the discussions show that the meaning of the houri and the model of companionship are not fixed. Through scriptural interpretation, Muslim discourse seeks to redefine the houri and understand her promise within the contemporary world. Here, then, are four different answers to the question of what women receive.

ANSWER: THE MISOGYNY OF ISLAM

The argument that Islam is inherently misogynistic is common in European and American texts. The claim that misogyny is evident in the treatment of women in paradise is seen as early as the sixteenth century, in Juan Andrés's polemic and du Loir's early modern travel writings. Even Byron uses the houri as a metaphor for the sexual interplay between men and women and Christian and Turk, and bemoans the treatment of Turkish women. The contention that the Islamic religion is systematically unfair to women is not just an American or European argument. In *Women in Islamic Paradise*, Fatima Mernissi argues that Islam is inherently misogynistic. For Mernissi, the problem lies in the expectations of paradise that privilege male pleasure over female potential. For her, this not only disadvantages women, it also stunts the potential of men. The only solution for Mernissi is to find alternative ways to conceptualize paradise.

Mernissi begins her book with a personal anecdote. She was watching a television show about paradise with a male colleague. As the imam in the show expounded on the rewards of paradise, her colleague became more and more excited, to the point that he spilled tea on his clothes. His elation was contrasted with her disapproval.[2] The book is a rejoinder to her colleague, who had chastised her for criticizing the imam's interpretation.

Mernissi argues that paradise is merely a realm for male desire, and all religions leave women out of visions of paradise:

> I decided to take a look at the Paradise I am promised after life if I behave well! I advise you to do the same if you are a Parsi, a Catholic, a Protestant, a Jew or. . . . You're in for a big surprise! Parsi, Catholic, Protestant, Jewish, and Moslem paradises are not designed to make women happy![3]

She challenges the reader to examine the traditions of paradise for herself and to form an organization: "The International Association of Women Interested in Designing Alternative Paradises." Through the book, she traces different ways of envisioning paradise and heavenly reward.

In the case of the Islamic paradise, Mernissi notes that males will be offered a houri, and houris are more enticing than real women. "What is more troublesome for banal earthly women like me is that it is very easy for these beauties to be eternally nice and pure, the houri does not have to make an effort to be so, she is naturally that way."[4] The houri sets up an impossible standard for earthly women that they can never achieve. Mernissi addresses the question of how many houris men are to receive. She notes that the Qur'an did not mention specific numbers, but al-Bukhari suggested two, al-Sindi suggested seventy-three, al-Suyuti suggested seventy, and al-Qadi 4,900 (with seventy on each bed and seventy beds). She reminds the reader that men can enjoy these numbers because they are promised eternal sexual vigor.[5]

Mernissi chides women for not engaging the Qur'an and developing a practice of scriptural interpretation. Women need to join in the process of renewal and reform with the aim of articulating what paradise for women would look like.

> Now that we have gone into mortal Imam's Paradise, we realize that male-female relations they have nothing to do with loving and peace and communication; we are deep into score and accounts and prowess. We are not in what I think of as a paradisiacal encounter. I see Paradise as a deep, deep breath taken in wide, wide horizons of peace. Paradise is when I wear the sun around my head like a necklace. Paradise is when others can sense that I am connected with stars, with moons, familiar and unfamiliar, with skies, the blue ones and the others.[6]

For Mernissi, the traditions about paradise show how necessary it is that women begin engaging the Qur'an in order to shape interpretations of religious texts. Only through such engagement can women claim their legitimacy as Muslim believers; they must present a vision of paradise that transcends a cosmology that privileges male desire.

Mernissi sees the figure of the houri as problematic for women's development. Because the houri is seen as a commodity designed for male consumption,[7] traditions of the houri hamper decision-making, particularly in relation to underprivileged women.[8] For Mernissi, the problem with the houri as a model is that she is a passive female, and the celebration of the houri furthers the expectation of passivity for women.

Women in the Muslim Unconscious (1984), written by Fatima Mernissi under the pseudonym Fatna Ait Sabbah, puts forward the claim that Islam stops women from realizing their potential because they are seen as designed for male pleasure, just as the houri is designed for male desire.[9] The pleasure entails not only sexual access to women, but also women's passivity that ensures male dominion. For Ait Sabbah, houris are passive objects for men who are mere consumers in paradise. Since neither the houri nor the male can procreate in paradise, male desire is already determined and inconsequential.[10] Paradise, then, is a realm that projects an ideal order of Muslim society. In that order, both men and women are passive beings without judgment. Men are consumed by desire for passive women, and the result of their desire is inconsequential. The houri not only demonstrates misogyny, but also reduces men's ability to choose, act, or exercise free will. In this argument, the beauty of the houri is a cosmic reward that traps both women and men.

Other scholars mirror Mernissi's argument about the privileging of male desire. Amina Wadud, who seeks to develop a feminist hermeneutics of the Qur'an, also cedes that the Qur'an promotes male sexuality: "The notorious virginal huris [houri] for men—even after they are dead, men's pleasure should not be forsaken (52.20, 55.72, 56.22)."[11] But she develops a more philosophical argument. After noting that the verses about houris date from the early Meccan period,[12] whereas verses from the later, Medinan period use the term *zawj* or companion,[13] Wadud turns to the larger significance of companionship. Cosmic companionship, in her framework, is the essence of human coupling that is an important step for the completion of the soul.[14] For Wadud, the final goal is more elevated than replicating and amplifying the possibilities of gratification on earth.[15]

The argument that the houris reveal the misogyny of Islam proceeds on the principle that paradise should offer more equal treatment of male and female believers, and that females should not be objectified into rewards. The mere appearance of a female companion as reward suggests a relationship of power between dismissive Muslim men and undervalued Muslim women. Unlike earlier writers who simply recognize that there is a lack of freedom for women in Muslim societies, Mernissi and Wadud are activists who call for engaging the Islamic scriptural tradition in order to raise women's standing.

ANSWER: ETERNITY WITH THEIR HUSBAND

The consensus in the classical Qur'anic commentaries was that in paradise a woman would receive her husband or her last husband if she had remarried. The same opinions appear in print and online discussions of the subject. Yet the contemporary commentators mirror the assumptions about equality that reformers continue to discuss. An excellent example of the twenty-first century's fusion of classical and contemporary expectations may be found in the Huda channel of Assim Luqman al-Hakeem of Saudi Arabia. He frequently appears on television and radio, and his website is a dynamic platform where Muslims world-wide ask questions, accessing his lectures in both English and Arabic. When Assim was asked about the *hur al-'in*, he responded that a woman will receive her husband and only him, "because by default women can only love one man."[16] Assim argues that God made men with the capac-ity to love more than one woman, but women are differ-ent by nature. He assures women that they will be happy in paradise and "they should not doubt Allah's generosity and reward to them." This line of argument echoes the clas-sical commentaries in placing a woman with her earthly husband; however, his explanation also hints that the hus-band may not be enough of a reward. It is for this reason that he affirms the power of God to reward in a way that will make women happy. Beyond faith in the promise of paradise, Assim reminds viewers that human wives will be more beautiful and have greater status than the *hur al-'in* because the houris are essentially "considered servants."[17] In this way, he places the houris in a category below the female believer who had agency on earth and will have sta-tus in paradise as a wife.

The assertion that women will be content with their reward in the afterlife is reiterated by Ustadh Nouman Ali Khan, a US-based teacher of Islam who established Bayyinah Television, which develops Arabic and Qur'anic curricula in English. In one interview, he repeats the idea of the different capacities of men and women, and offers an interesting perspective on why the rewards for women are not made explicit. For Nouman Ali Khan, houris were designed so young men would not be tempted by earthly women. He argues that young men are driven to think about women, and daily life is difficult for men because they constantly think about sex. This is made all the more difficult in the United States, whose women Khan deems promiscuous. But he urges the righteous to turn their eyes away and know that "Allah has better for me."[18] Houris, then, serve to turn desire away from earthly women and project it onto a more acceptable, spiritually infused object.

For Khan, men are wired to desire women, while women have a range of desires.[19] While the rewards of paradise for men are couched within the language of male desire, the rewards for women are located within the ineffable spiritual meaning of paradise. He assures women that they will not be disappointed: "You will have whatever you desire."[20]

The contention that women receive placement with their husbands accords with classical commentaries that promise a transformed mirror of earthly life. The twenty-first-century answers draw on supposed psychological and physical differences between men and women as a way to understand the difference in their rewards. These arguments mirror al-Awlaqi's claim that women do not require an equal reward because they are not the same in their constitutions and are not as sexually driven as men. Men are driven by desire, while women are satisfied with being reunited with their husbands or accepting the true reward of God's generosity.

ANSWER: HIGHER STATUS THAN THE HOURIS

While there has always been a comparison between the wife and the houri, the outcome of the comparison is not always clear. In terms of beauty, the houri is a purified version of the female. On the other hand, some commentators have argued that even if the houri is beauty embodied, women are nonetheless superior to houris. In this line of argument, houris are servants of the afterlife. They provide satisfaction for male desire, but they cannot be on the same level of women who have lived righteously during their earthly lives. Even if the houris are extolled in superlative terms, they are subordinate to wives because the houris, in effect, serve them as types of beautiful laborers.

In one remarkable exchange, a woman calls Sheikh al-Arifi during a question-and-answer television segment. Al-Arifi is a professor at King Saud University who has delivered the Friday khutbah at the al-Bawardi Mosque in Riyadh. His dynamic website can be accessed through Arabic, English, and Persian platforms.[21] During the call in question, the woman asks if it is permissible to pray that she will be reunited with her husband in paradise, but without the possibility of his receiving *hur al-'in*. Al-Arifi laughs and teases that she is after her husband in this world and in the hereafter, as well. He reassures her about her status: "If you enter jannah, you will find what pleases you (by the will of Allah). Whether there is *hur al-'in* or not; your status will be higher than that of *hur al-'in*."[22] Wives will, in effect, have greater enjoyment, happiness, and beauty compared to the *hur al-'in*.

The themes of the transformation of the self and the promise of companionship are found in other interpreters of the Qur'an. Amina Wadud asks a basic question: "Is there an essential difference between the women and men in the Qur'anic portrayal of the Hereafter?" Wadud argues for the equity of recompense, noting that certain significant Arabic terms (such as *nafs*) refer to both male and female essences. She translates the term *azwaj*, or companions, as "you and whoever is paired with you because of like nature." In Wadud's formulation, the *hur al-'in* are a distraction from the universal aims of love and companionship that are promised to all believers. Wadud transcends the conventional categories of houri and wife by focusing on the spiritual essence of companionship. Within this framework, everyone is elevated because they develop into true companions for each other.

ANSWER: MALE HOURIS

The question "What do women receive" reflects the sense that there should be equality between male and female rewards. Interestingly, there are Muslim interpreters who suggest the possibility of male houris. The interpretation depends in part on identifying the gender of the noun *hur*. Some have posited that the term can be used for both male and female companions. According to this argument, the canonical tradition has misinterpreted the term as restricted to a female companion, and houris should be understood as "pure, chaste and beautiful companions that both good men, as well as good women will be rewarded with, without discrimination."[23] The website of the former Saudi grand mufti 'Abd al-Aziz ibn Baz (d.

1999) addresses this argument for equality under the question, "What sex is the *hur al-'in*?"[24]

Zakir Naik of the Islamic Research Foundation is based in India, but his English-language lectures on Islam have been broadcast around the world on the Internet and through *peacetv*, an Islamic Internet television channel.[25] In 2013, he was named Islamic Personality of the Year by Sheikh Mohammed bin Rashid al-Maktoum, the ruler of Dubai. In 2015, he won the King Faisal International Prize for Service to Islam from King Salman bin Abdulaziz al-Saud.[26] In the question-and-answer segment of one of his lectures, he is asked by a woman about the *hur al-'in*. His explanation alludes to the specific Qur'anic verses, and suggests that the word is properly understood as the plural of "big white beautiful eyes," which is interpreted as spouse or companion. For Naik, the word has no gender. He concludes, "For the man, he will get a good lady with big beautiful eyes and for a woman she will get a good man with big beautiful eyes."[27]

The way in which the lectures and question-and-answer sessions about houris use humor or modesty when talking about the possibility of sex in paradise is fascinating. Mufti Menk of Harare, Zimbabwe,[28] promises in a lecture to try to keep the discussion "decent," pointing out that typically people do not talk about sexual matters openly. He notes that when he discusses sex (even if there are no women in the room), it is possible to feel shy and actually blush. Each of his points is met with nervous, appreciative laughter from the male audience.[29]

There is often an awkwardness when a female questions a male authority. Ustadh Noman jokes about the tendency for women to say that "another" wants to ask a seemingly embarrassing question.[30] Yasir Qadhi of the US-based al-Maghrib Institute addresses this issue directly in his answer to a woman who asked him on behalf of her friend, "You said that there are beautiful women for men in paradise. Are there beautiful men for women?" Yasir Qadhi praises the questioner's modesty:

> Mash'allah very brave question from the sister but in her braveness she wrote the question and handed it over and didn't ask it herself and this is a sign of modesty as well al-hamdulillah that's good. Modesty should not prevent you from seeking knowledge so I think the ideal methodology. That she wanted to learn but she didn't want to identify herself so she wrote the question down. Excellent.[31]

After emphasizing the difference between men and women in terms of modesty, he addresses the question.

> This is [a] very honest question, and it needs to be asked. Many of the people are confused why does Allah *subhanahu wa ta'ala* talk about beautiful women for the men, and he does not talk about handsome men for the women. Will not the women also be blessed with a mate and spouse in *al-janna*? And the reason for this is that generally speaking it is not in the nature of women that these types of details be exposed and told. Look, even the sister did not want to be known and identified, and this is a sign of perfection that the woman wants to be modest. These types of issues do not form public conversation and so the Qur'an does not emphasize this point, it doesn't publicize it, but the reality is, as the prophet *subhan* Allah said . . . there is nobody in paradise who will remain single.[32]

Yasir Qadhi says that women will not feel jealousy that their husbands have been awarded houris. If women do not have a spouse in paradise, there will be a creation for them. They will not feel envious about the houris. Women, too, will have a creation, but it is not described. Qadhi concludes, "Our goal is to get to *al-janna*. Once we are there, we will be given everything in it as well. Don't worry, once you get to *al-janna*, you will have all that you desire."[33]

THE WOMAN'S QUESTION

Interpretations of the houri play a role in formulating propositions about Islamic values. For some writers, the houri is evidence of the consuming nature of Muslim male sexuality. Journalists and bloggers suggest that the houri as a reward demonstrates that Muslim men are scripturally ignorant, but sexually driven to pathological ends. For the early modern Spanish and French writers, the houri suggests that Muslim men devalue Muslim women by extending the practice of polygamy into the afterlife. Still other writers understand the houri as a standard for feminine beauty. English writers in the eighteenth and nineteenth centuries held up the houri as a universal ideal for Muslim and even Christian and Jewish women. For European and American writers, the houri has always been linked with feminine beauty—whether illicit or pure. By contrast, in Islamic texts the houri is an aesthetic reward that demonstrates the splendor of paradise. As a reward, the houri has had many functions. She demonstrates God's power in the Qur'an and hadiths, provides motivation for battle in *fada'il al-jihad* traditions, offers inspiration for singing slave girls, and is used to ridicule the idea of literal rewards in the afterlife. Ironically, it is in online jihadi videos that the houri's meaning is the most formulaic. She is a metaphor for cosmic perfection and signifies the possibility of a better life earned through violence.

The question about gender parity is a decidedly twentieth- and twenty-first-century concern. The range of answers suggests that theological authority takes different forms. Answers to the women's question capture the informal nature of contemporary discussion, reflect diffused authority, and show the creative process of interpretation that conveys religious messages, texts, and agendas. Authority is still invoked, captured through the television channels created on the Internet. These channels reflect the back-and-forth nature of popular discourse as well as the challenge and invocation of authority.

The writers, journalists, and bloggers of Chapter 1 argue that Islam does not have a tradition of scriptural interpretation. They have focused on the wrong question. The important question is not "virgins or white grapes?" The more meaningful question is "what do women receive?" It is this question that shows how interpretations of Islamic theology are still being developed and debated. This question also draws on different sources of authority and through media like online channels. "What do women receive?" is not merely a straightforward question; it is a way to access the vibrant intellectual and cultural life of Muslims who are engaged with scriptural interpretation.

CONCLUSION

THE HOURI APPEARS IN THE historical record, becomes "useful to think with,"[1] and then fades away, only to reappear in another context or genre. For those who are animated by discussions about cosmic promise and the feminine ideal, however, the figure of the houri continues to raise many questions. This book is a record of these questions.

If we consider the questions in chronological order, they illuminate the roles for women in their respective societies. Qurʾanic commentators asked, "What is a houri?" and "Is she better than wives?" These questions suggest that Muslim men and women were considering paradise through the lens of their earthly social worlds and trying to understand how the reconfigured cosmos would affect their everlasting lives. In the Qurʾan, the houri is an ambiguous reward. In Qurʾanic commentaries, theological manuals, jihadi meditations, and poetry, however, the houri has multiple dimensions. The houri has been viewed as a companion (like the male *wildan* and *ghilman*), a nurse tending to the wounded, a sensual reward, a bride earned through warfare, a form of entertainment like a singing slave girl, and a subject of parody for those who think that God's creations can be understood literally.

In early modern European frameworks, the dominant questions were informed by fear and admiration of the Ottoman Empire. Judgments concerning Turks often involved ideas about the treatment of women. The questions were often articulated as "What is the houri?" or "Do Muslim women have souls?" It was in reflections on theology, gender, and religious polemic between the sixteenth and seventeenth centuries that the terms *hora*, *horhin*, and ultimately "houri" were introduced. The houri provoked French and English interpreters to question the status of women in Muslim societies and to perceive women as devalued by Muslim men.

In the nineteenth and twentieth centuries, there was not a questioning of the houri, as much as a use of the houri to represent a feminine ideal. This cosmopolitan aesthetic drew inspiration from the Muslim East, but it could be achieved whether a woman was English, American, Jewish, or Christian. Like the houri, the ideal female was alluring yet modest, physically beautiful yet spiritually pure. In Islamic texts, the houri embodied a model of cosmic perfection. In nineteenth- and twentieth-century English texts, she did something else. She became a universal model for feminine beauty. By the nineteenth century, references to houris had become more numerous, and a typology of the houri emerged. Sometimes, she was an oppressed Muslim woman; other times, she was a celebrated Christian woman. The houri represented both the patriarchal structures that shaped women's lives and guidance for women to adhere to codes of purity.

Because of the mention of the houri in the letter attributed to Mohamed Atta, after September 11 the question of reward became more widely discussed. "What does Mohamed Atta receive?" became a driving question that used the houri as a way to refute the value of Islam in the twenty-first century. The digital age, with its capacity to reach new audiences, has allowed for multiple interpretations of the houri. In online media and polemics after September 11th, the houri came to represent the idea that Islam is inherently violent. Consumers of jihadi videos are encouraged to develop affective ties in online communities through images, chants, and symbols. The focus on the houri as a motive for violence obscures other robust interpretations. The meaning of the houri is debated in the dynamic media of online radio, television, and YouTube channels. In reformist websites, the houri becomes a rhetorical symbol to guide listeners through online tours of paradise.

The ongoing discussions of the question "What do women receive?" suggest dynamic, creative scriptural interpretations. It is significant that the question arises from contemporary expectations of parity of rewards for male and female believers. The desire for parity is what leads to the imaginative possibility of a male houri. Previous centuries never assumed that the reward of paradise should take the same form for men and women. Questioning what women receive shows that interpretation of the houri is still evolving.

The question raised at the beginning of the book ("What does Mohamed Atta receive?") and the question posed at the end of the book ("What do women receive?") are products of different worldviews. The question about Mohamed Atta seeks assurance that religious violence will not be rewarded. The second question seeks confirmation of the possibility of equal treatment between men and women in Islamic religious systems. The final chapter discusses the very scriptural interpretation that writers cited in the first chapter claimed did not exist in Muslim societies.

The houri is not an earthly woman, but in trying to understand her constitution, interpreters conflate the cosmic being with everyday women. For classical Qur'anic interpreters, the houri had an unsettled relationship with earthly wives. For European interpreters, the houri showed how Muslim women are devalued and desired. For contemporary Muslim commentators, the houri can represent a standard of perfection or misogyny. In interpretations that suggest that the houri is either male or female, the possibility of perfected companionship is a reward for all. The ways that the houri is configured reveal assumptions about gender and religion in respective societies. She can symbolize heavenly purity, an earthly impulse for violence, and a feminine model for women whose earthly lives do not allow them to achieve cosmic perfection.

The houri often appears in new formats. We have focused on discourse about houris in Arabic, English, and French texts, but there is houri material in Bengali, Indonesian, and Urdu, among other languages and platforms. There is no fixed body of literature about the contemporary houri because her meaning continues to be debated. Indeed, the houri remains a persistent figure, linked with enduring questions about the promise of paradise and the ideal feminine form.

The human desire to imagine the next world is powerful. When we compartmentalize our histories, we are unable to see the ways that certain figures prove compelling across time and space. The houri, as a cosmic being who stands outside the structures of time, has a considerable past and potential future interpretation. Reflections about women are a vital component of our cosmic imagining—what makes them pure, ideal, and perfected. It is a feminine being that has been used to develop arguments about the nature of a religion, the judgment of a society, and the future of a people.

Within their own contexts, writers have articulated the houris they desire. The figure of the houri was never just about religious reward. Instead, she provides a way to reflect upon asymmetries of power in this world and the next. The texts in this book use feminine beings to understand social relations between men and women. It is ironic that English and Americans writers, who have long claimed superiority over Muslim societies and Islam, nevertheless fashion houris for their own purposes. These many forms of the houri show us the dynamic ways in which people have imagined themselves, their societies, and their idealized forms of women in collective cosmic futures.

NOTES

Introduction

1. Shai Secunda, *The Iranian Talmud: Reading the Bavli in the Sasanian Context* (Philadelphia: University of Pennsylvania Press, 2014), 123 and Charles Wendell, "The Denizens of Paradise," *Humaniora Islamica* 2 (1974): 29–30.
2. Wendell, "The Denizens of Paradise," 31.
3. Wendell, "The Denizens of Paradise," 30.
4. Emran El-Badawi, *The Qur'an and the Aramaic Gospel Traditions* (New York and London: Routledge Press, 2013), 27.
5. Wendell, "The Denizens of Paradise," 29.
6. Wendell, "The Denizens of Paradise," 31.

Chapter 1

1. "Full Text of Notes Found after Hijackings," *New York Times*, September 29, 2001, http://www.nytimes.com/2001/09/29/national/29SFULL-TEXT.html?pagewanted=print (accessed March 1, 2015); "Last Words of a Terrorist." *The Guardian.* September 30, 2001. https://www.theguardian.com/world/2001/sep/30/terrorism.september113.
2. *United States of America v. Zacarias Moussaoui.* Criminal No. 01-455-A. Prosecution Trial Exhibits. BS01101 and BS01101T,

http://www.vaed.uscourts.gov/notablecases/moussaoui/exhibits/prosecution (accessed February 15, 2015).

3. Bob Woodward, "In Hijacker's Bags, a Call to Planning, Prayer, and Death," *Washington Post*, November 18, 2007, A01.

4. Hans G. Kippenberg and Tilman Seidensticker, eds., *The 9/11 Handbook: Annotated Translation and Interpretation of the Attacker's Spiritual Manual* (London and Oakville: Equinox, 2006), 4.

5. Nerina Rustomji, "American Visions of the Houri," *Muslim World* 97, no. 1 (January 2007): 90–91.

6. The annotated translation is Kippenberg and Seidensticker, eds., *The 9/11 Handbook*. Other translations include Kanan Makiya and Hassan Mneimneh's "Manual for a Raid," *New York Review of Books* 49, no. 1 (January 17, 2002): 18–21; David Cook, *Understanding Jihad* (Berkeley: University of California Press, 2005), 195–202.

7. "Full Text of Notes Found after Hijackings."

8. "Full Text of Notes Found after Hijackings."

9. "Full Text of Notes Found after Hijackings."

10. "Full Text of Notes Found after Hijackings."

11. "Full Text of Notes Found after Hijackings."

12. "Full Text of Notes Found after Hijackings."

13. "Full Text of Notes Found after Hijackings."

14. "Full Text of Notes Found after Hijackings."

15. Makiya and Mneimneh, "Manual for a 'Raid.'"

16. Juan Cole, "Al-Qaeda's Doomsday Document and Psychological Manipulation," presented at "Genocide and Terrorism: Probing the Mind of the Perpetrator," Yale Center for Genocide Studies, New Haven, CT, April 9, 2003. http://hdl.handle.net/2027.42/156040

    Mark Clayton, "Reading into the Mind of a Terrorist: A Document Carefully Crafted for the 9-11 Hijackers May Be a Template for Terrorism, Say Some Academics," *Christian Science Monitor*, October 10, 2003.

17. "Full Text of Notes Found after Hijackings," Part I, no. 8.

18. "Full Text of Notes Found after Hijackings," Part I, no. 9.

19. "Full Text of Notes Found after Hijackings," Second Step.

20. "Full Text of Notes Found after Hijackings," Part III.

21. Kippenberg and Seidensticker, eds., *The 9/11 Handbook*, 21.
22. Kippenberg and Seidensticker, eds., *The 9/11 Handbook*, second stage, no. 13, third stage, no. 10.
23. Kippenberg and Seidensticker, eds., *The 9/11 Handbook*, first stage, no. 8.
24. ABC News Digital, "*Handwritten Letter Instructed Hijackers*," September 29, 2001. https://abcnews.go.com/US/story?id=92398&page=1.
25. Gustave Niebuhr, "Injunctions to Pray, Instructions to Kill," *New York Times*, September 29, 2001.
26. Bruce Hoffman, *Inside Terrorism* (New York: Columbia University Press, 2006), 159.
27. Hoffman, *Inside Terrorism*, 162.
28. Hoffman, *Inside Terrorism*, 163.
29. Alex Strick van Linschoten and Felix Kuehn, eds., *Poetry of the Taliban* (London: C. Hurst, 2002), 171.
30. "Albanian National Sentenced to 16 Years for Attempting to Support Terrorism," United States Department of Justice, Office of Public Affairs. https://www.justice.gov/opa/pr/albanian-national-sentenced-16-years-attempting-support-terrorism (accessed July 15, 2018).
31. Liz Robbins, "Man Accused of Trying to Join Jihadists," *New York Times*, September 10, 2011, A22.
32. Mark Juergensmeyer, *Terror in the Mind of God: The Global Rise of Religious Violence* (Berkeley: University of California Press, 2003), 201.
33. Juergensmeyer, *Terror in the Mind of God*, 199.
34. Robert Pape, *Dying to Win: The Strategic Logic of Suicide Bombing* (New York: Random House, 2005), 199–216.
35. Juergensmeyer, *Terror in the Mind of God*, 201.
36. Juergensmeyer, *Terror in the Mind of God*, 201.
37. Stefan Wild, "Lost in Philology? The Virgins of Paradise and the Luxenberg Hypothesis," in *The Qur'an in Context*, eds. Angelika Neuwirth, Nicolai Sinai, and Michael Marx (Leiden: Brill, 2009), 632.
38. Walid Saleh, "The Etymological Fallacy and Qur'anic Studies: Muhammad, Paradise, and Late Antiquity," in *The Qur'an in Context: Historical and Literary Investigations into*

the Qur'anic Milieu, eds. Angelika Neuwirth, Nicolai Sinai, and Michael Marx (Leiden: Brill, 2009), 670.

39. Fred Donner, "The Qur'an in Recent Scholarship: Challenges and Desiderata"; Wild, "Lost in Philology?"; Saleh, "The Etymological Fallacy and Qur'anic Studies."

40. For the bibliography of reviews of Luxenberg, see Emran Iqbal El-Badawi, *The Qur'an and the Aramaic Gospel Traditions* (London and New York: Routledge, 2014), 27–29.

41. Angelika Neuwirth, "Qur'an and History: A Disputed Relationship. Some Reflections on Qur'anic History and History in the Qur'an," *Journal of Qur'anic Studies* V, no. 1 (2003): 1–18.

42. Pew Research Religion and Public Life Project, Religious Landscape Survey, http://religions.pewforum.org/reports# (accessed February 15, 2015).

43. Fred Donner, "The Historian, the Believer, and the Qur'an," in *New Perspectives on the Qur'an*, ed. Gabriel Said Reynolds (London and New York: Routledge, 2011), 25–37.

44. Christoph Luxenberg, *The Syro-Aramaic Reading of the Koran: A Contribution to the Decoding of the Language of the Koran* (Verlag Hans Schiler, 2007), 251.

45. Wild, "Lost in Philology?," 643.

46. Neuwirth, "Qur'an and History."

47. Ibn Warraq, "Virgins? What Virgins?" *Guardian*, January 12, 2002. https://www.theguardian.com/books/2002/jan/12/books.guardianreview5

48. Ibn Warraq, http://ibnwarraq.com/category/institute-for-the-secularisation-of-islamic-society/ (accessed July 15, 2018).

49. Ibn Warraq, "Virgins? What Virgins?".

50. Ibn Warraq, "Virgins? What Virgins?"

51. Ibn Warraq, "Virgins? What Virgins?"

52. Ibn Warraq, "Virgins? What Virgins?"

53. Ibn Warraq, "Virgins? What Virgins?"

54. Alexander Stille, "Scholars Scrutinize the Koran's Origins: A Promise of Moist Virgins or Dried Fruit?" *New York Times and International Herald Tribune*, March 4, 2002. https://www.nytimes.com/2002/03/02/arts/scholars-are-quietly-offering-new-theories-of-the-koran.html

55. Stefan Theil, "Challenging the Qur'an," *Newsweek*, July 27, 2003. https://www.newsweek.com/challenging-quran-139447
56. Theil, "Challenging the Qur'an."
57. "Pakistan Bans Newsweek's Quran Issue," *World News Daily*, July 26, 2003. https://www.ifex.org/bangladesh/2003/08/05/latest_issue_of_newsweek_magazine/. Accessed July 15, 2015.
58. "Newsweek Story on Islam Banned," *Chicago Tribune*, July 29, 2003, 6.
59. Reporters without Borders: For Press Freedom, "Newsweek Banned over Article on the Koran," July 30, 2003. https://rsf.org/en/news/newsweek-banned-over-article-koran
60. Muhammad Sayed Tantawy, "Origins of the Quran," *Dawn*, October 3, 2003. https://www.dawn.com/news/1065100
61. Nicholas Kristof, "Martyrs, Virgins and Grapes," *New York Times*, August 4, 2004. https://www.nytimes.com/2004/08/04/opinion/martyrs-virgins-and-grapes.html
62. Kristof, "Martyrs, Virgins and Grapes."
63. Kristof, "Martyrs, Virgins and Grapes."
64. Kristof, "Martyrs, Virgins and Grapes."
65. Nicholas Kristof, "Islam, Virgins and Grapes." New York Times, August 9, 2009 https://www.nytimes.com/2009/04/23/opinion/23kristof.html
66. Sometimes, the syndication would offer a revised title. For example, Nicholas Kristof, "Martyrs, Virgins and Grapes: Towards an Islamic Reformation," *Sarasota Herald-Tribune*, August 5, 2004, 13A.
67. Steve Martin, "Seventy-two Virgins," *The New Yorker*, January 29, 2007, 42–43.
68. "The Islamic Heaven: A Pornographic Brothel," http://www.moriel.org/articles/discernment/islam/islamic_heaven.htm (accessed July 15, 2015).
69. Christian Video 4 Free, "72 Virgins for Martyrs in Heaven—Myth or Truth?" http://www.christianvideo4free.com/christians-of-asia-network/72-virgins-for-martyrs-in-heaven-myth-or-truth-, posted June 4, 2011 (accessed February 15, 2015).
70. Vocativ. http://www.vocativ.com/world/ukraine-world/jihadi-jokesters-waging-holy-war-hot-ukrainian-ladies/, posted March 14, 2014 (accessed February 15, 2015).

71. "Another Idiot in Pakistan" https://m.blog.daum.net/mallam/ 1688?np_nil_b=1 (accessed July 15, 2018), and "Full Metal Jacket . . . around Penis of Suicide Bomber," https://www.liveleak.com/view?t=86e_1387152923 (accessed July 15, 2018).

72. The Global Edition, "Female Taliban Suicide Bomber Hates the Idea of Virgins in Heaven," http://www.theglobaledition.com/ female-taliban-suicide-bomber-hates-the-idea-of-virgins-in-heaven/, updated June 26, 2012 (accessed February 15, 2015).

73. Avi Perry, *72 Virgins: Countdown to Terror Attack on US Soil* (Paramus, NJ: Gradient, 2009), 18.

74. Perry, *72 Virgins: Countdown to Terror Attack on US Soil*, 275.

75. Martin Amis, "The Last Days of Muhammad Atta," in *The Second Plane: September 11: Terror and Boredom* (New York and Toronto: Alfred A. Knopf, 2008), 100.

Chapter 2

1. I am grateful for Dohra Ahmad and Kathleen Lubey for their careful reading and suggestions in this chapter.

2. Geraldine Heng, "Sex, Lies, and Paradise: The Assassins, Prester John, and the Fabulation of Civilizational Identities," *Differences* 23, no. 1 (2012): 1–31; Suzanne Conklin Akbari, *Idols in the East: European Representations of Islam and the Orient, 1100–1450* (Ithaca, NY: Cornell University Press, 2012), 260.

3. Horace Walpole, *The Yale Edition of Horace Walpole's Correspondence*, Letter to Sir Horace Mann, February 28, 1745 (New Haven, CT: Yale University Press, 1937–1983), 11–13, online edition (accessed February 15, 2015).

4. Sharon Kinoshita and Siobhain Bly Calkin, "Saracens as Idolaters in European Vernacular Literatures," in *Christian-Muslim Relations: A Bibliographical History*, ed. David Thomas (Brill Online, 2015) (accessed February 23, 2015).

5. Kinoshita and Calkin, "Saracens as Idolaters in European Vernacular Literatures."

6. Siobhain Bly Calkin, *Saracens and the Making of English Identity: The Auchinleck Manuscript* (New York and London: Routledge, 2005), 4.

7. Zachary Zuwiyya, "*Confusión o confutación de la secta Mahomética*, Confusion or confutation of the sect of Muhammad," in *Christian-Muslim Relations: A Bibliographical History*, eds. David Thomas and John A. Chesworth, Vol. 6 (Leiden: Brill, 2014), 83–84.

8. Johannes Andreas Maurus, *The Confusion of Muhamed's sect or a confutation of the Turkish Alcoran. Being a discovery of many secret policies and practices in that religion, not till now revealed. Written originally in Spanish, by Johannes Andreas Maurus, who was one of their bishops and afterwards turned Christian. Translated into English by Joshua Notstock* (London: H. Blunden, 1652), 158, Early English Books Online (accessed February 15, 2015).

9. Maurus, trans. Joshua Notstock, *Confusion of Muhamed's sect*, 162–163.

10. Maurus, trans. Joshua Notstock, *Confusion of Muhamed's sect*, 162–163.

11. Maurus, trans. Joshua Notstock, *Confusion of Muhamed's sect*, 165.

12. Maurus, trans. Joshua Notstock, *Confusion of Muhamed's sect*, 166.

13. Richmond Barbour, *Before Orientalism: London's Theatre of the East, 1576–1626* (Cambridge: University of Cambridge, 2003), 3.

14. Nabil Matar, *Turks, Moors, and Englishmen in the Age of Discovery* (New York: Columbia University Press, 1999), 4.

15. Bernadette Andrea, *Women and Islam in Early Modern English Literature* (Cambridge: Cambridge University Press, 2007), 27–28.

16. Nabil Matar, *Islam in Britain 1558–1685* (Cambridge: Cambridge University Press, 1998), 190.

17. Matar, *Turks, Moors, and Englishmen in the Age of Discovery*, 15.

18. Jonathan Burton, *Traffic and Turning: Islam and English Drama, 1579–1624* (Cranbury, NJ: University of Delaware Press, 2005), 16.

19. Sophia Rose Arjana, *Muslims in the Western Imagination* (New York: Oxford, 2015), 76.

20. Anna Suranyi, *The Genius of the English Nation: Travel Writing and National Identity in Early Modern England* (Newark, NJ: University of Delaware Press, 2008), 19.
21. Suranyi, *The Genius of the English Nation*, 21.
22. Suranyi, *The Genius of the English Nation*, 21.
23. Suranyi, *The Genius of the English Nation*, 137.
24. Suranyi, *The Genius of the English Nation*, 128.
25. Suranyi, *The Genius of the English Nation*, 32.
26. Suranyi, *The Genius of the English Nation*, 32.
27. Suranyi, *The Genius of the English Nation*, 70.
28. Saree Makdisi, *Making England Western: Occidentalism, Race, and Imperial Culture* (Chicago: University of Chicago, 2014), xvi.
29. Michael Harrigan, *Veiled Encounters: Representing the Orient in 17th-Century French Travel Literature* (Amsterdam and New York: Rodopi, 2008), 153.
30. Harrigan, *Veiled Encounters*, 138–139.
31. Harrigan, *Veiled Encounters*, 140.
32. Harrigan, *Veiled Encounters*, 141.
33. Harrigan, *Veiled Encounters*, 153.
34. I am grateful to Michael Harrigan for his assistance in researching du Loir's origins.
35. Harrigan, *Veiled Encounters*, 13.
36. Nicolas du Loir, *Les Voyages du Sieur du Loir* (Paris: Chez Gervais Closvzier, 1654), 166.
37. Du Loir, *Les Voyages*, 170–174.
38. Du Loir, *Les Voyages*, 176.
39. Du Loir, *Les Voyages*, 178.
40. Du Loir, *Les Voyages*, 178.
41. "Houri," *Dictionnaire de l'Académie Française*, 4th edition (Paris: Chez la Vve B. Brunet, 1762), 889. The ARTFL Project Edition (accessed February 15, 2015).
42. Mohja Kahf, *Western Representations of the Muslim Woman: From Termagant to Odalisque* (Austin: University of Texas Press, 1999), 111.
43. Lisa Lowe, *Critical Terrains: French and British Orientalisms* (Ithaca, NY, and London: Cornell University Press, 1991), 38.
44. Humberto Garcia, *Islam and the English Enlightenment, 1670–1840* (Baltimore, MD: Johns Hopkins University Press, 2012), 60–61.

45. Alain Grosrichard, *Sultan's Court: European Fantasies of the East*, trans. Liz Heron (London: Verso, 1998), 125–126.
46. Lady Mary Wortley Montagu, *Letters of the Right Honourable Lady M-y W-y M-e*. Letter 33, "To the Countess of—," Adrianopolis, April 18, 1717 (London: Thomas Martine, 1790). Project Gutenberg Edition, release date: January 15, 2006.
47. Montagu, *Letters*, Letter 33, "To the Countess of—," Adrianopolis, April 18, 1717.
48. Montagu, *Letters*, Letter 33, "To the Countess of—," Adrianopolis, April 18, 1717.
49. Montagu, *Letters*, Letter 33, "To the Countess of—," Adrianopolis, April 18, 1717.
50. Montagu, *Letters*, Letter 35, "To the Abbot—," Constantinople, May 29, 1717.
51. Joan DelPlato, *Multiple Wives, Multiple Pleasures* (Madison, NJ: Fairleigh Dickinson University Press, 2002), 88–89.
52. Roderick Cavaliero, *Ottomania: The Romantics and the Myth of the Islamic Orient* (London and New York: I. B. Tauris, 2010), 42.
53. Horace Walpole, *The Yale Edition of Horace Walpole's Correspondence*, Letter to Sir Horace Mann, February 13, 1743 (New Haven, CT: Yale University Press, 1937–1983), online edition (accessed February 15, 2015).
54. Walpole, *Correspondence*, Letter to Sir Horace Mann, February 28, 1745.
55. Walpole, *Correspondence*, Letter to Mason, October 11, 1778.
56. Walpole, *Correspondence*, Letter to Mason, January 17, 1780.
57. Ghazi Nassir, *Samuel Johnson's Attitude Toward Islam: A Study of His Oriental Readings and Writings* (Lewiston, NY: Edwin Mellen Press, 2012), 108.
58. Samuel Johnson, *Irene: A Tragedy* (London: J. Dodsley, 1781), 68. Eighteenth Century Collections Online (accessed February 15, 2015).
59. Katherine Hodges Adams, "A Study of Samuel Johnson's Irene." Florida State University (ProQuest UMI Dissertations Publishing, 1981), 92–93.
60. Johnson, *Irene: A Tragedy*, 7.

Chapter 3

1. I am grateful to Dohra Ahmed and Kathleen Lubey for their careful reading and suggestions in this chapter.
2. Charlotte Brontë, *Jane Eyre* (New York: The Modern Library, 1993), 401–402.
3. Joyce Zonana, "The Sultan and the Slave: Feminist Orientalism and the Structure of Jane Eyre," *Signs: Journal of Women in Culture and Society* 18, no. 3 (Spring 1993): 597–598.
4. Zonana, "The Sultan and the Slave," 596.
5. William Beckford, *The History of the Caliph Vathek* (London: J. Johnson, 1786), 2, Eighteenth Century Collections Online (accessed February 18, 2015).
6. Beckford, *The History of the Caliph Vathek*, 5.
7. Mohammed Sharafuddin, *Islam and Romantic Orientalism* (London and New York: I. B. Tauris, 1994), xxxii.
8. Sharafuddin, *Islam and Romantic Orientalism*, xxxi.
9. "Slippers: A Turkish Tale," Chapter 1, *The Monthly Mirror, Reflecting Men and Manners*, Vol. 19 (London: J. Wright, 1805), 223.
10. "Wealth, Wisdom, and Virtue: An Eastern Tale," in *Gleanings of Wit Being A Choice Collection of Tales, Anecdotes, Occurrences and Various Pieces in Prose and Verse Interspersed with Many Original Pieces Never before published from the Worlds of an Old Military Officer* (London: J. Ginger, 1805), 196–197.
11. Edward Said, *Orientalism* (New York: Verso, 1978), 22.
12. Lord Byron, *Childe Harold's Pilgrimage* (New York: Lovell Brothers, 1890), canto I, stanza lxix, HathiTrust Digital Library (accessed February 15, 2015).
13. Lord Byron, *The Bride of Abydos: A Turkish Tale* (London: John Murray, 1814), canto II, stanza iixiii, lines 692–693, HathiTrust Digital Library (accessed February 15, 2015).
14. Lord Byron, *The Bride of Abydos*, canto I, stanza v, lines 146–147.
15. Lord Byron, *The Bride of Abydos*, canto II, stanza vii, lines 112–113.
16. Lord Byron, *The Siege of Corinth* (Paris: B. Cormon and Black, 1835), stanza vii, HathiTrust Digital Library (accessed February 15, 2015).

17. Lord Byron, *The Giaour: A Fragment of a Turkish Tale* (London: John Murray 1814), lines 480–486, HathiTrust Digitial Library (accessed February 15, 2015).

18. Lord Byron, *The Giaour*, lines 480–486.

19. Lord Byron, *The Giaour*, lines 1045–1047.

20. Lord Byron, *The Giaour*, lines 738–744.

21. Lord Byron, *Don Juan* (Boston: Phillips, Sampson, 1858), canto viii, stanza cxi, HathiTrust Digital Library (accessed February 15, 2015).

22. Lord Byron, *Don Juan*, canto viii, stanza cxii.

23. Lord Byron, *Don Juan*, canto viii, stanza cxiv.

24. Lord Byron, *Don Juan*, canto viii, stanza cxv.

25. Said, *Orientalism*, 2–3.

26. Andrew Warren, *The Orient and the Young Romantics* (Cambridge: Cambridge University Press, 2014), 3.

27. Sir Charles Morell, *The Tales of the Genii or, the Delightful Lessons of Horam the Son of Asmar faithfully translated from the Persian Manuscript, and Compared with the French and Spanish Editions Published at Paris and Madrid* (London: J. Wilkie, 1786), 27.

28. "A Visit to Jerusalem by an American," *The Gentleman's Magazine* V. 1, ed. William E. Burton (Philadelphia: Charles Alexander, 1837), 264.

29. "Light of the Harem," in Lord George Gordon Byron, *The Gallery of Byron Beauties: Ideal Pictures of the Principal Female Characters in Lord Byron's Poems. From the original paintings by eminent artists* (New York: D. Appleton, 1867), n.p.

30. "Gulnare," in Lord George Gordon Byron, *The Gallery of Byron Beauties*, n.p.

31. "Marion," "Inez," and "Generva" in Lord George Gordon Byron, *The Gallery of Byron Beauties*, n.p.

32. Suzanne Conklin Akbari, *Idols in the East: European Representations of Islam and the Orient, 1100–1450* (Ithaca, NY: Cornell University Press, 2012), 260.

33. Akbari, *Idols in the East*, 278.

34. John Viktor Tolan, *Saracens: Islam in the Medieval European Imagination* (New York: Columbia University Press, 2002), 283.

35. Royall Tyler, *The Algerine Captive*, ed. Don L. Cook (New Haven, CT: College and University Press, 1970), 142.

36. Tyler, *The Algerine Captive*, 140.

37. Sir Walter Scott, *Ivanhoe*, ed. Graham Tulloch (Edinburgh: Edinburgh University Press, 1998), 72.

38. Sir Walter Scott, *Ivanhoe*, 71–72.

39. John Keats, *The Complete Poetical Works of John Keats*, eds. Horace Elisha Scudder and Harry Buxton Forman (Boston and New York: Houghton Mifflin, 1899), 430.

40. Mary Wollstonecraft Shelley, *Falkner*, Vol. II (London: Saunders and Otley, 1837), 177–178, Hathitrust Digital Library (accessed February 15, 2015).

41. David Theo Hines, *The Life, Adventures and Opinions of David Theo Hines South Carolina Master of Arts and, Sometimes, Doctor of Medicine* (New York: Bradley and Clark, 1840), 16.

42. "Female Beauty of the Mind," *The Universalist and the Ladies' Repository*, ed. Henry Bacon (Boston: Abel Tompkins, 1837), 198.

43. "Star of Love," *Ladies' Companion: A Monthly Magazine embracing Every department of literature, embellished with Original Engravings, and Music arranged for the piano forte, harp, and guitar*, Vol. 13 (New York: William W. Snowden, 1840), 31.

44. "Star of Love," 32.

45. "Star of Love," 32.

46. Todd Fine, Afterword to *Book of Khalid*, Ameen Rihani (Brooklyn, NY: Melville House, 2016), 322–323.

47. Ameen Fares Rihani, *The Book of Khalid: A Critical Edition* (Syracuse, NY: Syracuse University Press), 2016, 83.

48. Jacob Berman, *American Arabesque: Arabs, Islam, and the Nineteenth Century Imaginary* (New York: New York University Press), 2012, 199.

49. Rihani, *The Book of Khalid*, 84–85.

Chapter 4

1. Some material from this chapter is drawn from Nerina Rustomji, *The Garden and the Fire: Heaven and Hell in Islamic Culture* (New York: Columbia University Press, 2009); "Are Houris Heavenly Concubines?" in *Songs and Sons: Women, Slavery*

and Social Mobility in the Medieval Islamic World, eds. Matthew Gordon and Kathryn Hain (New York: Oxford University Press, 2017), 266–277; "Beauty in the Garden: Aesthetics and the *Wildan, Ghilman,* and *Hur,*" in *Roads to Paradise*, eds. Sebastian Guenther and Todd Lewis (Leiden: Brill, 2017), 295–310.

2. Kevin A. Reinhart, "The Here and the Hereafter in Islamic Religious Thought," in *Images of Paradise in Islamic Art*, eds. Sheila S. Blair and Jonathan M. Bloom (Austin: University of Texas Press, 1991), 16.

3. Ibn Ishaq, *Sirat Rasul Allah. Trans. as the Life of Muhammad: A Translation of Ishaq's Sirat Rasul Allah*, trans. A. Guillaume (London, Karachi, and New York: Oxford University Press, 1955), 93–94.

4. Robert Carter, *Sea of Pearls: Seven Thousand Years of the Industry That Shaped the Gulf* (London: Arabian, 2012), 29. I am grateful to Joel Walker for this reference.

5. Finbarr Barry Flood, *Great Mosque of Damascus: Studies on the Makings of an Umayyad Visual Culture* (Leiden, Boston, and Koln: Brill, 2001), 25.

6. al-Tabari *Jami'* 56.17, 76.19; Ibn Kathir *Tafsir* 56.17, 76.19; al-Mahalli and al-Suyuti *Tafsir al-jalalayn* 56.17; al-Tabarsi *Majma'* 56.17; and al-Qurtubi *al-Jami'*, 56.17, 76.19.

7. al-Tabari *Jami'* 76.19; Ibn Kathir *Tafsir* 76.19; al-Mahalli and al-Suyuti *Tafsir al-jalalayn* 76.19; and al-Qurtubi *al-Jami'*, 76.19.

8. al-Tabari *Jami'* 52.24; Ibn Kathir *Tafsir* 52.24; al-Mahalli and al-Suyuti *Tafsir al-jalalayn* 52.24; al-Tabarsi, *Majma'* 52.24.

9. al-Qurtubi *al-Jami'* 56.17; al-Zamakhshari *al-Kashshaf* 56.17; al-Tabarsi *Majma'* 56.17; al-Qurtubi *al-Jami'* 56.17.

10. Jerry Wright, "Masculine Allusion and the Structure of Satire in Early Abbasid Poetry," in *Homoeroticism in Classical Arabic Literature*, eds. Jerry W. Wright and Everett K. Rowson (New York: Columbia University, 1997), 12.

11. al-Tabari *Jami'* 44.54; al-Qurtubi *al-Jami'* 44.54.

12. al-Tabari *Jami'* 52.20; al-Mahalli and al-Suyuti *Tafsir al-jalalayn* 44.54; al-Tabarsi *Majma'* 56.17; and al-Qurtubi *al-Jami'*, 44.54.

13. Charles Wendell, "The Denizens of Paradise," 41.

14. al-Qurtubi *al-Jami'*, 44.54.

15. Nancy L. Segal, Aaron T. Goetz, and Alberto C. Maldonado, "The Whites of Our Eyes," *New York Times*, July 17, 2015 (accessed July 15, 2018). https://www.nytimes.com/2015/07/19/opinion/the-whites-of-our-eyes.html

16. al-Ghazali, *The Remembrance of Death and Afterlife (Selections from Ihya' 'ulum al-din)*, trans. T. J. Winter (Cambridge, UK: Islamic Texts Society, 1989), 130.

17. Ibn Habib, *Kitab Wasf al-Firdaws*, no. 208.

18. al-Ghazali, *The Remembrance of Death and Afterlife*, 130.

19. Aziz al-Azmeh, "Rhetoric of the Senses: A Consideration of Muslim Paradise Narratives," *Journal of Arabic Literature* 26 (1995): 220.

20. al-Tirmidhi, *al-Jami' al-sahih*, 4.2533.

21. Ibn Habib, *Kitab Wasf al-Firdaws*, no. 223.

22. al-Muhasibi, *Une vision humaine des fins dernières: le kitab al-tawahhum d'al-Muhasibi*. Trans. André Roman (Paris: Librairie Klincksieck, 1978), no. 160.

23. al-Qadi, *Daqa'iq al-akhbar*, 80. For authorship, see Roberto Tottoli, "Muslim Eschatological Literature and Western Studies," *Der Islam* 83 (2008): 452-77; Christian Lange, *Paradise and Hell in Islamic Ttraditions* (New York: Cambridge University Press, 2016), 24.

24. Ibn Habib, *Kitab Wasf al-Firdaws*, no. 203, 205.

25. Ibn Habib, *Kitab Wasf al-Firdaws*, no. 204.

26. Ibn Ishaq, *Sirat Rasul Allah*, 519.

27. Ibn Ishaq, *Sirat Rasul Allah*, 519.

28. Ibn Ishaq, *Sirat Rasul Allah*, 349–350.

29. Maher Jarrar, "The Martyrdom of Passionate Lovers: Holy War as a Sacred Wedding," in *Myths, Historical Archetypes, and Symbolic Figures in Arabic Literature: Towards a New Hermeneutic Approach: Proceedings of the International Symposium in Beirut*, June 25–30, 1996, ed. Angelika Neuwirth et al. (Stuttgart: Franz Steiner Verlag, 1999), 87–107.

30. Ibn al-Mubarak, *Kitab al-Jihad* (Cairo: Majma' al-Buhuth al-Islamiyah, 1979), no. 21, 22, 143.

31. Ibn al-Mubarak, *Kitab al-Jihad*, no. 23.

32. Ibn al-Mubarak, *Kitab al-Jihad*, no. 143.

33. Jarrar, "The Martyrdom of Passionate Lovers, 100.

34. Ibn al-Mubarak, *Kitab al-Jihad*, no. 21.

35. Ibn al-Mubarak, *Kitab al-Jihad*, no. 23.
36. Ibn al-Mubarak, *Kitab al-Jihad*, no. 143.
37. Ibn al-Mubarak, *Kitab al-Jihad*, no. 145.
38. Ibn al-Mubarak, *Kitab al-Jihad*, no. 148.
39. Ibn al-Mubarak, *Kitab al-Jihad*, no. 149.
40. Ibn al-Mubarak, *Kitab al-Jihad*, no. 150.
41. Ibn al-Mubarak, *Kitab al-Jihad*, no. 150.
42. Ibn al-Mubarak, *Kitab al-Jihad*, no. 150.
43. Ibn al-Mubarak, *Kitab al-Jihad*, no. 143.
44. Ibn Abi Zamanayn, *Kitab Qudwat al-Ghazi* (Beirut: Dar al-Gharb al-Islami, 1989), no. 111.
45. Ibn Abi Zamanayn, *Kitab Qudwat al-Ghazi*, no. 109, 110.
46. Ibn Abi Zamanayn, *Kitab Qudwat al-Ghazi*, no. 112.
47. Ibn al-Nahhas al-Dumyati, *Mashariʿ al-ashwaq ila masariʿ al-ʿushshaq fi al-jihad wa-fadaʾilihi*. Eds. Durish Muhammad ʿAli and Muhammad Khalid Istambuli (Beirut: Dar al-Bashaʾir al-Islamiyya, 2002), 129.
48. Asma Afsaruddin, "Dying in the Path of God: Reading Martyrdom and Moral Excellence in the Quran," in *Roads to Paradise: Eschatology and Concepts of the Hereafter in Islam*, eds. Sebastian Gunther, Todd Lawson, and Christian Mauder, Vol. 1 (Leiden and Boston: Brill, 2017), 179.
49. Ibn Habib, *Wasf al-firdaws* (Beirut: Dar al-Kutub al-ʿIlmiyya, 1987), no. 223, al-Tirmidhi, Muhammad. *Al-Jamiʿ al-sahih*, ed. Ibrahim ʾAtwa ʾAud (Cairo: Dar Ihyaʾ al-Turath al-ʿArabi, n.d.), 4.2564.
50. al-Tirmidhi, *al-Jamiʾ al-sahih* 4.2533.
51. al-Jahiz, *Risalat al-qiyan: The Epistle on Singing-Girls of Jahiz*, ed. A. F. L. Beeston (Warminster, UK: Aris & Phillips, 1980), 34.
52. Lisa Nielson, "Diversions of Pleasure: Singing Slave Girls and the Politics of Music in Early Islamic Courts (661–1000 CE)," Ph.D. dissertation, The University of Maine, 2010, 161–162.
53. Manuscrit supplément turc 190, Bibliothèque nationale, Paris, ca. 1500.
54. Zakariyya b. Muhammad al-Qazwini, *Kitab ʾAjaʾib al-makhluqat wa gharaʾib al-mawjudat*, Add. 7706, Fol. 60b, British Library, Mughal, early seventeenth century; Or. 7315, Fol. 50a, British Library, early seventeenth century; Or. 1371, Fol. 96a, British Library, mid-seventeenth century; Add.

16738, Fol. 55a, British Library, seventeenth century; Or. 13935, fol. 76a, British Library, mid-seventeenth century; Arthur M. Sackler Gallery, Smithsonian Institution, F1954.57, early fifteenth century.

55. Omar Khayyam, *The Rubaiyat of Omar Khayyam*, trans. Peter Avery and John Heath-Stubbs (New York: Penguin, 1979), no. 90, p. 69.

Chapter 5

1. I would like to thank Carla Bellamy, Amy Allocco, Lynn Huber, and Ruth Marshall for their stimulating comments at the CUNY Graduate Center symposium "The Politics of Eschatology and Religious Movements."
2. Scott Shane, "In 'Watershed Moment,' YouTube Blocks Extremist Cleric's Message," *New York Times*, November 17, 2017 (accessed December 1, 2017). https://www.nytimes.com/2017/11/12/us/politics/youtube-terrorism-anwar-al-awlaki.html
3. Charles Hirschkind, "Experiments in Devotion Online: The YouTube Khutba," *International Journal of Middle East Studies* 44 (2012): 6.
4. Hirschkind, "Experiments in Devotion Online."
5. Hirschkind, "Experiments in Devotion Online."
6. Nelly Lahoud, "A Cappella Songs (Anashid) in Jihadi Culture," in *Jihadi Culture*, ed. Thomas Hegghammer (Cambridge, UK: Cambridge University Press, 2017), 43.
7. Jonathan Pieslak, "A Musicological Perspective on Jihadi *anashid*," in *Jihadi Culture*, ed. Thomas Hegghammer (Cambridge, UK: Cambridge University Press, 2017), 76.
8. Jean-Pierre Filiu, *Apocalypse in Islam*, trans. M. B. DeBevoise (Berkeley: University of California Press, 2011), x; and David Cook, *Martyrdom in Islam* (Cambridge: Cambridge University Press, 2007), 150–171.
9. My visits were 1999–2000, 2003, 2004, and 2007.
10. Layla Mabruk, *'Alamat al-sa'a al-sughra wa-l-kubra* (Cairo: Mukhtar al-Islami), 1986.
11. 'Abd al-Ma'iz Khatab, *Nisa' min ahl al-nar* (Cairo: Dar al-khahbiya), 1997.

12. ʿAbd al-Maʾiz Khatab, *Nisaʾ min ahl al-janna* (Cairo: Dar al-khahbiya), n.d.
13. Rachid Abou Houdefya, "A Travel in Paradise!" https://www.youtube.com/watch?v=iiX6uZfOYhA, (accessed July 15, 2015).
14. Houdefya, "A Travel in Paradise!"
15. Ahmed Ali, "The Final Abode," https://www.youtube.com/watch?v=jpB0mFPzxnk, published January 6, 2012 (accessed July 15, 2015).
16. Ali, "The Final Abode."
17. Ali, "The Final Abode," (accessed July 15, 2015).
18. Ali, "The Final Abode."
19. Ali, "The Final Abode," 2.59–3.20.
20. Ali, "The Final Abode," 8.18–9.46.
21. Ali, "The Final Abode," 9.47–10.34.
22. Scott Shane, *Objective Troy: A Terrorist, a President, and the Rise of the Drone* (New York: Tim Duggan Books, 2015), 190.
23. Shane, *Objective Troy: A Terrorist, a President, and the Rise of the Drone*, 304.
24. Shane, *Objective Troy: A Terrorist, a President, and the Rise of the Drone*, 317.
25. Shane, *Objective Troy: A Terrorist, a President, and the Rise of the Drone*, 146.
26. Ali, "The Final Abode."
27. Anwar al-Awlaqi, "Tour of Jannah Paradise," https://www.youtube.com/watch?v=pL7TYYcmvpU (accessed July 15, 2015).
28. al-Awlaqi, "Tour of Jannah Paradise."
29. al-Awlaqi, "Tour of Jannah Paradise."
30. al-Awlaqi, "Tour of Jannah Paradise."
31. al-Awlaqi, "Tour of Jannah Paradise."
32. al-Awlaqi, "Tour of Jannah Paradise."
33. al-Awlaqi, "Tour of Jannah Paradise."
34. al-Awlaqi, "Tour of Jannah Paradise."
35. al-Awlaqi, "Tour of Jannah Paradise."
36. Bruce Hoffman, *Inside Terrorism* (New York: Columbia University Press, 2006), 180.
37. J. Friedman, "Call for 9/12 and 9/13 Newspapers," January 16, 2015, http://www.911memorial.org/blog/call-912-and-913-newspapers (accessed July 15, 2015).

38. Charles Hirschkind, "Experiments in Devotion Online," 18.

39. Philipp Holtmann, "Virtual Leadership: How Jihadists Guide Each Other in Cyberspace," in *New Approaches to the Analysis of Jihadism: Online and Offline*, ed. Rudiger Lohlker (Vienna University Press, 2012), 75.

40. Holtmann, "Virtual Leadership," 74.

41. Holtmann, "Virtual Leadership," 69.

42. Holtmann, "Virtual Leadership," 49.

43. Holtmann, "Virtual Leadership," 44–45.

44. Anwar Al-Awlaqi, "Hoor al-Ayn," https://www.youtube.com/watch?v=5noV0zM8H1w, 0–1.34 (accessed July 15, 2015).

45. al-Awlaqi, "Hoor al-Ayn," 1.25–2.47.

46. Muslim, *Sahih Muslim*, Arabic English, 8 vols., trans. Hameed Siddiqui (Delhi: Adam Publishers, 1999), Kitab al-Imara, Book 20, no. 4651.

47. al-Awlaqi, "Hoor al-Ayn," 0–1.34.

48. al-Awlaqi, "Hoor al-Ayn," 2.47–3.29.

49. Holtmann, "Virtual Leadership," 124.

50. Hirschkind, "Experiments in Devotion Online," 17.

51. Tilman Seidensticker, "Jihad Hymns (Nashids) as a Means of Self-motivation in the Hamburg Group," in *New Approaches to the Analysis of Jihadism: Online and Offline*, ed. Rudiger Lohlker (Vienna University Press, 2012), 77.

52. Jonathan Pieslak, *Radicalism and Music: An Introduction to the Music Cultures of Al-Qa'ida, Racist Skinheads, Christian-Affiliated Radicals, and Eco-Animal Rights Militants* (Middletown, CT: Wesleyan University Press, 2015), 197.

53. "Fil cenne huriya 2012 nasheed," https://www.youtube.com/watch?v=LgoGFWjFqM0&list=PLFm0RlJ3qO_0B1Vfnvm-dHuNuMrogsLzF&index=10; "Nasheed avec as shabab," https://www.youtube.com/watch?v=CJ-Y0kBqoiU (accessed July 15, 2015).

54. Thomas Seymat, "How Nasheeds Became the Soundtrack of Jihad," Euronews.com, http://www.euronews.com/2014/10/08/nasheeds-the-soundtrack-of-jihad/, August 10, 2014 (accessed July 15, 2015).

55. Behnam Said, "Hymns (Nasheeds): A Contribution to the Study of Jihadist Culture," *Studies in Conflict & Terrorism* 35 (2012): 864.

56. Alex Marshall. "How Isis Got Its Anthem," *The Guardian*, November 9, 2014, http://www.theguardian.com/music/2014/nov/09/nasheed-how-isis-got-its-anthem (accessed July 15, 2015).

57. "Nashiido Urduu Ah: Jannah Hoor al Ayn," https://www.youtube.com/watch?v=VXJKBrjXxhw&index=8&list=PLFm0RlJ3qO_0B1Vfnvm-dHuNuMrogsLzF (accessed July 15, 2015).

58. "Hur Al-Ayn Tunadini," https://www.youtube.com/watch?v=ChHg7sobJ90 (accessed July 15, 2015); "Hoor Al Ayn Nasheed—Eng Translation," https://www.youtube.com/watch?v=_dzqrNaYQyY (accessed July 15, 2015).

59. "Bi Jihadina," https://www.youtube.com/watch?v=0eewpBtZhIU (accessed July 15, 2015); "Bi Jihadina (ST francais)," https://www.youtube.com/watch?v=ofZgYkoV4ys (accessed July 15, 2015).

60. Katherine Boyle, "Islamist Nasheeds Embrace Modern Technology While Staying True to Ideals," *Washington Post*, July 15, 2013. https://www.washingtonpost.com/lifestyle/style/islamist-nasheeds-embrace-modern-technology-while-staying-true-to-ideals/2013/07/15/20d6c3a4-e8b0-11e2-aa9f-c03a72e2d342_story.html

61. "Beautiful Arabic Nasheed—Hoor al Ayn," https://www.youtube.com/watch?v=hlWRiEM7Zio (accessed July 15, 2015).

62. "Hur al ayn Aby Anza—Jihad Nasheed," https://www.youtube.com/watch?v=2bLRQ799A5Y (accessed July 15, 2015).

63. "Hur Al-Ayn Tunadini," https://www.youtube.com/watch?v=ChHg7sobJ90, published November 24, 2013 (accessed July 15, 2015).

64. "Nasheed Hur al-Ayn Tunadini in Syria," https://www.youtube.com/watch?v=FjgGmkaGhrg (accessed July 15, 2015).

65. "Young Mujahid Sings Hoor Al-Ayn Nasheed with His Brothers, Preparing to Meet Her," https://www.youtube.com/watch?v=vqd4DkUbykY (accessed July 15, 2015).

66. Christa Salamandra, "Arab Television Drama Production and the Islamic Public Sphere," in *Visual Culture in the Modern Middle East*, eds. Christiane Gruber and Sune Haugbolle (Bloomington: Indiana University Press, 2013), 267.

67. Salamandra, "Arab Television Drama Production and the Islamic Public Sphere," 266.

68. Salamandra, "Arab Television Drama Production and the Islamic Public Sphere," 267.

Chapter 6

1. Aziz al-Azmeh, "Rhetoric of the Senses: A Consideration of Muslim Paradise Narratives," *Journal of Arabic Literature* 26 (1995): 215.
2. Fatima Mernissi, *Women in Moslem Paradise* (New Delhi: Kali for Women, 1986), n.p.
3. Fatima Mernissi, *Women in Moslem Paradise*, n.p.
4. Fatima Mernissi, *Women in Moslem Paradise*, n.p.
5. Fatima Mernissi, *Women in Moslem Paradise*, n.p.
6. Fatima Mernissi, *Women in Moslem Paradise*, n.p.
7. Raja Rhouni, *Secular and Islamic Feminist Critiques in the Work of Fatima Mernissi* (Leiden and Boston: Brill, 2010), 186.
8. Rhouni, *Secular and Islamic Feminist Critiques in the Work of Fatima Mernissi*, 186.
9. Rhouni, *Secular and Islamic Feminist Critiques in the Work of Fatima Mernissi*, 186.
10. Rhouni, *Secular and Islamic Feminist Critiques in the Work of Fatima Mernissi*, 186–187.
11. Rhouni, *Secular and Islamic Feminist Critiques in the Work of Fatima Mernissi*, 261; and Amina Wadud, *Inside the Gender Jihad: Women's Reform in Islam* (Oxford: Oneword, 2006), 193.
12. Amina Wadud, *Qur'an and Woman: Rereading the Sacred Texts from a Woman's Perspective* (New York, Oxford: Oxford University Press, 1999), 54.
13. Wadud, *Qur'an and Women*, 54.
14. Wadud, *Qur'an and Women*, 59.
15. Wadud, *Qur'an and Women*, 59.
16. Assim Luqman Al Hakeem, Huda Television, "If Men Receive Houris (Women) in Paradise, What Will Women Receive?," published August 31, 2010, http://www.youtube.com/watch?v=0gPrmcQ_xgY (accessed July 15, 2017).
17. al Hakeem, "If Men Receive Houris (Women) in Paradise, What Will Women Receive?"

18. Nouman Ali Khan, "Why Is Allah Explicit about Hoor Al Ayn & What Will Women Get in Jannah," https://www.youtube.com/watch?v=VmTPlovGIt8 (accessed July 15, 2017).
19. Ali Khan, "Why Is Allah Explicit about Hoor Al Ayn."
20. Ali Khan, "Why Is Allah Explicit about Hoor Al Ayn."
21. Arifi website, http://arefe.ws/en/index.php?com=content&id=1 (accessed July 15, 2017).
22. Arifi channel, https://www.youtube.com/watch?v=JyGbmBu50ZY&list=PLFm0RlJ3qO_0B1Vfnvm-dHuNuMrogsLzF&index=4 (accessed July 15, 2017).
23. Nilofar Ahmed, "Are All 'Houris' Female?," Dawn, June 9, 2011, http://www.dawn.com/news/635343/are-all-houris-female (accessed July 15, 2017).
24. Bin Baz website, http://www.binbaz.org.sa/node/10354 (accessed July 15, 2017).
25. http://www.peacetv.tv/en-gb/# (accessed July 15, 2017).
26. Ben Hubbard, "Saudi Award Goes to Muslim Televangelist Who Harshly Criticizes U.S." *New York Times*, March 3, 2015, A4.
27. Zakir Naik, "Houris in Islam," http://www.youtube.com/watch?v=HWDzZSreVcc (accessed July 15, 2017).
28. Mufti Menk website, http://www.muftimenk.com (accessed July 15, 2017).
29. Mufti Menk website, http://www.muftimenk.com (accessed July 15, 2017).
30. Ali Khan, "Why Is Allah Explicit about Hoor Al Ayn."
31. Yasir Qadhi, "Are There Beautiful Men for Women in Paradise?," published January 11, 2008, https://www.youtube.com/watch?v=PMo8Q8U04hQ (accessed July 15, 2017).
32. Qadhi, "Are There Beautiful Men for Women in Paradise?"
33. Qadhi, "Are There Beautiful Men for Women in Paradise?"

Conclusion

1. Ali does not use this phrase in relation to houris, but enslaved persons. Kecia Ali, *Marriage and Slavery in Early Islam* (Cambridge, MA: Harvard University Press, 2010), 7.

BIBLIOGRAPHY

Engravings and Paintings

Byron, Lord George Gordon. *The Gallery of Byron Beauties: Ideal Pictures of the Principal Female Characters in Lord Byron's Poems. From the original paintings by eminent artists.* New York: D. Appleton, 1867. Call Number: B825B99 F7 1867. Rare Book & Manuscript Library, Columbia University in the City of New York.

Byron, Lord George Gordon. *The Gallery of Byron Beauties: Ideal Pictures of the Principal Female Characters in Lord Byron's Poems. From the original paintings by eminent artists.* London: W. Kent, 18–. Call Number: B825B99 F7 18–. Rare Book & Manuscript Library, Columbia University in the City of New York.

Ingres, Jean Auguste Dominque. *The Great Odalisque (La Grande Odalisque).* 1819. Oil on canvas, 91 x 162 cm. Inv.: RF 1158. Photo: Thierry Le Mage. © RMN-Grand Palais / Art Resource, NY.

Ingres, Jean Auguste Dominque. *The Turkish Bath.* 1862. Oil on wood, 110 x 110 cm; diam. 108 cm. RF 1934. Photo: Gérard Blot. © RMN-Grand Palais / Art Resource, NY.

Jazet, Jean Pierre Marie (1788–1871). Recueil. Oeuvre des Jazet. Bibliothèque nationale de France.

Manuscrit supplément turc 190. *Bibliothèque nationale*, Paris. Ca. 1500.

Maurin, Nicolas-Eustache (1799–1850). Recueil. Oeuvre des Maurin. Bibliothèque nationale de France.

al-Qazwini, Zakariyya b. Muhammad. *Kitab 'Aja'ib al-makhluqat wa ghara'ib al-mawjudat.* Add. 7706, Fol. 60b. British Library. Mughal, early seventeenth century.

al-Qazwini, Zakariyya b. Muhammad. Or. 7315, Fol. 50a. British Library, early seventeenth century.

al-Qazwini, Zakariyya b. Muhammad. Or. 1371, Fol. 96a. British Library, mid-seventeenth century.

al-Qazwini, Zakariyya b. Muhammad. Add. 16738, Fol. 55a. British Library, seventeenth century.

al-Qazwini, Zakariyya b. Muhammad. Or. 13935, fol. 76a. British Library, mid-seventeenth century.

al-Qazwini, Zakariyya b. Muhammad. Arthur M. Sackler Gallery. Smithsonian Institution. F1954.57, early fifteenth century.

al-Qazwini, Zakariyya b. Muhammad. 1972.3, folio 80 verso. Harvard University, seventeenth century.

Star of Love. *The Ladies' Companion.* October 1840, Vol. 13, Opp. p. 261. Engraving. General Research Division, The New York Public Library, Astor, Lenox, and Tilden Foundations.

Articles, Books, and Websites

Abou Houdefya, Imam Rachid. "A Travel in Paradise!" https://www.youtube.com/watch?v=iiX6uZfOYhA. Accessed July 15, 2015.

ABSNews Digital, "Handwritten Letter Instructed Hijackers," September 29, 2001. https://abcnews.go.com/US/story?id=923 98&page=1.

Ahmed, Nilofar. "Are All 'Houris' Female?" *Dawn.* June 9, 2011. http://www.dawn.com/news/635343/are-all-houris-female. Accessed July 15, 2017.

"Albanian National Sentenced to 16 Years for Attempting to Support Terrorism." United States Department of Justice, Office of Public Affairs. https://www.justice.gov/opa/pr/albanian-national-sentenced-16-years-attempting-support-terrorism. Accessed July 15, 2018.

Ali, Shaykh Ahmed. "The Final Abode." https://www.youtube.com/watch?v=qJzv3lFVpSk. Accessed July 15, 2015.

Amis, Martin. "The Last Days of Muhammad Atta." In *The Second Plane: September 11: Terror and Boredom*, by Martin Amis. New York and Toronto: Alfred A. Knopf, 2008. 93–122.

Astell, Mary. *A Serious Proposal to the Ladies, for the advancement of their true and greatest interest, in two parts. By a lover of her sex.* London: 1697 [1701] Eighteenth Century Collections Online. Accessed August 1, 2016.

"Another Idiot in Pakistan!" https://m.blog.daum.net/mallam/1688?np_nil_b=19 (accessed July 15, 2018).

al-Awlaqi, Anwar. "Hoor al-Ayn." https://www.youtube.com/watch?v=5noV0zM8H1w. Accessed July 15, 2015.

al-Awlaqi, Anwar. "Tour of Jannah Paradise." https://www.youtube.com/watch?v=pL7TYYcmvpU. Accessed July 15, 2015.

"Beautiful Arabic Nasheed–Hoor al Ayn," https://www.youtube.com/watch?v=hlWRiEM7Zio. Accessed July 15, 2015.

Beckford, William. *The History of the Caliph Vathek.* London: J. Johnson, 1786. Eighteenth Century Collections Online. Accessed February 18, 2015.

"Bi jihadina." https://www.youtube.com/watch?v=0eewpBtZhIU. Accessed July 15, 2015.

"Bi Jihadina (ST français)." https://www.youtube.com/watch?v=ofZgYkoV4ys. Accessed July 15, 2015.

Bin Baz website. http://www.binbaz.org.sa/node/10354. Accessed July 15, 2017.

Brontë, Charlotte. *Jane Eyre.* New York: The Modern Library, 1993.

Byron, Lord George Gordon. *The Bride of Abydos: A Turkish Tale.* London: John Murray, 1814. HathiTrust Digital Library. Accessed February 15, 2015.

Byron, Lord George Gordon. *Childe Harold's Pilgrimage.* New York: Lovell Brothers, 1890.

Byron, Lord George Gordon. *The Corsair.* New York: N. P. Willis, 1839–1840. Accessed February 15, 2015.

Byron, Lord George Gordon. *The Corsair, a tale. Lara, a tale.* Paris: Truchy, 1830. Accessed February 15, 2015.

Byron, Lord George Gordon. *Don Juan.* Boston: Phillips, Sampson, 1858. HathiTrust Digital Library. Accessed February 15, 2015.

Byron, Lord George Gordon. *The Giaour: A Fragment of a Turkish Tale*. London: John Murray, 1814. HathiTrust Digitial Library. Accessed February 15, 2015.

Byron, Lord George Gordon. *The Siege of Corinth*. Paris: B. Cormon and Black, 1835. Accessed February 15, 2015.

Chambers, Joseph R. "The Islamic Heaven: A Pornographic Brothel." http://www.moriel.org/articles/discernment/islam/islamic_heaven.htm. Accessed February 15, 2015.

Christian Video 4 Free. "72 Virgins for Martyrs in Heaven—Myth or Truth?" http://www.christianvideo4free.com/christians-of-asia-network/72-virgins-for-martyrs-in-heaven-myth-or-truth-. Posted June 4, 2011. Accessed February 15, 2015.

Dictionnaire de l'Académie Française, 4th edition. Paris: Chez la Vve B. Brunet, 1762. ARTFL Project Edition.

Du Loir, Nicolas. *Les Voyages du Sieur du Loir*. Paris: Chez Gervais Closvzier, 1654.

"Female Beauty of the Mind." In *The Universalist and the Ladies' Repository*. Ed. Henry Bacon. Boston: Abel Tompkins, 1837.

"Fil cenne huriya 2012 nasheed." https://www.youtube.com/watch?v=LgoGFWjFqM0&list=PLFm0RlJ3qO_0B1Vfnvm-dHuNuMrogsLzF&index=10. Accessed July 15, 2015.

Four-page hand-written Arabic letter found in luggage recovered at Logan Airport, Boston, Massachusetts. Exhibit No. BS 01101 in the trial of the *United States of America v. Zacarias Moussaoui*. http://www.vaed.uscourts.gov/notablecases/moussaoui/. Accessed February 15, 2015.

"Full Metal Jacket . . . around Penis of Suicide Bomber." https://www.liveleak.com/view?t=86e_1387152923. Accessed July 15, 2018.

"Full Text of Notes Found after Hijackings." *New York Times*, September 29, 2001. http://www.nytimes.com/2001/09/29/national/29SFULL-TEXT.html?pagewanted=print. Accessed March 1, 2015.

al-Ghazali. *The Remembrance of Death and Afterlife (Selections from Ihya' 'ulum al-din)*. Trans. T. J. Winter. Cambridge, UK: Islamic Texts Society, 1989.

The Global Edition. "Female Taliban Suicide Bomber Hates the Idea of Virgins in Heaven." http://www.theglobaledition.com/female-taliban-suicide-bomber-hates-the-idea-of-virgins-in-heaven/. Updated June 26, 2012. Accessed February 15, 2015.

Hagler, Joshua. "72 Virgins to Die For." February 5–March 1, 2009. Frey Gallery, San Francisco, 2008.

Hines, David Theo. *The Life, Adventures and Opinions of David Theo Hines South Carolina Master of Arts and, Sometimes, Doctor of Medicine.* New York: Bradley and Clark, 1840.

"Hoor Al Ayn Nasheed—Eng Translation." https://www.youtube.com/watch?v=_dzqrNaYQyY. Accessed July 15, 2015.

"Houri." *Dictionnaire de l'Académie Française,* 4th edition. Paris: Chez la Vve B. Brunet, 1762. The ARTFL Project Edition. Accessed February 15, 2015.

"Hur al ayn Aby Anza—Jihad Nasheed." https://www.youtube.com/watch?v=2bLRQ799A5Y. Accessed July 15, 2015.

"Hur Al-Ayn Tunadini." https://www.youtube.com/watch?v=Ch Hg7sobJ90. Accessed July 15, 2015.

Ibn Abi Zamanayn. *Kitab Qudwat al-Ghazi.* Beirut: Dar al-Gharb al-Islami, 1989.

Ibn al-Mubarak. *Kitab al-Jihad.* Cairo: Majma' al-Buhuth al-Islamiyah, 1979.

Ibn Habib. *Wasf al-Firdaws.* Beirut: Dar al-Kutub al-'Ilmiyya, 1987.

Ibn Ishaq. *Life of Muhammad: A Translation of Ishaq's Sirat Rasul Allah.* Trans. A. Guillaume. London: Oxford University Press, 1955.

Ibn Kathir, Isma'il. *Tafsir al-Qur'an al-karim.* Royal Aal al-Bayt Institute for Islamic Thought, Amman. http://www.aalalbayt.org. Accessed May 17, 2010.

Ibn al-Nahhas al-Dumyati. *Mashari' al-ashwaq ila masari' al-'ushshaq fi al-jihad wa-fada'ilihi.* Eds. Durish Muhammad 'Ali and Muhammad Khalid Istambuli. Beirut: Dar al-Basha'ir al-Islamiyya, 2002.

Ibn Warraq. "Institute for the Secularisation of Islamic Scoety website." http://ibnwarraq.com/category/institute-for-the-secularisation-of-islamic-society/. Accessed July 15, 2018.

Ibn Warraq, "Virgins? What Virgins?" *Guardian,* January 12, 2002. https://www.theguardian.com/books/2002/jan/12/books.guardianreview5. Accessed July 15, 2018.

al-Jahiz. *Risalat al-qiyan: The Epistle on Singing-Girls of Jahiz.* Ed. A. F. L. Beeston. Warminster, UK: Aris & Phillips, 1980.

Johnson, Samuel. *Irene: A Tragedy.* London: J. Dodsley, 1781. Eighteenth Century Collections Online. Accessed February 15, 2015.

Keats, John. *The Complete Poetical Works of John Keats*. Eds. Horace Elisha Scudder and Harry Buxton Forman. Boston and New York: Houghton Mifflin, 1899.

Khan, Nouman Ali "Why Is Allah Explicit about Hoor Al Ayn & What Will Women Get in Jannah," https://www.youtube.com/watch?v=VmTPlovGIt8, Accessed July 15, 2017.

Khatab, ʿAbd al-Maʿiz Khatab. *Nisaʾ min ahl al-janna*. Cairo: Dar al-khahbiya, n.d.

Khatab, ʿAbd al-Maʿiz Khatab. *Nisaʾ min ahl al-nar*. Cairo: Dar al-khahbiya, 1997.

Kippenberg, Hans G., and Tilman Seidensticker, eds. *The 9/11 Handbook: Annotated Translation and Interpretation of the Attacker's Spiritual Manual*. London and Oakville: Equinox, 2006.

Kristof, Nicholas. "Islam, Virgins and Grapes." New York Times, August 9, 2009. https://www.nytimes.com/2009/04/23/opinion/23kristof.html

Kristof, Nicholas. "Martyrs, Virgins and Grapes." *New York Times*, August 4, 2004. https://www.nytimes.com/2004/08/04/opinion/martyrs-virgins-and-grapes.html

Kristof, Nicholas. "Martyrs, Virgins and Grapes: Towards an Islamic Reformation." *Sarasota Herald-Tribune*. August 5, 2004. 13A.

Kundnani, Arun. *The Muslims Are Coming! Islamophobia, Extremism, and the Domestic War on Terror*. London and New York: Verso, 2014.

"Last Words of a Terrorist." *The Guardian*. September 30, 2001. https://www.theguardian.com/world/2001/sep/30/terrorism.september113. Accesssed July 15, 2015.

Luqman Al Hakeem, Sheikh Assim. "If Men Receive Houris (Women) in Paradise, What Will Women Receive?" Huda Television. Published August 31, 2010. http://www.youtube.com/watch?v=0gPrmcQ_xgY. Accessed July 15, 2017.

Luxenberg, Christoph. *Die syro-aramäische Lesart des Koran: Ein Beitrag zur Entschlüsselung der Koransprache*. Berlin: Das Arabische Buch, 2000.

Luxenberg, Christoph. *The Syro-Aramaic Reading of the Koran: A Contribution to the Decoding of the Language of the Koran*. Berlin: Hans Schiler, 2007.

Mabruk, Layla. *ʿAlamat al-saʿa al-sughra wa-l-kubra*. Cairo: Mukhtar al-Islami, 1986.

al-Mahalli, Muhammad, and ʿAbd al-Rahman al-Suyuti. *Tafsir al-jalalyn.* Trans. F. Hamza. Royal Aal al-Bayt Institute for Islamic Thought, Amman. http://www.aalalbayt.org. Accessed May 17, 2010.

Martin, Steve. "Seventy-two Virgins." *New Yorker,* January 29, 2007, 42–43.

Maurus, Johannes Andreas. *The Confusion of Muhamed's sect or a confutation of the Turkish Alcoran. Being a discovery of many secret policies and practices in that religion, not till now revealed. Written originally in Spanish, by Johannes Andreas Maurus, who was one of their bishops and afterwards turned Christian. Translated into English by Joshua Notstock.* London: H. Blunden, 1652. Early English Books Online. Accessed February 15, 2015.

Montagu, Lady Mary Wortley. *Letters of the Right Honourable Lady M-y W-y M-e.* London: Thomas Martine, 1790. Project Gutenberg Edition. Release date: January 15, 2006.

Montagu, Lady Mary Wortley. *The Turkish Embassy Letters.* Eds. Teresa Wefferman and Daniel O'Quinn. Buffalo and Petersborough: Broadview, 2013.

Morell, Sir Charles. *The Tales of the Genii or, the Delightful Lessons of Horam the Son of Asmar faithfully translated from the Persian Manuscript, and Compared with the French and Spanish Editions Published at Paris and Madrid.* London: J. Wilkie, 1786.

Mufti Menk website. http://www.muftimenk.com. Accessed July 15, 2017.

al-Muhasibi. *Une vision humaine des fins dernières: le kitab al-tawahhum d'al-Muhasibi.* Trans. André Roman. Paris: Librairie Klincksieck, 1978.

Muslim b. Hajjaj. *Sahih Muslim.* Arabic English. 8 vols. Trans. Hameed Siddiqui. Delhi: Adam, 1999.

"Nasheed avec as shabab." https://www.youtube.com/watch?v=CJ-Y0kBqoiU. Accessed July 15, 2015.

"Nasheed Hur al-Ayn Tunadini in Syria." https://www.youtube.com/watch?v=FjgGmkaGhrg. Accessed July 15, 2015.

"Nashiido Urduu Ah: Jannah Hoor al Ayn." https://www.youtube.com/watch?v=VXJKBrjXxhw&index=8&list=PLFm0RlJ3qO_0B1Vfnvm-dHuNuMrogsLzF. Accessed July 15, 2015.

Neele, Henry. "The Houri: A Persian Tale." *The Oriental Herald and Journal of General Literature 19*, no. 59. London: W. Lewer, 1828. 246–253.

"Newsweek Story on Islam Banned," *Chicago Tribune*, July 29, 2003. 6.

Niebuhr, Gustave. "Injunctions to Pray, Instructions to Kill." *New York Times*, September 29, 2001. https://www.nytimes.com/2001/09/29/us/a-nation-challenged-the-letter-injunctions-to-pray-and-orders-to-kill.html

Omar Khayyam. *The Rubaiyat of Omar Khayyam*. Trans. Peter Avery and John Heath-Stubbs. New York: Penguin, 1979.

Pardoe, Julia Sophia. *Romance of the Harem: A Novel*. Philadelphia: T. B. Peterson and Brothers, 1929.

Perry, Avi. *72 Virgins: Countdown to Terror Attack on US Soil*. Paramus, NJ: Gradient, 2009.

Planquette, Robert. *Le Paradis de Mahomet: Operette de trois actes de Henri Blondeau; musique de Robert Planquette*. Paris: Choudens, 1906. HathiTrust Digital Library. Accessed February 15, 2015.

Pressburg, Norbert. *What the Modern Martyr Should Know: Seventy-Two Grapes and Not a Single Virgin: The New Picture of Islam*. Create Space Independent Publishing Platform, 2012.

al-Qadi, ʿAbd al-Rahim. *Daqaʾiq al-akhbar fi dhikr al-janna wa-l-nar*. Cairo: Maktaba al-Saʾidiyya, n.d.

Qadhi, Yasir. "Are There Beautiful Men for Women in Paradise?" Published January 11, 2008. https://www.youtube.com/watch?v=PMo8Q8U04hQ. Accessed July 15, 2017.

al-Qurtubi, Muhammad. *Al-Jamiʿ li-ahkam al-Qurʾan*. Royal Aal al-Bayt Institute for Islamic Thought, Amman. http://www.aalalbayt.org. Accessed May 17, 2010.

Reinhart, A. Kevin. "The Here and the Hereafter in Islamic Religious Thought." In *Images of Paradise in Islamic Art*. Eds. Sheila S. Blair and Jonathan M. Bloom. Austin: University of Texas Press, 1991. 15–23.

Rihani, Ameen. *The Book of Khalid*. Illustrated by Kahlil Gibran. Brooklyn, NY: Melville House, first edition, 1911. Reprint 2012.

Rihani, Ameen Fares. *The Book of Khalid: A Critical Edition*. Syracuse, NY: Syracuse University Press, 2016.

Saint Ephrem. *Hymns on Paradise*. Trans. Sebastian Bock. Crestwood, NY: 1990.

Scott, Sir Walter. *Ivanhoe*. Edited by Graham Tulloch. Edinburgh: Edinburgh University Press, 1998.

Sheikh Arifi channel. https://www.youtube.com/watch?v=JyGbm Bu50ZY&list=PLFm0RlJ3qO_0B1Vfnvm-dHuNuMrogs LzF&index=4. Accessed July 15, 2017.

Sheikh Arifi website. http://arefe.ws/en/index.php?com=content& id=1. Accessed July 15, 2017.

Shelley, Mary Wollstonecraft. *Falkner*, Vol. II. London: Saunders and Otley, 1837. Hathitrust Digital Library. Accessed February 15, 2015.

"Slippers: A Turkish Tale." Chapter 1, *The Monthly Mirror, Reflecting Men and Manners* Vol. 19. London: J. Wright, 1805.

"Star of Love." *Ladies' Companion: A Monthly Magazine embracing Every department of literature, embellished with Original Engravings, and Music arranged for the piano forte, harp, and guitar*, Vol. 13. New York: William W. Snowden, 1840.

Stille, Alexander. "Scholars Scrutinize the Koran's Origins: A Promise of Moist Virgins or Dried Fruit?" *New York Times* and *International Herald Tribune*, March 4, 2002. https://www.nytimes.com/2002/03/02/arts/scholars-are-quietly-offering-new-theories-of-the-koran.html

al-Tabari, Muhammad. *Jami' al-bayan 'an ta'wil ay al-Qur'an*. Royal Aal al-Bayt Institute for Islamic Thought, Amman. http://www.aalalbayt.org. Accessed May 17, 2010.

al-Tabarsi, al-Fadl. *Majma' al-bayan fi tafsir al-Qur'an*. Royal Aal al-Bayt Institute for Islamic Thought, Amman. http://www.aalalbayt.org. Accessed May 17, 2010.

Tantawy, Muhammad Sayed. "Origins of the Qur'an." *Dawn*, October 3, 2003. https://www.dawn.com/news/1065100

Theil, Stefan. "Challenging the Qur'an." *Newsweek*, July 27, 2003. https://www.newsweek.com/challenging-quran-139447

al-Tirmidhi, Muhammad. *Al-Jami' al-sahih*, Ed. Ibrahim 'Atwa 'Aud, 4 vols. Cairo: Dar Ihya' al-Turath al-'Arabi, n.d.

Tyler, Royall. *The Algerine Captive*. Edited by Don L. Cook. New Haven, CT: College and University Press, 1970.

United States of America v. Zacarias Moussaoui. Criminal No. 01-455-A. Prosecution Trial Exhibits. BS01101 and BS01101T. http://www.vaed.uscourts.gov/notablecases/moussaoui/exhibits/prosecution.html.

"A Visit to Jerusalem by an American." *The Gentleman's Magazine*, V. 1. Ed. William E. Burton. Philadelphia: Charles Alexander, 1837.

Vocativ. http://www.vocativ.com/world/ukraine-world/jihadi-jokesters-waging-holy-war-hot-ukrainian-ladies/. Accessed February 15, 2015.

Walpole, Horace. *The Yale Edition of Horace Walpole's Correspondence*. New Haven, CT: Yale University Press, 1937–1983. Online edition. Accessed February 15, 2015.

"Wealth, Wisdom, and Virtue: An Eastern Tale." In *Gleanings of Wit being A Choice Collection of Tales, Anecdotes, Occurrences and various pieces in Prose and Verse Interspersed with Many Original Pieces Never before published from the Worlds of an Old Military Officer*. London: J. Ginger, 1805. 193–200.

"Young Mujahid Sings Hoor Al-Ayn Nasheed with His Brothers, Preparing to Meet Her." https://www.youtube.com/watch?v=vqd4DkUbykY. Accessed July 15, 2015.

al-Zamakhshari, Mahmud. *Al-Kashshaf 'an haqa'iq al-tanzil wa-'uyun al-aqawal fi wujuh al-ta'wil*. Royal Aal al-Bayt Institute for Islamic Thought, Amman. http://www.aalalbayt.org. Accessed May 17, 2010.

Secondary Sources

Abdulla, Rasha A. "Islam, Jihad, and Terrorism in Post 9/11 Arabic Discussion Boards." *Journal of Computer-Mediated Communication* 12, no. 3 (April 2007): 1063–1081.

Abu-Lughod, Lila. *Do Muslim Women Need Saving?* Cambridge, MA, and London: Harvard University Press, 2013.

Adams, Katherine Hodges. "A Study of Samuel Johnson's Irene." Florida State University. ProQuest UMI Dissertations Publishing, 1981.

Afsaruddin, Asma. "Dying in the Path of God: Reading Martyrdom and Moral Excellence in the Qur'an." In *Roads to Paradise: Eschatology and Concepts of the Hereafter in Islam.* Eds. Sebastian Gunther, Todd Lawson, and Christian Mauder. Vol. 1. Leiden and Boston: Brill, 2017. 162–180.

Afsaruddin, Asma. *Striving in the Path of God: Jihad and Martyrdom in Islamic Thought.* Oxford: Oxford University Press, 2013.

Ahmed, Sharbari Z. "Raisins Not Virgins." In *The Ocean of Mrs. Nagai: Stories,* by Sharbari Z. Ahmed. Dhaka: Daily Star Books, 2013. 602–979.

Aidi, Hisham. *Rebel Music: Race, Empire, and the New Muslim Youth Culture.* New York: Vintage, 2014.

Ait Sabbah, Fatna. *Woman in the Muslim Unconscious.* New York: Pergamon Press, 1984.

Akbari, Suzanne Conklin, *Idols in the East: European Representations of Islam and the Orient, 1100–1450.* Ithaca, NY: Cornell University Press, 2012.

Alam, Muzaffar, and Sanjay Subrahamanyam. *Indo-Persian Travels in the Age of Discoveries 1400–1800.* Cambridge, UK: Cambridge University Press, 2007.

"Albanian National Sentenced to 16 Years for Attempting to Support Terrorism." United States Department of Justice, Office of Public Affairs. https://www.justice.gov/opa/pr/albanian-national-sentenced-16-years-attempting-support-terrorism. Accessed July 15, 2018.

Ali, Kecia. *Sexual Ethics and Islam: Feminist Reflections on Qur'an, Hadith, and Jurisprudence.* Oxford: Oneworld, 2006.

Anderson, Jon. "New Media, New Publics: Reconfiguring the Public Sphere in Islam." *Social Research* 70, no. 3, Islam: The Public and Private Spheres (Fall 2003): 887–906.

Andrea, Bernadette. *Women and Islam in Early Modern English Literature.* Cambridge, UK: Cambridge University Press, 2007.

Arjana, Sophia Rose. *Muslims in the Western Imagination.* New York: Oxford, 2015.

al-Azmeh, Aziz. "Rhetoric of the Senses: A Consideration of Muslim Paradise Narratives." *Journal of Arabic Literature* 26 (1995): 215–231.

Bach, Rebecca Ann. *Colonial Transformations: The Cultural Production of the New Atlantic World, 1580–1640.* New York: Palgrave, 2000.

El-Badawi, Emran. *The Qur'an and the Aramaic Gospel Traditions.* New York and London: Routledge Press, 2014.

Baepler, Paul. *White Slaves, African Masters: An Anthology of American Barbary Captivity Narratives.* Chicago and London: University of Chicago Press, 1999.

Barbour, Richmond. *Before Orientalism: London's Theatre of the East, 1576–1626.* Cambridge, UK: University of Cambridge, 2003.

Barlas, Asma. *"Believing Women" in Islam: Unreading Patriarchal Interpretations of the Qur'an.* Austin: University of Texas Press, 2002.

Bauer, Karen. *Gender Hierarchy in the Qur'an: Medieval Interpretations, Modern Responses.* Cambridge, UK: Cambridge University Press, 2015.

Beaty, Jerome. *Misreading Jane Eyre: A Postformalist Paradigm.* Columbus: Ohio State University Press, 1996.

Beckles, Colin A. "Black Liberation and the Internet: A Strategic Analysis." *Journal of Black Studies* 31, no. 3, Special Issue: Africa: New Realities and Hopes (2001): 311–324.

Behdad, Ali. *Belated Travelers: Orientalism in the Age of Colonial Dissolution.* Durham, NC, and London: Duke University Press, 1994.

Berg, Maggie. *Jane Eyre: Portrait of a Life.* Boston: Twayne, 1987.

Berko, Anat. *The Path to Paradise: The Inner World of Suicide Bombers and Their Dispatches.* Trans. Elizabeth Yuval. Westport, CT, and London: Praeger Security International, 2007.

Berman, Jacob. *American Arabesque: Arabs, Islam, and the Nineteenth Century Imaginary.* New York: New York University Press, 2012.

Bloom, Mia. *Dying to Kill: The Allure of Suicide Terror.* New York: Columbia University Press, 2005.

Bly Calkin, Siobhain Bly. *Saracens and the Making of English Identity: The Auchinleck Manuscript.* New York and London: Routledge, 2005.

Boekhoff-Van der Voort, et al., eds. *The Transmission and Dynamics of the Textual Sources of Islam: Essays in Honor of Harald Motzki.* Leiden: Brill, 2011.

Bolt, David, Julia Miele Rodas, and Elizabeth J. Donaldson, eds. *The Madwoman and the Blindman: Jane Eyre, Discourse, and Disability*. Columbus: Ohio State University Press, 2012.

Bone, Drummond, ed. *The Cambridge Companion to Byron*. Cambridge, UK: Cambridge University Press, 2004.

Borromea, Elisabetta. *Voyageurs occidentaux dans l'Empire ottoman, 1600–1644: Inventaire des récits et études sur les itinéraires, les monuments remarqués et les populations rencontrées: Roumélie, Cyclades, Crimée*. Paris and Istanbul: Maisonneuve & Larose and Institit français d'études anatoliennes, 2007.

Boyle, Katherine. "Islamist Nasheeds Embrace Modern Technology While Staying True to Ideals." *Washington Post*, July 15, 2013. https://www.washingtonpost.com/lifestyle/style/islamist-nasheeds-embrace-modern-technology-while-staying-true-to-ideals/2013/07/15/20d6c3a4-e8b0-11e2-aa9f-c03a72e2d342_story.html

Brewer, John. *The Pleasures of the Imagination: English Culture in the Eighteenth Century*. London: Harper Collins, 1997.

Brinkerhoff, Jennifer M. *Digital Diasporas: Identity and Transnational Engagement*. Cambridge, UK, and New York: Cambridge University Press, 2009.

Brotton, Jerry. *The Sultan and the Queen: The Untold Story of Elizabeth and Islam*. New York: Viking, 2016.

Bunt, Gary. "#islam, Social Networking and the Cloud." In *Islam in the Modern World*. Eds. Jeffrey T. Kenney and Ebrahim Moosa. London: Routledge, 2013. 177–208.

Bunt, Gary. *iMuslims: Rewiring the House of Islam*. Chapel Hill: University of North Carolina Press, 2009.

Bunt, Gary. *Islam in the Digital Age: E-jihad, Online Fatwas and Cyber Islamic Environments*. London and Sterling: Pluto Press, 2003.

Bunt, Gary. "Surfing Islam: Ayatollahs, Shayks, and Hajjis on the Superhighway." In *Religion on the Internet: Research Prospects and Promises*. Eds. Jeffery K. Hadden and Douglas E. Cowan. New York: Elsevier Science, 2000. 127–151.

Bunt, Gary. *Virtually Islamic: Computer-Mediated Communication and Cyber Islamic Environments*. Cardiff: University of Wales Press, 2000.

Burton, Jonathan. *Traffic and Turning: Islam and English Drama 1579–1624*. Newark: University of Delaware Press, 2005.

Campbell, Heidi A. *When Religion Meets New Media*. London and New York: Routledge, 2010.

Campbell, Heidi, ed. *Digital Religion: Understanding Religious Practice in New Media Worlds*. Abingdon, Oxon, and New York: Routledge, 2013.

Carter, Robert. *Sea of Pearls: Seven Thousand Years That Shaped the Gulf*. London: Arabian, 2012.

Cavaliero, Roderick. *Ottomania: The Romantics and the Myth of the Islamic Orient*. London and New York: I. B. Tauris, 2010.

Chaudhry, Ayesha. *Domestic Violence and the Islamic Tradition*. Oxford: Oxford University Press, 2013.

Chew, Samuel C. *The Crescent and the Rose*. New York: Octagon Books, 1965.

Cheong, Pauline Hope, ed. *Digital Religion, Social Media, and Culture: Perspectives, Practices, and Futures*. New York: Peter Lang, 2012.

Clayton, Mark. "Reading into the Mind of a Terrorist: A Document Carefully Crafted for the 9-11 Hijackers May Be a Template for Terrorism, Say Some Academics." *Christian Science Monitor*, October 10, 2003. https://www.csmonitor.com/2003/1030/p11s01-legn.html

Clifford, Stephanie. "Terrorism Case against Pakistani Man Is Going to Jury." *New York Times*, March 3, 2015. A22.

Clifford, Stephanie. "Testifying in His Own Defense, Terror Suspect Starts Strong before Faltering." *New York Times*, February 26, 2015. Accessed July 15, 2015. https://www.nytimes.com/2015/02/27/nyregion/testifying-in-his-own-defense-terror-suspect-starts-strong-before-faltering.html

Clifford, Stephanie. "U.S. Jury Convicts Man Charged in a British Bomb Plot." *New York Times*, March 4, 2015. Accessed July 15, 2015. https://www.nytimes.com/2015/03/05/nyregion/abid-naseer-terror-suspect-found-guilty-on-all-counts-in-2009-bomb-plot.html

Cochran, Peter. *Byron and Orientalism*. Newcastle, UK: Cambridge Scholars Press, 2006.

Cole, Juan. "Al-Qaeda's Doomsday Document and Psychological Manipulation." Presented at "Genocide and Terrorism: Probing the Mind of the Perpetrator," Yale Center for Genocide Studies,

New Haven, CT, April 9, 2003. http://hdl.handle.net/2027.42/
156040

http://interlinkconsulting.com/Bonus_Info/Doomsday%20
Document-Atta%27s%20Letter%20and%20Al%20Qaeda-
Comment%20by%20Dr.%20Juan%20Cole.pdf. Accessed July
15, 2015.

Connell, Philip, and Nigel Leask. *Romanticism and Popular Culture
in Britain and Ireland*. Cambridge, UK: Cambridge University
Press, 2009.

Cook, David. *Contemporary Muslim Apocalyptic Literature*.
Syracuse, NY: Syracuse University Press, 2005.

Cook, David. *Martyrdom in Islam*. Cambridge, UK: Cambridge
University Press, 2007.

Cook, David. *Studies in Muslim Apocalyptic*. Princeton, NJ: The
Darwin Press, Inc., 2002.

Cook, David. *Understanding Jihad*. Berkeley: University of
California Press, 2005.

Cook, David, and Olivia Allison. *Understanding and Addressing
Suicide Bombing: Faith and Politics of Martyrdom Operations*.
Westport, CT, and London: Praeger Security International, 2007.

cooke, miriam and Bruce Lawrence, eds. *Muslim Networks: From
Hajj to Hip Hop*. Chapel Hill: University of North Carolina, 2005.

Davis, John. *The Landscape of Belief: Encountering the Holy Land
in Nineteenth Century American Art and Culture*. Princeton,
NJ: Princeton University Press, 1996.

De Sondy, Amanullah. *The Crisis of Islamic Masculinities*. London
and New York: Bloomsbury, 2013.

DelPlato, Joan. *Multiple Wives, Multiple Pleasures*. Madison, NJ,
and Teaneck, NJ: Fairleigh Dickinson University Press, 2002.

Dimmock, Matthew. *New Turkes: Dramatizing Islam and the
Ottomans in Early Modern England*. Aldershot, UK, and
Burlington, VT: Ashgate, 2005.

Donner, Fred. "The Historian, the Believer, and the Qur'an." In *New
Perspectives on the Qur'an*. Ed. Gabriel Said Reynolds. London
and New York: Routledge, 2011. 25–37.

Donner, Fred. "The Qur'an in Recent Scholarship: Challenges and
Desiderata." In *The Qur'an in Its Historical Context*. Ed. Gabriel
Said Reynolds. London and New York: Routledge, 2008. 29–50.

Eagleton, Terry. *Myths of Power: A Marxist Study of the Brontes.* New York: Barnes & Noble, 1975.

Ervine, Jonathan. "Lil Maaz's Mange du kebab: Challenging Cliches or Serving up an Immigrant Stereotype for Mass Consumption Online?" In *Music, Culture, and Identity in the Muslim World.* Ed. Kamal Salhi. London and New York: Routledge, 2014. 261–280.

Ferjani, Riadh. "Religion and Television in the Arab World: Towards a Communication Studies Approach." *Middle East Journal of Culture & Communication* 3 (2010): 82–100.

Festa, Lynn. *Sentimental Figures of Empire in Eighteenth Century Britain and France.* Baltimore, MD: John Hopkins University Press, 2006.

Filiu, Jean-Pierre. *Apocalypse in Islam.* Trans. M. B. DeBevoise. Berkeley: University of California Press, 2011.

Fine, Todd. Afterword to *Book of Khalid*, Ameen Rihani. Brooklyn, NY: Melville House, 2016. 317–325.

Firestone, Reuven. *Jihad: The Origin of Holy War in Islam.* New York and Oxford: Oxford University Press, 1999.

Flood, Finnbar. *Great Mosque of Damascus: Studies of the Makings of an Umayyad Visual Culture.* Boston: Brill, 2011.

Friedman, J. "Call for 9/12 and 9/13 Newspapers." January 16, 2015. http://www.911memorial.org/blog/call-912-and-913-newspapers. Accessed July 15, 2015.

Fulford, Tim, and Peter J. Kitson, eds. *Romanticism and Colonialism.* Cambridge, UK: Cambridge University Press, 1998.

Garcia, Humberto. *Islam and the English Enlightenment, 1670–1840.* Baltimore, MD: John Hopkins University Press, 2012.

Goffman, Daniel. *Britons in the Ottoman Empire: 1642–1660.* Seattle: University of Washington Press, 1998.

Gordon, Matthew, and Kathryn Hain. *Concubines and Courtesans: Women and Slavery in Islamic History.* Oxford: Oxford University Press, 2017.

Gräf, Bettina. "Sheikh Yusuf al-Qaradawi in Cyberspace." *Die Welt des Islams* 47, no. 3–4, 2007. http://www.digitalislam.eu/book.do?articleId=2154. Accessed July 15, 2015.

Griffith, Sidney. "Christian Lore and the Arabic Qur'an: The 'Companions of the Cave' in Surat al-Kahf and in Syriac Christian

Tradition." In *The Qur'an in Its Historical Context*. Ed. Gabriel Said Reynolds. London and New York: Routledge, 2008. 109–137.

Grosrichard, Alain. *Sultan's Court: European Fantasies of the East*. Trans. Liz Heron. London: Verso, 1998.

Haddad, Emily A. *Orientalist Poetics: The Islamic Middle East in Nineteenth Century English and French Poetry*. Aldershot, UK, and Burlington, VT: Ashgate, 2002.

Hadfield, Andrew. *Amazons, Savages, and Machiavels: Travel and Colonial Writings in English, 1550–1630: An Anthology*. New York: Oxford University Press, 2001.

Hadfield, Andrew. *Literature, Travel, and Colonial Writing in the English Renaissance 1545–1625*. New York: Clarendon Press, 1998.

Halevi, Leor. "The Consumer Jihad: Boycott Fatwas and Nonviolent Resistance on the World Wide Web." *International Journal of Middle Eastern Studies*. 44, no. 1 (2012): 45–70.

Harrigan, Michael. *Veiled Encounters: Representing the Orient in 17th-Century French Travel Literature*. Amsterdam and New York: Rodopi, 2008.

Heng, Geraldine. "Sex, Lies, and Paradise: The Assassins, Prester John, and the Fabulation of Civilizational Identities." *Differences* 23, no. 1 (2012): 1–31.

Herding, Maruta. "The Borders of Virtual Space: New Information Technologies and European Islamic Youth Culture." *Journal of Postcolonial Writing* 49, no. 5 (2013): 552–564.

Herrera, Linda. *Revolution in the Age of Social Media*. London and New York: Verso, 2014.

Herrera, Linda. "Youth and Citizenship in the Digital Age: A View from Egypt." *Harvard Educational Review* 82, no. 3 (2012): 333–353.

Hidayatullah, Aysha. *Feminist Edges of the Qur'an*. New York: Oxford, 2014.

Hirschkind, Charles. "Experiments in Devotion Online: The YouTube Khutba." *International Journal of Middle East Studies* 44 (2012): 5–21.

Hirschkind, Charles. "From the Blogosphere to the Street: Social Media and Egyptian Revolution." *Oriente Moderno*, Nuova serie,

91, no. 1, Between Everyday Life and Political Revolution: The Social Web in the Middle East (2011): 61–74.

Ho, Kong-Chong, Randy Kluver, and Kenneth C. C. Yang. *Asia.com: Asia Encounters the Internet*. London and New York: Routledge Curzon, 2003.

Hodgson, Barbara. *Dreaming of East: Western Women and the Exotic Allure of the Orient*. Vancouver, BC, and Berkeley, CA: Publishers Group West, 2005.

Hoffman, Bruce. *Inside Terrorism*. New York: Columbia University Press, 2006.

Hoffmann, Thomas, and Göran Larsson. *Muslims and the New Information and Communications Technologies*. Dordrecht: Springer, 2013.

Holtmann, Philipp. "Virtual Leadership: How Jihadists Guide Each Other in Cyberspace." In *New Approaches to the Analysis of Jihadism: Online and Offline*. Ed. Rudiger Lohlker. Vienna: University Press, 2012. 63–124.

Hubbard, Ben. "Saudi Award Goes to Muslim Televangelist Who Harshly Criticizes U.S." *New York Times*, March 3, 2015, A4.

Inhorn, Marcia. *The New Arab Man: Emergent Masculinities, Technologies, and Islam in the Middle East*. Princeton, NJ, and Oxford: Princeton University Press, 2012.

Jamal, Amal. *The Arab Public Sphere in Israel: Media Space and Cultural Resistance*. Bloomington: Indiana University Press, 2009.

Jarrar, Maher. "The Martyrdom of Passionate Lovers: Holy War as a Sacred Wedding." In *Myths, Historical Archetypes, and Symbolic Figures in Arabic Literature: Towards a New Hermeneutic Approach: Proceedings of the International Symposium in Beirut, June 25–30, 1996*. Ed. Angelika Neuwirth et al. Stuttgart: Franz Steiner Verlag. 1999. 87–107.

Jenkins, Eugenia Zuroski. *A Taste for China: English Subjectivity and the Prehistory of Orientalism*. New York: Oxford University Press, 2013.

Juergensmeyer, Mark. *Terror in the Mind of God: The Global Rise of Religious Violence*. Berkeley: University of California Press, 2003.

Kabbani, Rana. *Europe's Myths of Orient: Devise and Rule*. Basingstoke, UK: Macmillan, 1986.

Kahf, Mohja. *Western Representations of the Muslim Woman: From Termagant to Odalisque.* Austin: University of Texas Press, 1999.

Kalmar, Ivan. *Early Orientalism: Imagined Islam and the Notion of Sublime Power.* London and New York: Routledge, 2012.

Kaul, Suvir. *Poems of Nation, Anthems of Empire: English Verse in the Long Eighteenth Century.* Charlottesville and London: University Press of Virginia, 2000.

Keefe, Robert. *Charlotte Bronte's World of Death.* Austin: University of Texas, 1979.

Khanmohamadi, Shirin. *In Light of Another's Word: European Ethnography in the Middle Ages.* Philadelphia: University of Pennsylvania Press, 2014.

Khosrokhavar, Farhad. *Suicide Bombers: Allah's New Martyrs.* Trans. David Macey. London and Ann Arbor, MI: Pluto Press, 2005.

Kidawi, Abdur Raheem. *Orientalism in Lord Byron's "Turkish Tales."* Lewiston and Lampeter: Mellen University Press, 1995.

King, Amy. *Bloom: The Botanical Vernacular in the English Novel.* Oxford and New York: Oxford University Press, 2003.

Kinoshita, Sharon, and Siobhain Bly Calkin. "Saracens as Idolaters in European Vernacular Literatures." In *Christian-Muslim Relations: A Bibliographical History.* Ed. David Thomas. Brill Online, 2015. Accessed February 23, 2015.

Kippenberg, Hans G., and Tilman Seidensticker, Eds. *The 9/11 Handbook: Annotated Translation and Interpretation of the Attacker's Spiritual Manual.* London and Oakville: Equinox, 2006.

Koester, Nancy. *Introduction to the History of Christianity in the United States.* Minneapolis: Fortress Press, 2015.

Korte, Barbara. *English Travel Writing from Pilgrimages to Postcolonial Expectations.* Trans. Catherine Matthias. New York: St. Martin's Press, 2000.

Kundnani, Arun. *The Muslims Are Coming! Islamaphobia, Exteremism, and the Domestic War on Terror.* London and Brooklyn, NY: Verso, 2014.

Lahoud, Nelly. "A Cappella Songs (Anashid) in Jihadi Culture." In *Jihadi Culture.* Ed. Thomas Hegghammer. Cambridge, UK: Cambridge University Press, 2017. 42–62.

Laisram, Pallavi Pandit. *Viewing the Islamic Orient: British Travel Writers of the Nineteenth Century.* London and New York: Routledge, 2006.

Lamptey, Jerusha Tanner. *Never Wholly Other: A Muslima Theology of Religious Pluralism*. New York: Oxford University Press, 2014.

Lange, Christian. *Paradise and Hell in Islamic Traditions*. New York: Cambridge University Press, 2016.

Langman, Lauren. "From Virtual Public Spheres to Global Justice: A Critical Theory of Internetworked Social Movements." *Sociological Theory* 23, no. 1 (2005): 42–74.

Larsson, Göran. *Muslims and New Media: Historical and Contemporary Debates*. Surrey, UK, and Burlington, VT: Ashgate, 2011.

Lee, Rachel C., and Sau-ling Cynthia Wong. *Asian America.net: Ethnicity, Nationalism and Cyberspace*. New York: Routledge, 2003.

Lennon, Joseph. *Irish Orientalism: A Literary and Intellectual History*. Syracuse, NY: Syracuse University Press, 2004.

Lewis, Reina. *Rethinking Orientalism: Women, Travel, and the Ottoman Harem*. New Brunswick, NJ: Rutgers University Press, 2004.

Lincoln, Bruce. *Holy Terrors: Thinking about Religion after September 11*. Chicago: University of Chicago Press, 2003.

Lohlker, Rüdiger. *Jihadism: Online Discourses and Representations*. Göttingen: Vienna University Press, 2013.

Lowe, Lisa. *Critical Terrains: French and British Orientalisms*. Ithaca, NY, and London: Cornell University Press, 1991.

Lynch, Gordon. *Between Sacred and Profane: Researching Religion and Popular Culture*. London and New York: I. B. Tauris, 2007.

Mabro, Judy. *Veiled Half-Truths: Western Travellers' Perceptions of Middle Eastern Women*. London and New York: I. B. Tauris and St. Martin's Press, 1991.

Maclean, Gerald, and Nabil Matar. *Britain and the Islamic World, 1558–1713*. Oxford: Oxford University Press, 2011.

Makdisi, Saree. *Making England Western: Occidentalism, Race, and Imperial Culture*. Chicago and London: University of Chicago Press, 2014.

Makdisi, Saree. *Romantic Imperialism: Universal Empire and the Culture of Modernity*. Cambridge, UK: Cambridge University Press, 1998.

Makiya, Kanan, and Hassan Mneimneh's "Manual for a Raid." *New York Review of Books* 49, no. 1 (January 17, 2002): 18–21 and https://www.nybooks.com/articles/2002/01/17/manual-for-a-raid/ Accessed March 1, 2015.

Marandi, Seyed Mohammed. "The Bride of the East." In *Byron and Orientalism*. Ed. Peter Cochran. Newcastle, UK: Cambridge Scholars Press, 2006. 215–231.

Marr, Timothy. *The Cultural Roots of American Islamicism*. New York: Cambridge University Press, 2006.

Marshall, Alex. "How Isis Got Its Anthem." *The Guardian*, November 9, 2014. http://www.theguardian.com/music/2014/nov/09/nasheed-how-isis-got-its-anthem. Accessed July 15, 2015.

Matar, Nabil. *Islam in Britain 1558–1685*. Cambridge, UK: Cambridge University Press, 1998.

Matar, Nabil. *Turks, Moors, and Englishmen in the Age of Discovery*. New York: Columbia University Press, 1999.

Matar, Nabil, ed. *Henry Stubbe and the Beginnings of Islam*. New York: Columbia University Press, 2014.

Maynard, John. *Charlotte Bronte and Sexuality*. Cambridge, UK: Cambridge University Press, 1984.

McClintock, Anne. *Imperial Leather: Race, Gender, and Sexuality in the Colonial Context*. New York: Routledge, 1995.

McDayter, Ghislaine. *Byromania and the Birth of Celebrity Culture*. Albany: State University of New York Press, 2009.

McJannet, Linda. *The Sultan Speaks: Dialogue in English Plays and Histories about the Ottoman Turks*. New York: Palgrave Macmillan, 2007.

Melman, Billie. *Women's Orients: English Women and the Middle East, 1718–1918*, 2nd edition. Hampshire and London: Macmillan Press, 1995.

Mernissi, Fatima. *Scheherazade Goes West: Different Cultures, Different Harems*. New York, London, Toronto, Sydney, and Singapore: Washington Square Press, 2001.

Meyer, Susan. *Imperialism at Home: Race in Victorian Women's Fiction*. Ithaca, NY: Cornell University Press, 1996.

Miller, Flagg. *The Audacious Ascetic: What the Bin Laden Tapes Reveal about al-Qa'ida*. London: Hurst, 2015.

Mitchell, Marea, and Dianne Osland. *Representing Women and Female Desire from Arcadia to Jane Eyre*. Hampshire, UK, and New York: Palgrave Macmillian, 2005.

Moghadam, Assaf. *The Globalization of Martyrdom*. Baltimore, MD: Johns Hopkins University Press, 2008.

Moglen, Helen. *Charlotte Bronte: The Self Conceived*. New York: W. W. Norton, 1976.

Mohanty, Chandra Talpade. *Feminism without Borders*. Durham, NC, and London: Duke University Press, 2003.

Mulholland, James. *Sounding Imperial: Poetic Voice and the Politics of Empire, 1730–1820*. Baltimore MD: Johns Hopkins University Press, 2013.

Naik, Zakir. "Houris in Islam." http://www.youtube.com/watch?v=HWDzZSreVcc. Accessed July 15, 2017.

Nash, Geoffrey. *Writing Muslim Identity*. London and New York: Continuum, 2012.

Nassir, Ghazi. *Samuel Johnson's Attitude Toward Islam: A Study of His Oriental Readings and Writings*. Lewiston, NY: Edwin Mellen Press, 2012.

el-Nawawy, Mohammed, and Sahar Khamis. *Islam Dot Com: Contemporary Islamic Discourses in Cyberspace*. New York: Palgrave Macmillan, 2009.

Neuwirth, Angelika. "Qur'an and History—A Disputed Relationship: Some Reflections on Qur'anic History and History in the Qur'an." *Journal of Qur'anic Studies* V, no. 1 (2003): 1–18.

"Newsweek Story on Islam Banned." *Chicago Tribune*, July 29, 2003. 6.

Nielson, Lisa. "Diversions of Pleasure: Singing Slave Girls and the Politics of Music in Early Islamic Courts (661–1000 CE): Their Influence, History and Cultural Roots as Seen through the Kitab al-Muwashsha (Book of Brocade), of Ibn al-Washsha, The Risala al-Qiyan (Epistle of the Singing Girls) of al-Jahiz, and the Dhamm al-Mahahi (Censure of Instruments of Diversion) of Ibi'l Dunya." Ph.D. dissertation, University of Maine, 2010.

Nussabaum, Felicity. *Torrid Zones: Maternity, Sexuality, and Empire in Eighteenth Century English Narratives*. Baltimore, MD: John Hopkins University Press, 1995.

Obaid, Hammood Khalid. *Topicality and Representation: Islam and Muslims in Two Renaissance Plays*. Newcastle upon Tyne: Cambridge Scholars, 2013.

Oliver, Susan. *Scott, Byron, and the Poetics of Cultural Encounter*. New York: Palgrave Macmillan, 2005.

Oueijan, Naji. *Lord Byron's Oriental World*. Piscataway, NJ: Gorgias Press, 2011.

Ouzgane, Lahoucine, ed. *Islamic Masculinities*. New York and London: Zed Books, 1988.

"Pakistan Bans Newsweek's Qur'an Issue." *World News Daily*, July 26, 2003. https://www.ifex.org/bangladesh/2003/08/05/latest_issue_of_newsweek_magazine/. Accessed July 15, 2015.

Pape, Robert. *Dying to Win: The Strategic Logic of Suicide Bombing*. New York: Random House, 2005.

Peirce, Leslie. *Empress of the East: How a European Slave Girl Became Queen of the Ottoman Empire*. New York: Basic Books, 2017.

Percy, William. *William Percy's Mahomet and His Heaven: A Critical Edition*. Ed. Matthew Dimmock. Aldershot, UK, and Burlington, VT: Ashgate, 2006.

Pew Research Religion and Public Life Project. *Religious Landscape Survey*. http://religions.pewforum.org/reports#. Accessed February 15, 2015.

Phillips, Kim. *Before Orientalism: Asian Peoples and Cultures of European Travel Writing 1245–1510*. Philadelphia: University of Pennsylvania Press, 2013.

Pieslak, Jonathan. "A Musicological Perspective on Jihad *anashid*." In *Jihadi Culture*. Ed. Thomas Hegghammer. Cambridge, UK: Cambridge University Press, 2017. 63–81.

Pieslak, Jonathan. *Radicalism and Music: An Introduction to the Music Cultures of Al-Qa'ida, Racist Skinheads, Christian-Affiliated Radicals, and Eco-Animal Rights Militants*. Middletown, CT: Wesleyan University Press, 2015.

Porter, Bernard. *The Absent-Minded Imperialists: Empire, Society, and Culture in Britain*. Oxford: Oxford University Press, 2004.

Pratt, Mary. *Imperial Eyes: Travel Writing and Transculturation*. London: Routledge, 1992.

Pyrhönenŋë, Hera. *Bluebeard Gothic: Jane Eyre and Its Progeny*. Toronto: University of Toronto Press, 2010.

Reporters without Borders: For Press Freedom. "Newsweek Banned over Article on the Koran." July 30, 2003. https://rsf. org/en/news/newsweek-banned-over-article-koran

Rhouni, Raja. *Secular and Islamic Feminist Critiques in the Work of Fatima Mernissi*. Leiden and Boston: Brill, 2010.

Robbins, Liz. "Man Accused of Trying to Join Jihadists." *New York Times*, September 10, 2011. A22.

Roberts, Mary. *Intimate Outsiders: The Harem in Ottoman and Orientalist Art and Travel Literature*. Durham, NC, and London: Duke University Press, 2007.

Rosenthal, Franz. "Reflections on Love in Paradise." In *Love and Death in the Ancient Near East: Essays in Honor of Marvin H. Pope*. Eds. John H. Marks and Robert M. Good. Guilford, CT: Four Quarters, 1987. 247–254.

Russell, Adrienne, and Nabil Echchaibi, Eds. *International Blogging: Identity, Politics, and Networked Publics*. New York: Peter Lang, 2009.

Rustomji, Nerina. "American Visions of the Houri." *Muslim World* 97, no. 1 (January 2007): 79–92.

Rustomji, Nerina. "Are Houris Heavenly Concubines?" In *Songs and Sons: Women, Slavery and Social Mobility in the Medieval Islamic World*. Eds. Matthew Gordon and Kathryn Hain. New York: Oxford University Press, 2017. 266–277.

Rustomji, Nerina. "Beauty in the Garden: Aesthetics and the *Wildan, Ghilman*, and *Hur*." In *Roads to Paradise*. Eds. Sebastian Guenther and Todd Lewis. Leiden: Brill, 2017. 295–310.

Rustomji, Nerina. *The Garden and the Fire: Heaven and Hell in Islamic Culture*. New York: Columbia University Press, 2009.

Said, Behnam. "Hymns (Nasheeds): A Contribution to the Study of Jihadist Culture." *Studies in Conflict & Terrorism* 35 (2012): 863–879.

Said, Edward. *Orientalism*. New York: Verso, 1978.

Salamandra, Christa. "Arab Television Drama Production and the Islamic Public Sphere." In *Visual Culture in the Modern Middle East: Rhetoric of an Image*. Eds. Christiane Gruber and Sune Haugbolle. Bloomington: Indiana University Press, 2013.

Saleh, Walid. "The Etymological Fallacy and Qurʾanic Studies: Muhammad, Paradise, and Late Antiquity." In *The Qurʾan in Context: Historical and Literary Investigations into the Qur'anic Milieu*. Eds. Angelika Neuwirth, Nicolai Sinai, and Michael Marx. Leiden: Brill, 2009. 649–698.

Sapra, Rahul. *The Limits of Orientalism: Seventeenth-Century Representations of India*. Newark: University of Delaware Press, 2011.

Sati, Mohamed A. "Internet Islam: An Analysis of U.S.-Based Websites Dedicated to Promoting an Islamic Viewpoint in the Post 9/11 World." Ohio University dissertation, 2009.

Sawma, Gabriel. *The Qur'an: Misinterpreted, Mistranslated, and Misread: The Aramaic Language of the Qur'an*. Plainsboro, NJ: GMS, 2006.

Schanzer, Jonathan, and Steven Miller. *Facebook Fatwa: Saudi Clerics, Wahhabi Islam and Social Media*. Washington, DC: Foundation for Defense of Democracies, 2012.

Schlek, Julia. *Telling True Tales of Islamic Lands: Forms of Mediation in English Travel Writing, 1575–1630*. Selinsgrove, PA: Susquehanna University Press, 2011.

Secunda, Shai. "The Construction, Composition, and Idealization of the Female Body in Rabbic Literature and Parallel Iranian Texts." *Nashim: A Journal of Jewish Women's Studies and Gender Issues* 23. Ed. Rachel Harris (Spring–Fall 2012): 60–86.

Secunda, Shai. *The Iranian Talmud: Reading the Bavli in the Sasanian Context*. Philadelphia: University of Pennsylvania Press, 2014.

Segal, Nancy L., Aaron T. Goetz, and Alberto C. Maldonado. "The Whites of Our Eyes." *New York Times*, July 17, 2015. Accessed July 15, 2018. https://www.nytimes.com/2015/07/19/opinion/the-whites-of-our-eyes.html

Seidensticker, Tilman. "Jihad Hymns (Nashids) as a Means of Self-motivation in the Hamburg Group." In *New Approaches to the Analysis of Jihadism: Online and Offline*. Ed. Rudiger Lohlker. Goettingen: Vienna University Press, 2012. 71–78.

Sell, Jonathan. *Rhetoric and Wonder in English Travel Writing, 1560–1613*. Hampshire, UK: Ashgate, 2006.

Seymat, Thomas. "How Nasheeds Became the Soundtrack of Jihad." *Euronews.com*. August 10, 2014. http://www.euronews.com/2014/10/08/nasheeds-the-soundtrack-of-jihad/. Accessed July 15, 2015.

Shane, Scott. "In 'Watershed Moment,' YouTube Blocks Extremist Cleric's Message." *New York Times*, November 17, 2017.

Accessed December 1, 2017. https://www.nytimes.com/2017/11/12/us/politics/youtube-terrorism-anwar-al-awlaki.html

Shane, Scott. *Objective Troy: A Terrorist, a President, and the Rise of the Drone.* New York: Tim Duggan Books, 2015.

Sharafuddin, Mohammed. *Islam and Romantic Orientalism.* London and New York: I. B. Tauris, 1994.

Shelton, Taylor, Matthew Zook, and Mark Graham. "The Technology of Religion: Mapping Religious Cyberscapes." *The Professional Geographer* 64, no. 4 (2011): 602–617.

Smith, Byron Porter. *Islam in English Literature.* Ed. and with an Introduction by S. B. Bushrui and Anahid Melikian. Delmar, NY: Caravan Books, 1977 (2nd edition); first edition, 1939.

Sokefeld, Martin. "Alevism Online: Re-Imaging a Community in Virtual Space." *Diaspora: A Journal of Transnational Studies* 11, no. 1 (2002): 85.

Spector, Shelia A. *Byron and the Jews.* Detroit: Wayne State University Press, 2010.

Spivak, Gayatri Chakravorty. "Three Women's Texts and a Critique of Imperialism." *Critical Inquiry* 12 (1985): 243–261.

Stanivukovic, Goran V. *Remapping the Mediterranean World in Early Modern English Writings.* New York: Palgrave Macmillan, 2007.

Steinitz, Oren. "The Attitude Towards the Other in Jewish and Islamic Religious Websites." University of Calgary dissertation, July 2014.

Stenersen, Anne. "A History of Jihad Cinematography." In *Jihadi Culture.* Ed. Thomas Hegghammer. Cambridge, UK: Cambridge University Press, 2017. 108–127.

Stewart, Devin. "Notes on Medieval and Modern Emendations of the Qur'an." In *The Qur'an in Its Historical Context.* Ed. Gabriel Said Reynolds. New York and London: Routledge. 225–245.

Strick van Linschoten, Alex, and Felix Kuehn, eds. *Poetry of the Taliban.* Trans. Mirwais Rahmany and Hamid Stanikzai. London: C. Hurst, 2002.

Suranyi, Anna. *The Genius of the English Nation: Travel Writing and National Identity in Early Modern England.* Newark: University of Delaware Press, 2008.

Taha-Hussein, Moënis. *Le Romantisme francais et l'Islam.* Beirut: Dar al-Maaref, 1961.

Tantawy, Muhammad Sayed. "Origins of the Qur'an." *Dawn,* October 3, 2003. https://www.dawn.com/news/1065100

Tartoussieh, Karim. "Virtual Citizenship: Islam, Culture, and Politics in the Digital Age." *International Journal of Cultural Policy* 17, no. 2 (2011): 198–208.

Teo, Hsu-Ming. *Desert Passions: Orientalism and Romance Novels.* Austin: University of Texas Press, 2012.

Third, Amanda. *Gender and the Political: Deconstructing the Female Terrorist.* New York: Palgrave Macmillan, 2014.

Thomas, Sue. *Imperialism, Reform, and the Making of Englishness in Jane Eyre.* Hampshire, UK, and New York: Palgrave Macmillian, 2009.

Thompson, C. W. *French Romantic Travel Writing: Chateaubriand to Nerval.* Oxford: Oxford University Press, 2012.

Tolan, John Viktor. *Saracens: Islam in the Medieval European Imagination.* New York: Columbia University Press, 2002. 283.

Tottoli, Roberto. "Muslim Eschatological Literature and Western Studies." *Der Islam* 83 (2008): 452–477.

Turner, Bryan S. "Religious Authority and the New Media." *Theory, Culture & Society Theory Culture Society* 24, no. 2 (2007): 117–134.

Tuson, Penelope. *Western Women Travelling East, 1716-1916.* Oxford: Arcadian Library, 2014.

Vogel, Lester. *To See a Promised Land: Americans and the Holy Land in the Nineteenth Century.* University Park: Pennsylvania University Press, 1993.

Vitkus, Daniel. *Turning Turk: English Theater and the Multicultural Mediterranean 1570-1630.* New York: Palgrave Macmillan, 2003.

Wadud, Amina. *Inside the Gender Jihad: Women's Reform in Islam.* Oxford: Oneworld, 2006.

Wadud, Amina. *Qur'an and Woman: Rereading the Sacred Texts from a Woman's Perspective.* New York and Oxford: Oxford University Press, 1999.

Warren, Andrew. *The Orient and the Young Romantics.* Cambridge, UK: Cambridge University Press, 2014.

Wendell, Charles. "The Denizens of Paradise." *Humaniora Islamica* 2 (1974): 29–59.

Wentz, Abdel Ross. *History of the Gettysburg Theological Seminary of the General Synod of the Evangelical Lutheran Church in the United States and of the United Lutheran Church in America, Gettysburg, Pennsylvania, 1826–1926.* Philadelphia: United Lutheran, 1927.

Wicker, Brian, ed. *Witnesses to Faith? Martyrdom in Christianity and Islam.* Aldershot, UK, and Burlington, VT: Ashgate, 2006.

Wild, Stefan. "Lost in Philology? The Virgins in Paradise and the Luxenberg Hypothesis." In *The Qur'an in Context.* Eds. Angelika Neuwirth, Nicolai Sinai, and Michael Marx. Leiden: Brill, 2010. 625–648.

Woodward, Bob. "In Hijacker's Bags, a Call to Planning, Prayer, and Death." *Washington Post*, November 18, 2007. A01.

Wright, Jerry W. "Masculine Allusion and the Structure of Satire in Early Abbasid Poetry." In *Homoeroticism in Classical Arabic Literature.* Eds. Jerry W. Wright and Everett K. Rowson. New York: Columbia University, 1997. 1–23.

Wright, Lawrence. *The Looming Tower: Al-Qaeda and the Road to 9/11.* New York: Knopf, 2006.

Yothers, Brian. *The Romance of the Holy Land in American Travel Writing, 1790–1876.* Aldershot, UK: Ashgate, 2007.

Youngs, Tim. *The Cambridge Introduction to Travel Writing.* New York: Cambridge University Press, 2013.

Zaman, Saminaz. "From Imam to Cyber-Mufti: Consuming Identity in Muslim America." *Muslim World* 98, no. 4 (2008): 465–474.

Zeevi, Dror. *Producing Desire: Changing Sexual Discourse in the Ottoman Middle East, 1500–1900.* Berkeley, Los Angeles, and London: University of California Press, 2006.

Zonana, Joyce. "The Sultan and the Slave: Feminist Orientalism and the Structure of *Jane Eyre*." *Signs: Journal of Women in Culture and Society* 18, no. 3 (Spring 1993): 592–617.

Zuwiyya, Zachary. "*Confusión o confutación de la secta Mahomética,* Confusion or Confutation of the Sect of Muhammad." In *Christian-Muslim Relations: A Bibliographical History.* Eds. David Thomas and John A. Chesworth. Vol. 6. Leiden: Brill, 2014. 83–84.

INDEX

For the benefit of digital users, indexed terms that span two pages (e.g., 52–53) may, on occasion, appear on only one of those pages.

Figures are indicated by *f* following the page number

Abdulmutallab, Umar Farouk, 135
Abedzai, Mawlawi
    Samiullah, 22–23
Abu Nuwas, poetry of, 101–2
Abu Shukheudem, Sheikh, 22
Abu Zayd, Nasr Hamid,
    36–37
afterlife
    parodies and ridiculing
        depiction of, 38–39
    sensuality of Islamic
        paradise, 77–82
    See also paradise
afterlife, promise of
    digital Islamic
        afterworlds, 123–26
    eschatological manuals, 126–27
    houri, current significance
        of, 148

nashid, as motivation for
    jihad, 144–47
    virtual jihad, 139–44
    virtual jihad, audience
        for, 147–48
    See also paradise, virtual
        tours of
Ait Sabbah, Fatna, 154
Algerine Captive, The (Tyler), 65–
    66, 77–79
al- Hur al- 'in, television serial, 148
Ali, Ahmed, 132–35
al-janna (Garden of
    paradise), 97–98
al-nar (Fire of hell), 93, 97–98
Amerindians
    British pre-colonial contact
        with, 47–48
    European demonization of, 49

American literature, metaphor of
the houri in, 85–91
The Book of Khalid
(Rihani), 89–90
David Theo Hines, 85–86
"Female Beauty of the
Mind," 85–86
models of femininity, 88–91
"Star of Love," 86–87, 88*f*
American perspectives, 6–7
Amis, Martin, 41–42
Andrae, Tor, 30–31
Andrés, Juan, 46–47, 52, 151–52
Anzour, Najdat Ismail, 148
al-Arifi, Sheikh, television
program of, 158
Assassins, sect, 25–26, 43–44
Atta, Mohamed, purported letter
by, 7, 15*f*
American reactions to, 16–17
discovery and contents, 13–17
distribution of, 16
and houri as reward, 166–67
meaning and reward of
mission, 19–20
narrative regarding, 42
reactions to, 20–21
sections and contents, 17–21
See also "Last Days of Mohamed
Atta" (Amis)
Auchinleck Manuscript, 45–46
al-Awlaqi, Anwar, 135–39, 141–
44, 147

Battle of Uhud, 111–13
Beckford, William, 66–67
Behn, Aphra, 59
Berg, Nicholas, 140
Bible, critical scholarship and
interpretations of, 27–31
Blount, Henry, 51
Book of John Mandeville, 77

Book of Khalid, The
(Rihani), 89–90
Boston Marathon bombing, 135
Bride of Abydos, The (Byron), 68–
69, 74, 75*f*
British literature
houri, as model of feminine
beauty, 58–62
houri, nineteenth-century,
references to, 65–66
introduction of houri in, 43–44
Jane Eyre, depiction of
romance, 63–65
Lady Mary Montagu, letters
of, 54–56
Ottoman Empire, nineteenth-
century representations
of, 64–65
representations of Muslim
Middle East in, 44–50
travel writing and Muslim
Middle East, 50–51
See also Byron, George Gordon
Lord; European perspectives
Brontë, Charlotte, 63–65
Byron, George Gordon Lord, 67–
77, 151–52
Childe Harold's Pilgrimage, 68
Don Juan, 69, 70–72
The Giaour, 68–70
literary influence of, 72–77
Turkish Tales, 66–67, 68–69

cartoons, and ridicule of the
houri, 37–40
Castle of Otranto, The
(Walpole), 58–59
"Challenging the Qur'an"
(Theil), 34–35
Chanson de Roland, 45–46
Charlie Hebdo, 2015 attack on
offices of, 135

Childe Harold's Pilgrimage
  (Byron), 68
Christianity, origins of houri in, 5
Christian literary characters,
  depicted as houri, 84–85
Cole, Juan, on letter by September
  11, 2001 hijackers, 19
comedy, and tales of the
  houri, 37–40
companion, houri as, 8–9, 107–
  8, 111
companionship, in paradise,
  102–7
  and completion of the soul,
  154–55, 159
configurations of houri, 168
*Confusión o confutación de la secta
  Mahomética y del Alcorán*
  (Andrés), 43–44, 46–47
conversion stories, 115
Cook, David, 126
Cook, Michael, 29
Corsair, The (Byron), 68–69
cosmological composition, of
  houri, 107–8, 110–11
cosmological imagery, and poetry
  on martyrdom, 23–24
Crone, Patricia, 29

*Daqaʾiq al-akhbar fi dhikr al-janna
  wa-l-nar* (al-Qadi)
daughters, as characters in oriental
  tales, 67
descriptions, of houri
  conventional, 1
  variations of, 10–11
digital afterworlds, promise
  of, 123–26
  common themes, 123–25
  dynamic nature of, 124
  houri, current significance
  of, 148

nashid, as affect, 144–47
online constituencies, 125–26
virtual jihad, 139–44
  See also paradise, virtual
  tours of
diplomacy, and European contact
  with Muslim Middle
  East, 47–49
Don Juan (Byron), 65–66,
  69, 70–72
du Loir, Nicolas, 52–54, 151–52
  introduction of *houri* in travel
  writings, 43–44
Dying to Win (Pape), 24–25

Elizabethan period,
  representations of Muslim
  Middle East in, 47–49
England, emergence of racial and
  cultural identity in, 51
engravings
  and images of Islamic paradise,
  79, 80–81, 82*f*
  "Star of Love," 88*f*
entertainment, and rewards of
  paradise, 117–22
Ephrem the Syrian, *Hymns of
  Paradise,* 30–31
eschatological manuals
  descriptions of houri in, 109–11
  tours of afterworld, 123
  and promise of afterworld,
  126–27, 128*f*
etymology of *houri,* 95–96
European perspectives, 6, 8
  painting, and images of women
  in the harem, 57
  and travel writing, 50–57
  See also British literature;
  French literature
eyes, in descriptions of houri, 95–
  96, 105

Falkner a Novel (Wollstonecraft
Shelley), 84–85
"Female Beauty of the
Mind," 85–86
Filiu, Jean-Pierre, 126
"Final Abode, The," 132–35
Fire
as central tenet in Islamic
history, 97–99
Fires of hell, Qur'anic
allusions to, 93
Foley, James, 140
fountains in paradise, 93–94
French literature
introduction of houri in, 43–44
Nicolas du Loir, travel writing
of, 52–54
representations of Muslim
Middle East in, 44–50
travel writing and Muslim
Middle East, 51–57
See also European perspectives

Galland, Antoine, 53–54
Gallery of Byron Beauties, The, 74,
75*f*, 76*f*
Garden
alternative ways for women to
conceptualize, 151–55
as central tenet in Islamic
history, 97–99
companionship in, 102–8, 111,
154–55, 159
as described in paradise, 96
entertainment, as reward
in, 117–22
expectations of earthly women
for, 149–51
labor, experiences of, 99–102
male desires and, 151–53
as reflection of ideal Muslim
society, 154

rewards granted to women
in, 155–57
sacred wedding in, 111–17
sensuality of Islamic
afterlife, 107–11
social rank and status in, 110
status of women in, 158–59
See also Paradise
Gebir (Landor), 66–67
gender parity, and tradition of
houri, 9–10, 163
Generall Historie of the Turks
(Knolles), 51
ghilman (male youths in paradise),
94–95, 99–102, 119–20
Giaour, The (Byron), 68–70,
74, 75*f*
Great Odalisque, The, 57*f*, 57

hadiths, descriptions of houri in,
96, 107–11
Hagarism (Crone & Cook), 29
al-Hakeem, Assim
Luqman, 155–56
Harrigan, Michael, 52
Hasan, Nidal Malik, 135
Hashbajrami, Agron, 23–24
hell, Qur'anic allusions to, 93
"Hereafter Books, The," 135–
39, 147
hijackers, September 11, 2001
letter by, 7, 15*f*
American reactions to,
16–17
authorship and
distribution of, 16
discovery and contents, 13–17
meaning and reward of
mission, 19–20
narrative regarding, 42
reactions to, 20–21
sections and contents, 17–21

Hines, David Theo, 85–86
Hirshkind, Charles, 125–
    26, 144–45
Historie of the Turkes
    (Knolles), 59–60
History of the Caliph Vathek
    (Beckford), 66–67
Hoffman, Bruce, on terrorism and
    the houri, 22
Holtmann, Philip, 140–41
hora, introduction of term, 43–
    44, 45–50
horhin, introduction of term, 43–
    44, 45–50
Houdeyfa, Rachid Abou, 131–32
houri
    Christian literary characters
        as, 84–85
    configurations of, 168
    cosmological composition of,
        107–8, 110–11
    current significance of, 148
    described in virtual tours of
        paradise, 132–33
    description of, 1, 95–96, 105
    descriptions in eschatological
        manuals, 109–11
    descriptions in hadiths,
        96, 107–11
    etymology of term, 95–96
    evolving concept of, 121–
        22, 165–69
    as female martyrs, 22
    interpretations of, 1–2, 162–70
    introduction of term, 43–
        44, 53–54
    Jewish literary characters
        as, 82–84
    in Lord Byron's *Don
        Juan,* 70–72
    in Lord Byron's *The
        Giaour,* 69–70

male houri, possibility
    of, 159–62
material *vs.* spiritual aspects
    of, 5–6
as model of feminine beauty,
    58–62, 166
as models of femininity, 88–91
multiple dimensions of, 165
non-Muslim women as, 82–85
origins of, 3–6
and poetry on
    martyrdom, 22–24
prevalence of, 2
and redirecting desires of
    men, 156–57
representations in European
    literature, 45–50
as servants of the afterlife, 158
and status of women in
    paradise, 158–59
terminology referring to, 10–
    11, 113–14
terrorism and the, 21–24
transformation in nineteenth-
    century British literature,
    66, 72–77
typology of, 166
Hymns of Paradise (Ephrem the
    Syrian), 30–31

Ibn Abi Zaminayn, *Qudwat al-
    Ghazi,* 113
Ibn al-Mubarak, *Kitab al-
    Jihad,* 113
Ibn Baz, Abd al-Aziz, 159–60
Ibn Habib, descriptions of houri
    by, 109, 149–50
Ibn Ishaq, *Sirat Rasul Allah,* 97–98,
    111–13, 114–15
Ibn al-Nahhas, compendium of
    jihad traditions, 113, 115–
    16, 141

Ibn Warraq, and the "white grape" theory, 32–34
Ingres, Jean-Auguste-Dominique, 57*f*, 57, 58*f*
Inside Terrorism (Hoffman), 22
Inspire magazine, 135
Institution for Secularization of Islamic Society, 32
interpretations, of houri, 162–63
   conflicting, 1–2
introduction in United States, 2–3
Irene (Johnson), 59–61
"Islam, Virgins and Grapes" (Kristof), 36–37
"Islamic Heaven: A Pornographic Brothel," and ridiculing depiction of afterlife, 38–39
Islamic perspectives, 6–7
   paradise, tradition of houri in, 8–9
Islamic society
   Institution for Secularization of Islamic Society, 32
Islamic State, The, 145
Island of Doctor Moreau, The (Wells), 65–66
Ivanhoe (Scott), 65–66, 82–84

jahannam (hell), 93
al-Jahiz, singing of houri, 118–19
Jane Eyre (Brontë), 63–65
Jazet, Jean-Pierre-Marie, 79, 80–81, 82*f*
Jewish literary characters, depicted as houri, 82–84
jihad
   houri and descriptions of, 113–15, 141–44
   media and twenty-first-century jihad, 140
   virtual jihad, 139–44

virtual jihad, audience for, 147–48
Johnson, Boris, 41
Johnson, Samuel, 59–61, 66–67
Judaism, origins of houri in, 4–5
Juergensmeyer, Mark, mindset of religious violence, 24–26
Julius, Jens, 40
Jyllands-Posten, editorial cartoon in, 40

al-Kasabeh, Moaz, 140
Keats, John, 84
Kitab 'aja'ib al-makhluqat wa ghara'ib al-mawjudat (al-Qazwini), 120–21
Kitab al-Jihad (Ibn al-Mubarak), 113
Kitab al-Tawahhum (al-Muhasibi), 109–10
Kitab Qudwat al-Ghazi (Ibn Abi Zaminayn), 113, 115
Kitab wasf al-firdaws (Ibn Habib), 109, 149–50
Knolles, Richard, 51, 59–60
Kouachi, Saïd and Chérif, 135
Kristof, Nicholas, 1–2, 36–37
   "Martyrs, Virgins and Grapes" (Kristof), 1–2, 36–37

labor, and experiences in paradise, 99–102
   servants, characteristics of, 119–21
Lalla Rookh (Moore), 66–67
Landor, Walter Savage, 66–67
Lara (Byron), 68–69
"Last Days of Mohamed Atta" (Amis), 41–42
Les Dames de Byron, 74, 75*f*, 76*f*
Lesser and Greater Signs of the Hour, The, 127, 128*f*

Les Voyages du Sieur du Loir (du Loir), 52–54
letter, by September 11, 2001 hijackers, 7, 15*f*
American reactions to, 16–17
authorship and distribution of, 16
discovery and contents, 13–17
and houri as reward, 166–67
meaning and reward of mission, 19–20
narrative regarding, 42
reactions to, 20–21
sections and contents, 17–21
literature
and houri as model of feminine beauty, 58–62, 166
introduction of houri in, 43–44
representations of Muslim Middle East, 44–50, 90–91
tradition of houri in Romantic literature, 8
travel writing, and representations of Muslim Middle East, 50–57
See also American literature, metaphor of the houri in; British literature; French literature
lithographs, and images of Islamic paradise, 79–81, 80*f*, 81*f*
Luxenberg, Christoph, 26–34, 36–37

Makdisi, Saree, 51
male houri, possibility of, 159–62
Mandeville, John, 43–44
marriage
and companionship of houri in paradise, 103, 105–7, 111, 137–39, 141–44

sacred wedding in paradise, 111–17
and status of earthly women in paradise, 158–59
Martin, Steve, comedic parody, 38
martyrdom
houri as female martyrs, 22
poetry on, 23
"Martyrs, Virgins and Grapes" (Kristof), 1–2, 36–37
Mashari ʿ al-ashwaq (Ibn al-Nahhas), 113, 115–16, 141
Matar, Nabil, 47–49
material aspects of houri, 5–6
Maurin, Nicolas Eustache, 79–80, 80*f*, 81*f*
media
and twenty-first-century jihad, 140, 141
responses to "white grape" theory, 31–37
Menk, Mufti- 160
Mernissi, Fatima, 151–55
Mir Haydar, illustrated manuscripts, 120–21
misogyny, and what women may receive in paradise, 151–55
Montagu, Lady Mary, 54–56
Montesquieu, Charles-Louis de Secondat, baron de La Brède et de, 53–54, 66–67
Moore, Thomas, *Lalla Rookh*, 66–67
Moors, 44–45, 46
Moussaoui, Zacarias, 14
Mughal India, Elizabethan England and, 47–48
al-Muhasibi, descriptions of houri by, 109–10

Muslims, literary representations
of, 44–50, 90–91
and adversarial European
relationships, 48–50
in Elizabethan period, 47–49
and expanded perceptions of
Islam, 61–62
Lady Mary Montagu, letters
of, 54–56
Nicolas du Loir, travel writing
of, 52–54
pre-colonial contacts and, 47–49
travel writing and, 50–57

Naik, Zakir, 160
nashid
and devotional exercise, 125–26
imagery accompanying, 145–47
as motivation for jihad, 144–47
news media, responses to "white
grape" theory, 31–37
Newsweek, reaction to publication
of "Challenging the
Qur'an," 35–36
1001 Nights (Galland
translation), 53–54
Nouman Ali Khan, Ustadh, 156–
57, 160–61

odalisque, in representations of the
harem, 56
Omar Khayyam, 121–22
Orientalism (Said), 47
oriental tale, nineteenth-century
genre of, 66–77
Childe Harold's Pilgrimage
(Byron), 68
daughters, theme of
beautiful, 67
Don Juan (Byron), 69, 70–72
The Giaour (Byron), 69–70
introduction of, 66–67

proliferation of, 72–77
The Tales of the Genii, 72–73
Turkish Tales (Byron), 66–
67, 68–69
origins of houri, 3–6
Qur'anic allusions to, 93–97
"Origins of the Qur'an, The"
(Tantawy), 35–36
Oroonoko (Behn), 59
Ottoman Empire
Elizabethan England and, 47–48
and introduction of houri, 166
nineteenth-century literary
and artistic representations
of, 64–65

painting, and images of women in
the harem, 57
Pape, Robert, women and religious
violence, 24–25
paradise
alternative ways for women to
conceptualize, 151–55
companionship in, 102–8, 111,
154–55, 159
entertainment, as reward
in, 117–22
expectations of earthly women
for, 149–51
Garden described in, 96
labor in, 99–102
male desires and, 151–53
male youths and servers in, 94–
95, 99–102
notions of time in, 100
pearl, as descriptor of youth and
beauty, 99–100
Qur'anic allusions to, 93–94
as reflection of ideal Muslim
society, 154
rewards granted to women
in, 155–57

sacred wedding in, 111–17
sensuality of Islamic afterlife,
77–82, 107–11
social rank and status in, 101,
105–7, 110
status of women in, 158–59
tradition of houri in, 8–9
See also Garden
paradise, virtual tours of, 131–39
"A Travel in Paradise,"
131–32
earthly women described in,
133–35, 137–39
houri described in, 132–33
online videos and lectures,
features of paradise, 135–39
online videos and lectures,
objectives of, 131
speakers and narrators, 131–35
"The Final Abode," 132–35
"The Hereafter Books," 135–39
Pardoe, Julia Sophia, 66–67
parody, and tales of the houri, 37–
40, 58–59
pearl, as descriptor of youth and
beauty, 99–100
Pearl, Daniel, 140
Perry, Avi, 41
Persia, Elizabethan England
and, 47–48
Persian Letters (Montesquieu), 53–
54, 66–67
perspectives, European and
American, 6–7, 8
perspectives, Islamic, 6–7
paradise, tradition of houri
in, 8–9
poetry
celebrating wine with,
101–2
and promise of virgins in
paradise, 23

Polo, Marco, on Assassins, 25–
26, 43–44
Pressburg, Norbert, 38–39
prevalence, of houri, 2
purity, and companionship of
houri in paradise, 104–5

Qadhi, Yasir, 160–62
al-QadiS, descriptions of houri
by, 110
al-Qa'ida, 22–24
al-Qa'ida in the Arabian
Peninsula, 9, 135
al-Qazwini, compendium of
marvels, 120–21
qiyan, singing slave girl,
118–22
Qur'an
companionship, themes of
heavenly, 102–7
critical scholarship and
interpretations of, 27–31
feminist hermeneutics
of, 154–55
Fire, allusions to, 97
Garden, allusions to, 97
hell, allusions to, 93
houri, allusions to, 93–97
linguistic analysis, 26–27, 29–
30, 31
paradise, allusions to, 93–94
paradise, male youths and
servers in, 94–95
Qur'anic commentaries,
descriptions of houri in, 6, 8,
100–1, 103, 105–7
Qur'anic Studies
(Wansborough), 28–29
al-Qutb, Sayyid, 141

Rasselas- (Johnson), 66–67
recruitment, jihadist, 9, 22–23, 33

*Relation of a Journey begun: An:
    Dom:1610, A* (Sandys), 51
rewards, in paradise, 93–97
    companionship, 102–7
    entertainment, 117–22
    the Garden, 97–99
    houri as heavenly reward, 8–9,
        22–23, 166–67
    literal *vs.* metaphorical, 79
    sacred wedding, 111–17
    sensuality, 107–11
    servants and leisure, 99–102
Rihani, Ameen, 89–90
Risalat al-qiyan (Al-Jahiz),
    118–19
Romance of the Harem
    (Pardoe), 66–67
Romantic literature, tradition of
    houri in, 8, 89–91

Safavid Persia, Elizabethan
    England and, 47–48
Safiye, Ottoman queen
    mother, 47–48
Said, Edward, 47, 67–68, 72
Salamandra, Christa, 148
salsabil (fountain in
    paradise), 93–94
Sandys, George, 51
Saracens, in British
    worldview, 44–45
"Scholars Are Quietly Offering
    New Theories of the Koran"
    (Stille), 34
Scott, Walter, *Ivanhoe,* 65–
    66, 82–84
Seidensticker, Tilman, 144–45
sensuality, and depiction of Islamic
    afterlife, 77–82, 107–11
servants
    characteristics in
        paradise, 119–21

houri as servant of the
    afterlife, 158
Seventy-Two Virgins, 41
sexual deviancy, and ridiculing
    depiction of Islamic
    afterlife, 38–39
sexuality, and religious
    violence, 24–26
Shahzad, Faisal, 135
Shelley, Mary
    Wollstonecraft, 84–85
Siege of Corinth, The
    (Byron), 68–69
singing, and voice of houri in
    paradise, 117–22
Sirat Rasul Allah (Ibn Ishaq), 97–
    98, 111–13, 114–15
slave girl, houri as singing, 118–22
"Slippers, The," 67
social rank and status, in Garden
    of paradise, 101, 105–7, 110
Sotloff, Steven, 140
Southey, Robert, 66–67
spiritual aspects of houri, 5–6
"Star of Love," 86–87, 88*f*
Stille, Alexander, 34
suicide bombers, ridiculing
    depiction of, 39–40
Syro-Aramaic Reading of the Koran
    (Luxenberg), 26–34

Taliban, and poetry on
    martyrdom, 23
Tales of the Genii, The, 72–73
Tantawy, Mohammad
    Sayed, 35–36
terminology, variations on, 10–
    11, 113–14
Terror in the Mind of God
    (Juergensmeyer), 24–26
terrorism, and the houri, 21–
    24, 35–36

frustration and sexuality, 24–26
terrorism, media and spectacle
    of, 140
Thalaba (Southey), 66–67
Theil, Stefan, 34–35
time, in Garden of paradise, 100
trade, and European contact with
    Muslim Middle East, 47–49
"Travel in Paradise, A," 131–32
Travels (Mandeville), 43–44
travel writing, and representations
    of Muslim Middle East, 50–57
    and lived experiences of
        women, 56–57
    popularity of travel literature, 51
Tsarnaev, Dzhokhar and
    Tamerlan, 135
Turkish Bath, The, 57, 58*f*
Turkish Tales (Byron), 66–
    67, 68–69
Turkish women, depiction in travel
    writing, 52–53
    Lady Mary Montagu, letters
        of, 52–54
    du Loir, Nicolas, letters of 52–54
Turks, in British worldview, 44–45
    as literary villains, 49–50
    pre-colonial contacts, 47–49
Tyler, Royall, *The Algerine Captive*,
    65–66, 77–79

Uhud, Battle of, 111–13
    Battle of Uhud, 111–12

virginity, and companionship of
    houri in paradise, 104–5
Virgins? What Virgins? (Ibn
    Warraq), 32–34
virtual jihad, 139–44
    audience for, 147–48
"Visit to Jerusalem by an
    American, A," 73

visual arts
    engravings, and images of
        Islamic paradise, 79, 80–
        81, 82*f*
    engravings, "Star of Love," 88*f*
    The Gallery of Byron Beauties,
        74, 75*f*, 76*f*
    lithographs, and images of
        Islamic paradise, 79–81,
        80*f*, 81*f*
    painting, and images of women
        in the harem, 57
vocalization
    and devotional exercise, 125–26
    imagery accompanying, 145–47
    as motivation for jihad, 144–47
voice of houri, and entertainment
    in paradise, 117–22
Voltaire (Francois-Marie
    Arouet), 66–67
Voyage to the Levant (Blount), 51

Wadud, Amina, 154–55, 159
Walpole, Horace, 58–59
Wansborough, John, 28–29
Warren, Andrew, 72
"Wealth, Wisdom, and Virtue," 67
wedding, sacred in
    paradise, 111–17
Wells, H. G., *The Island of Doctor
    Moreau*, 65–66
Wendell, Charles, on origins of
    houri, 5
*What the Modern Martyr Should
    Know* (Pressburg), 38–39
"white grape" theory
    media responses to, 31–37
    and perceptions of Islam, 26–31
Why I Am Not a Muslim (Ibn
    Warraq), 32–34
wildan (male youths in paradise),
    94–95, 99–102, 119–20

wine, celebrating with poetry, 101–2
Wollstonecraft Shelley,
    Mary, 84–85
women
    alternative ways to conceptualize
        paradise, 151–55
    engagement with religious
        renewal and reform, 153–55
    expectations of earthly women
        for paradise, 149–51
    and religious violence,
        24–25
    rewards granted in
        paradise, 155–57
    status in paradise, 158–59
Women in Islamic Paradise
    (Mernissi), 151–54

Women in the Muslim Unconscious
    (Mernissi), 154
Women of the People of Fire,
    127, 129*f*
Women of the People of the Garden,
    127, 130*f*
Woodward, Bob, article on letter
    by September 11, 2001
    hijackers, 14–16

Yonge, William, 60
YouTube clips, and digital Islamic
    afterworlds, 125–26

Zonana, Joyce, 64
Zoroastrianism, origins of houri
    in, 4

8/21

DISCARD